Hands-On Intelligent Agents with OpenAI Gym

A step-by-step guide to develop AI agents using deep reinforcement learning

Praveen Palanisamy

BIRMINGHAM - MUMBAI

Hands-On Intelligent Agents with OpenAI Gym

Commissioning Editor: Sunith Shetty
Acquisition Editor: Divya Poojari
Content Development Editor: Eisha Dsouza
Technical Editor: Ishita Vora
Copy Editor: Safis Editing
Project Coordinator: Namrata Swetta
Proofreader: Safis Editing
Indexer: Mariammal Chettiyar
Graphics: Jisha Chirayil
Production Coordinator: Deepika Naik

First published: July 2018

Production reference: 1300718

Published by Packt Publishing Ltd.
Livery Place
35 Livery Street
Birmingham
B3 2PB, UK.

ISBN 978-1-78883-657-9

www.packtpub.com

To Sulo, my loving mom, for all the sacrifices she has made and for doing the best she could. To my Dad, for his support during my early growth period. To the living entity that bears the sun and the moon.

– Praveen Palanisamy

`mapt.io`

Mapt is an online digital library that gives you full access to over 5,000 books and videos, as well as industry leading tools to help you plan your personal development and advance your career. For more information, please visit our website.

Why subscribe?

- Spend less time learning and more time coding with practical eBooks and Videos from over 4,000 industry professionals

- Improve your learning with Skill Plans built especially for you

- Get a free eBook or video every month

- Mapt is fully searchable

- Copy and paste, print, and bookmark content

PacktPub.com

Did you know that Packt offers eBook versions of every book published, with PDF and ePub files available? You can upgrade to the eBook version at `www.PacktPub.com` and as a print book customer, you are entitled to a discount on the eBook copy. Get in touch with us at `service@packtpub.com` for more details.

At `www.PacktPub.com`, you can also read a collection of free technical articles, sign up for a range of free newsletters, and receive exclusive discounts and offers on Packt books and eBooks.

Contributors

About the author

Praveen Palanisamy works on developing autonomous intelligent systems. He is currently an AI researcher at General Motors R&D. He develops planning and decision-making algorithms and systems that use deep reinforcement learning for autonomous driving. Previously, he was at the Robotics Institute, Carnegie Mellon University, where he worked on autonomous navigation, including perception and AI for mobile robots. He has experience developing complete, autonomous, robotic systems from scratch.

I want to thank the people who contribute to the open source development of OpenAI Gym and PyTorch.
I also would like to thank the Packt team, specifically Rushi, Eisha, and Ishita, for helping me throughout the authoring process.

About the reviewer

Sudharsan Ravichandiran is a data scientist, researcher, artificial intelligence enthusiast, and YouTuber (search for Sudharsan reinforcement learning). He completed his bachelors in information technology at Anna University. His area of research focuses on practical implementations of deep learning and reinforcement learning, which includes natural language processing and computer vision. He also authored bestseller *Hands-On Reinforcement Learning with Python*, published by Packt Publishing.

Packt is searching for authors like you

If you're interested in becoming an author for Packt, please visit `authors.packtpub.com` and apply today. We have worked with thousands of developers and tech professionals, just like you, to help them share their insight with the global tech community. You can make a general application, apply for a specific hot topic that we are recruiting an author for, or submit your own idea.

Table of Contents

Preface   1

Chapter 1: Introduction to Intelligent Agents and Learning Environments   7
   What is an intelligent agent?   8
   Learning environments   8
   What is OpenAI Gym?   9
   Understanding the features of OpenAI Gym   16
      Simple environment interface   16
      Comparability and reproducibility   17
      Ability to monitor progress   17
   What can you do with the OpenAI Gym toolkit?   18
   Creating your first OpenAI Gym environment   18
      Creating and visualizing a new Gym environment   20
   Summary   20

Chapter 2: Reinforcement Learning and Deep Reinforcement Learning   21
   What is reinforcement learning?   22
   Understanding what AI means and what's in it in an intuitive way   23
      Supervised learning   24
      Unsupervised learning   24
      Reinforcement learning   25
   Practical reinforcement learning   25
      Agent   26
      Rewards   26
      Environment   26
      State   27
      Model   29
      Value function   29
         State-value function   29
         Action-value function   30
      Policy   30
   Markov Decision Process   30
   Planning with dynamic programming   31
   Monte Carlo learning and temporal difference learning   31
   SARSA and Q-learning   32
   Deep reinforcement learning   32
   Practical applications of reinforcement and deep reinforcement learning algorithms   34
   Summary   35

Chapter 3: Getting Started with OpenAI Gym and Deep Reinforcement Learning	37
  Code repository, setup, and configuration	37
    Prerequisites	39
    Creating the conda environment	40
    Minimal install – the quick and easy way	41
    Complete install of OpenAI Gym learning environments	43
      Instructions for Ubuntu	43
      Instructions for macOS	43
      MuJoCo installation	44
      Completing the OpenAI Gym setup	44
  Installing tools and libraries needed for deep reinforcement learning	47
    Installing prerequisite system packages	48
    Installing Compute Unified Device Architecture (CUDA)	48
    Installing PyTorch	49
  Summary	51

Chapter 4: Exploring the Gym and its Features	53
  Exploring the list of environments and nomenclature	53
    Nomenclature	55
    Exploring the Gym environments	57
  Understanding the Gym interface	58
  Spaces in the Gym	63
  Summary	67

Chapter 5: Implementing your First Learning Agent - Solving the Mountain Car problem	69
  Understanding the Mountain Car problem	70
    The Mountain Car problem and environment	70
  Implementing a Q-learning agent from scratch	72
    Revisiting Q-learning	75
    Implementing a Q-learning agent using Python and NumPy	76
      Defining the hyperparameters	76
      Implementing the Q_Learner class's __init__ method	77
      Implementing the Q_Learner class's discretize method	78
      Implementing the Q_Learner's get_action method	79
      Implementing the Q_learner class's learn method	79
      Full Q_Learner class implementation	80
  Training the reinforcement learning agent at the Gym	81
  Testing and recording the performance of the agent	82
  A simple and complete Q-Learner implementation for solving the Mountain Car problem	83
  Summary	87

Chapter 6: Implementing an Intelligent Agent for Optimal Control using Deep Q-Learning	89

Improving the Q-learning agent   91
  Using neural networks to approximate Q-functions   92
    Implementing a shallow Q-network using PyTorch   93
      Implementing the Shallow_Q_Learner   94
      Solving the Cart Pole problem using a Shallow Q-Network   95
  Experience replay   98
    Implementing the experience memory   99
    Implementing the replay experience method for the Q-learner class   101
  Revisiting the epsilon-greedy action policy   103
    Implementing an epsilon decay schedule   104
Implementing a deep Q-learning agent   105
  Implementing a deep convolutional Q-network in PyTorch   106
  Using the target Q-network to stabilize an agent's learning   107
  Logging and visualizing an agent's learning process   109
    Using TensorBoard for logging and visualizing a PyTorch RL agent's progress   110
  Managing hyperparameters and configuration parameters   111
    Using a JSON file to easily configure parameters   112
    The parameters manager   112
  A complete deep Q-learner to solve complex problems with raw pixel input   114
The Atari Gym environment   121
  Customizing the Atari Gym environment   122
    Implementing custom Gym environment wrappers   122
      Reward clipping   123
      Preprocessing Atari screen image frames   124
      Normalizing observations   125
      Random no-ops on reset   127
      Fire on reset   128
      Episodic life   129
      Max and skip-frame   130
    Wrapping the Gym environment   131
Training the deep Q-learner to play Atari games   132
  Putting together a comprehensive deep Q-learner   133
  Hyperparameters   136
  Launching the training process   137
  Testing performance of your deep Q-learner in Atari games   138
Summary   139
Chapter 7: Creating Custom OpenAI Gym Environments - CARLA Driving Simulator   141
  Understanding the anatomy of Gym environments   142
    Creating a template for custom Gym environment implementations   143
    Registering custom environments with OpenAI Gym   145
  Creating an OpenAI Gym-compatible CARLA driving simulator environment   145
    Configuration and initialization   147
      Configuration   148
      Initialization   148
    Implementing the reset method   149

Customizing the CARLA simulation using the CarlaSettings object 150
Adding cameras and sensors to a vehicle in CARLA 150
Implementing the step function for the CARLA environment 153
Accessing camera or sensor data 154
Sending actions to control agents in CARLA 154
Continuous action space in CARLA 155
Discrete action space in CARLA 156
Sending actions to the CARLA simulation server 157
Determining the end of episodes in the CARLA environment 159
Testing the CARLA Gym environment 160
Summary 163

Chapter 8: Implementing an Intelligent - Autonomous Car Driving Agent using Deep Actor-Critic Algorithm 165
The deep n-step advantage actor-critic algorithm 166
Policy gradients 166
The likelihood ratio trick 168
The policy gradient theorem 169
Actor-critic algorithm 170
Advantage actor-critic algorithm 171
n-step advantage actor-critic algorithm 172
n-step returns 173
Implementing the n-step return calculation 175
Deep n-step advantage actor-critic algorithm 177
Implementing a deep n-step advantage actor critic agent 177
Initializing the actor and critic networks 178
Gathering n-step experiences using the current policy 182
Calculating the actor's and critic's losses 183
Updating the actor-critic model 184
Tools to save/load, log, visualize, and monitor 185
An extension - asynchronous deep n-step advantage actor-critic 186
Training an intelligent and autonomous driving agent 187
Training and testing the deep n-step advantage actor-critic agent 187
Training the agent to drive a car in the CARLA driving simulator 191
Summary 192

Chapter 9: Exploring the Learning Environment Landscape - Roboschool, Gym-Retro, StarCraft-II, DeepMindLab 193
Gym interface-compatible environments 194
Roboschool 195
Quickstart guide to setting up and running Roboschool environments 197
Gym retro 199
Quickstart guide to setup and run Gym Retro 200
Other open source Python-based learning environments 202
StarCraft II - PySC2 203
Quick start guide to setup and run StarCraft II PySC2 environment 204
Downloading the StarCraft II Linux packages 205
Downloading the SC2 maps 205

Installing PySC2 | 206
Playing StarCraftII yourself or running sample agents | 206
DeepMind lab | 207
DeepMind Lab learning environment interface | 208
reset(episode=-1, seed=None) | 208
step(action, num_steps=1) | 208
observations() | 208
is_running() | 209
observation_spec() | 209
action_spec() | 210
num_steps() | 211
fps() | 211
events() | 211
close() | 211
Quick start guide to setup and run DeepMind Lab | 211
Setting up and installing DeepMind Lab and its dependencies | 212
Playing the game, testing a randomly acting agent, or training your own! | 212
Summary | 213

Chapter 10: Exploring the Learning Algorithm Landscape - DDPG (Actor-Critic), PPO (Policy-Gradient), Rainbow (Value-Based) | 215
Deep Deterministic Policy Gradients | 216
Core concepts | 217
Proximal Policy Optimization | 218
Core concept | 219
Off-policy learning | 219
On-policy | 220
Rainbow | 222
Core concept | 222
DQN | 223
Double Q-Learning | 223
Prioritized experience replay | 224
Dueling networks | 224
Multi-step learning/n-step learning | 225
Distributional RL | 226
Noisy nets | 228
Quick summary of advantages and applications | 229
Summary | 230

Other Books You May Enjoy | 231

Index | 235

Preface

This book will guide you through the process of implementing your own intelligent agents to solve both discrete- and continuous-valued sequential decision-making problems with all the essential building blocks to develop, debug, train, visualize, customize, and test your intelligent agent implementations in a variety of learning environments, ranging from the Mountain Car and Cart Pole problems to Atari games and CARLA – an advanced simulator for autonomous driving.

Who this book is for

If you're a student, a game/machine learning developer, or an AI enthusiast looking to get started building intelligent agents and algorithms to solve a variety of problems using learning environments with the OpenAI Gym interface, this book is for you. You will also find this book useful if you want to learn how to build deep reinforcement learning-based, artificially intelligent agents to solve problems in your domain of interest. Though the book covers all the basic concepts that you need to know, some working knowledge of Python will help you get the most out of it.

What this book covers

Chapter 1, *Introduction to Intelligent Agents and Learning Environments*, which enables the development of several AI systems. It sheds light on the important features of the toolkit, which provides you with endless opportunities to create autonomous intelligent agents to solve several algorithmic tasks, games, and control tasks. By the end of this chapter, you will know enough to create an instance of a Gym environment using Python yourself.

Chapter 2, *Reinforcement Learning and Deep Reinforcement Learning*, provides a concise explanation of the basic terminologies and concepts in reinforcement learning. The chapter will give you a good understanding of the basic reinforcement learning framework for developing AI agents. The chapter will also introduce deep reinforcement learning and provide you with a flavor of the types of advanced problem the algorithms enable you to solve.

Chapter 3, *Getting Started with OpenAI Gym and Deep Reinforcement Learning*, jumps right in and gets your development machine/computer ready with all the required installations and configurations needed for using the learning environments as well as PyTorch for developing deep learning algorithms.

Chapter 4, *Exploring the Gym and its Features*, walks you through the inventory of learning environments available with the Gym library starting with the overview of how the environments are classified and named which will help you choose the correct version and type of environments from the 700+ learning environments available. You will then learn to explore the Gym, test out any of the environment you would like to, understand the interface and description of various environments.

Chapter 5, *Implementing your First Learning Agent – Solving the Mountain Car problem*, explains how to implement an AI agent using reinforcement learning to solve the mountain car problem. You will implement the agent, train it, and see it improve on its own. The implementation details will enable you to apply the concepts to develop and train an agent to solve various other tasks and/or games.

Chapter 6, *Implementing an Intelligent Agent for Optimal Control using Deep Q-Learning*, covers various methods to improve Q-learning including action-value function approximation using deep neural network, experience replay, target networks and also the necessary utilities and building-blocks that are useful for training and testing deep reinforcement learning agents in general. You will implement a DQN based intelligent agent for taking optimal discrete control actions and train it to play several Atari games and watch the agent's performance.

Chapter 7, *Creating Custom OpenAI Gym Environments – Carla Driving Simulator*, will teach you how to convert a real-world problem into a learning environment with interfaces compatible with the OpenAI Gym. You will learn the anatomy of Gym environments and create your custom learning environment based on the Carla simulator that can be registered with the Gym and used for training agents that we develop.

Chapter 8, *Implementing an Intelligent & Autonomous Car Driving Agent using Deep Actor-Critic Algorithm*, teaches you the fundamentals of the Policy Gradient based reinforcement learning algorithms and helps you intuitively understand the deep n-step advantage actor-critic algorithm. You will then learn to implement a super-intelligent agent that can drive a car autonomously in the Carla simulator using both the synchronous as well as asynchronous implementation of the deep n-step advantage actor-critic algorithm.

Chapter 9, *Exploring the Learning Environment Landscape – Roboschool, Gym-Retro, StarCraft-II, DeepMindLab*, takes you beyond the Gym and shows you around other well developed suite of learning environments that you can use to train your intelligent agents. You will understand and learn to use the various Roboschool environments, the Gym Retro environments, the very popular Star Craft II environment and the DeepMind Lab environments.

Chapter 10, *Exploring the Learning Algorithm Landscape – DDPG (Actor-Critic), PPO (Policy-Gradient), Rainbow (Value-Based),* Provides insights into latest deep reinforcement learning algorithms with their fundamentals demystified based on what you learned in the previous chapters of this book. You will get a quick understanding of the core concepts behind the best algorithms in the three different classes of deep reinforcement learning algorithms namely: The actor-critic based Deep Deterministic Policy Gradient (DDPG) algorithm, the Policy Gradient based Proximal Policy Optimization (PPO) and the value based Rainbow algorithm.

To get the most out of this book

The following will be required:

- Some working knowledge of Python programming in order to understand the syntax, module imports, and library installations
- Some experience with Linux or macOS X command line for basic tasks, such as navigating the filesystem and running Python scripts

Download the example code files

You can download the example code files for this book from your account at www.packtpub.com. If you purchased this book elsewhere, you can visit www.packtpub.com/support and register to have the files emailed directly to you.

You can download the code files by following these steps:

1. Log in or register at www.packtpub.com.
2. Select the **SUPPORT** tab.
3. Click on **Code Downloads & Errata**.
4. Enter the name of the book in the **Search** box and follow the onscreen instructions.

Once the file is downloaded, please make sure that you unzip or extract the folder using the latest version of:

- WinRAR/7-Zip for Windows
- Zipeg/iZip/UnRarX for Mac
- 7-Zip/PeaZip for Linux

The code bundle for the book is also hosted on GitHub at https://github.com/ PacktPublishing/Hands-On-Intelligent-Agents-with-OpenAI-Gym. In case there's an update to the code, it will be updated on the existing GitHub repository.

We also have other code bundles from our rich catalog of books and videos available at https://github.com/PacktPublishing/. Check them out!

Download the color images

We also provide a PDF file that has color images of the screenshots/diagrams used in this book. You can download it here: http://www.packtpub.com/sites/default/files/ downloads/HandsOnIntelligentAgentswithOpenAIGym_ColorImages.pdf.

Conventions used

There are a number of text conventions used throughout this book.

CodeInText: Indicates code words in text, database table names, folder names, filenames, file extensions, pathnames, dummy URLs, user input, and Twitter handles. Here is an example: "Mount the downloaded WebStorm-10*.dmg disk image file as another disk in your system."

A block of code is set as follows:

```python
#!/usr/bin/env python
import gym
env = gym.make("Qbert-v0")
MAX_NUM_EPISODES = 10
MAX_STEPS_PER_EPISODE = 500
```

When we wish to draw your attention to a particular part of a code block, the relevant lines or items are set in bold:

```python
for episode in range(MAX_NUM_EPISODES):
    obs = env.reset()
    for step in range(MAX_STEPS_PER_EPISODE):
        env.render()
```

Any command-line input or output is written as follows:

```
$ python get_observation_action_space.py 'MountainCar-v0'
```

Bold: Indicates a new term, an important word, or words that you see onscreen. For example, words in menus or dialog boxes appear in the text like this. Here is an example: "Select **System info** from the **Administration** panel."

Warnings or important notes appear like this.

Tips and tricks appear like this.

Get in touch

Feedback from our readers is always welcome.

General feedback: Email `feedback@packtpub.com` and mention the book title in the subject of your message. If you have questions about any aspect of this book, please email us at `questions@packtpub.com`.

Errata: Although we have taken every care to ensure the accuracy of our content, mistakes do happen. If you have found a mistake in this book, we would be grateful if you would report this to us. Please visit `www.packtpub.com/submit-errata`, selecting your book, clicking on the Errata Submission Form link, and entering the details.

Piracy: If you come across any illegal copies of our works in any form on the Internet, we would be grateful if you would provide us with the location address or website name. Please contact us at `copyright@packtpub.com` with a link to the material.

If you are interested in becoming an author: If there is a topic that you have expertise in and you are interested in either writing or contributing to a book, please visit `authors.packtpub.com`.

Reviews

Please leave a review. Once you have read and used this book, why not leave a review on the site that you purchased it from? Potential readers can then see and use your unbiased opinion to make purchase decisions, we at Packt can understand what you think about our products, and our authors can see your feedback on their book. Thank you!

For more information about Packt, please visit `packtpub.com`.

Introduction to Intelligent Agents and Learning Environments

1

Greetings! Welcome to the first chapter of this book. This book will introduce you to the awesome OpenAI Gym learning environment and guide you through an exciting journey to get you equipped with enough skills to train state-of-the-art, artificial intelligence agent-based systems. This book will help you develop hands-on experience with reinforcement learning and deep reinforcement learning through practical projects ranging from developing an autonomous, self-driving car to developing Atari game-playing agents that can surpass human performance. By the time you complete the book, you will be in a position to explore the endless possibilities of using artificial intelligence to solve algorithmic tasks, play games, and fix control problems.

The following topics will be covered in this chapter:

- Understanding intelligent agents and learning environments
- Understanding what OpenAI Gym is all about
- Different categories of tasks/environments that are available, with a brief description of what each category is suitable for
- Understanding the key features of OpenAI Gym
- Getting an idea about what you can do with the OpenAI Gym toolkit
- Creating and visualizing your first Gym environment

Let's start our journey by understanding what an intelligent agent is.

What is an intelligent agent?

A major goal of artificial intelligence is to build intelligent agents. Perceiving their environment, understanding, reasoning and learning to plan, and making decisions and acting upon them are essential characteristics of intelligent agents. We will begin our first chapter by understanding what an intelligent agent is, from the basic definition of agents, to adding intelligence on top of that.

An *agent* is an entity that acts based on the observation (perception) of its environment. Humans and robots are examples of agents with physical forms.

 A human, or an animal, is an example of an agent that uses its organs (eyes, ears, nose, skin, and so on) as sensors to observe/perceive its environment and act using their physical body (arms, hands, legs, head, and so on). A robot uses its sensors (cameras, microphones, LiDAR, radar, and so on) to observe/perceive its environment and act using its physical robotic body (robotic arms, robotic hands/grippers, robotic legs, speakers, and so on).

Software agents are computer programs that are capable of making decisions and taking actions through interaction with their environment. A software agent can be embodied in a physical form, such as a robot. *Autonomous agents* are entities that make decisions autonomously and take actions based on their understanding of and reasoning about their observations of their environment.

An *intelligent agent* is an autonomous entity that can learn and improve based on its interactions with its environment. An intelligent agent is capable of analyzing its own behavior and performance using its observations.

In this book, we will develop intelligent agents to solve sequential decision-making problems that can be solved using a sequence of (independent) decisions/actions in a (loosely) Markovian environment, where feedback in the form of reward signals is available (through percepts), at least in some environmental conditions.

Learning environments

A learning environment is an integral component of a system where an intelligent agent can be trained to develop intelligent systems. The learning environment defines the problem or the task for the agent to complete.

A problem or task in which the outcome depends on a sequence of decisions made or actions taken is a sequential decision-making problem. Here are some of the varieties of learning environments:

- Fully observable versus partially observable
- Deterministic versus stochastic
- Episodic versus sequential
- Static versus dynamic
- Discrete versus continuous
- Discrete state space versus continuous state space
- Discrete action space versus continuous action space

In this book, we will be using learning environments implemented using the OpenAI Gym Python library, as it provides a simple and standard interface and environment implementations, along with the ability to implement new custom environments.

In the following subsections, we will get a glimpse of the OpenAI Gym toolkit. This section is geared towards familiarizing a complete newbie with the OpenAI Gym toolkit. No prior knowledge or experience is assumed. We will first try to get a feel for the Gym toolkit and walk through the various environments that are available under different categories. We will then discuss the features of Gym that might be of interest to you, irrespective of the application domain that you are interested in. We'll then briefly discuss what the value proposition of the Gym toolkit is and how you can utilize it. We will be building several cool and intelligent agents in subsequent chapters, building on top of the Gym toolkit. So, this chapter is really the foundation for all that. We will also be quickly creating and visualizing our first OpenAI Gym environment towards the end of this chapter. Excited? Let's jump right in.

What is OpenAI Gym?

OpenAI Gym is an open source toolkit that provides a diverse collection of tasks, called environments, with a common interface for developing and testing your intelligent agent algorithms. The toolkit introduces a standard **Application Programming Interface** (**API**) for interfacing with environments designed for reinforcement learning. Each environment has a version attached to it, which ensures meaningful comparisons and reproducible results with the evolving algorithms and the environments themselves.

The Gym toolkit, through its various environments, provides an episodic setting for reinforcement learning, where an agent's experience is broken down into a series of episodes. In each episode, the initial state of the agent is randomly sampled from a distribution, and the interaction between the agent and the environment proceeds until the environment reaches a terminal state. Do not worry if you are not familiar with reinforcement learning. You will be introduced to reinforcement learning in `Chapter 2`, *Reinforcement Learning and Deep Reinforcement Learning*.

Some of the basic environments available in the OpenAI Gym library are shown in the following screenshot:

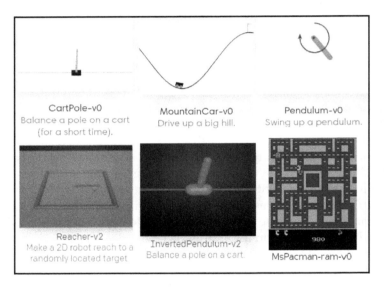

Examples of basic environments available in the OpenAI Gym with a short description of the task

At the time of writing this book, the OpenAI Gym natively has about 797 environments spread over different categories of tasks. The famous Atari category has the largest share with about 116 (half with screen inputs and half with RAM inputs) environments! The categories of tasks/environments supported by the toolkit are listed here:

- Algorithmic
- Atari
- Board games
- Box2D
- Classic control

- Doom (unofficial)
- Minecraft (unofficial)
- MuJoCo
- Soccer
- Toy text
- Robotics (newly added)

The various types of environment (or tasks) available under the different categories, along with a brief description of each environment, is given next. Keep in mind that you may need some additional tools and packages installed on your system to run environments in each of these categories. Do not worry! We will go over every single step you need to do to get any environment up and running in the upcoming chapters. Stay tuned!

We will now see the previously mentioned categories in detail, as follows:

- **Algorithmic environments**: They provide tasks that require an agent to perform computations, such as the addition of multi-digit numbers, copying data from an input sequence, reversing sequences, and so on.
- **Atari environments**: These offer interfaces to several classic Atari console games. These environment interfaces are wrappers on top of the **Arcade Learning Environment** (**ALE**). They provide the game's screen images or RAM as input to train your agents.
- **Board games**: This category has the environment for the popular game Go on 9 x 9 and 19 x 19 boards. For those of you who have been following the recent breakthroughs by Google's DeepMind in the game of Go, this might be very interesting. DeepMind developed an agent named AlphaGo, which used reinforcement learning and other learning and planning techniques, including Monte Carlo tree search, to beat the top-ranked human Go players in the world, including Fan Hui and Lee Sedol. DeepMind also published their work on AlphaGo Zero, which was trained from scratch, unlike the original AlphaGo, which used sample games played by humans. AlphaGo Zero surpassed the original AlphaGo's performance. Later, AlphaZero was published; it is an autonomous system that learned to play chess, Go, and Shogi using self-play (without any human supervision for training) and reached performance levels higher than the previous systems developed.

- **Box2D**: This is an open source physics engine used for simulating rigid bodies in 2D. The Gym toolkit has a few continuous control tasks that are developed using the Box2D simulator:

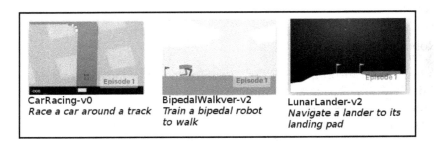

CarRacing-v0
Race a car around a track

BipedalWalkver-v2
Train a bipedal robot to walk

LunarLander-v2
Navigate a lander to its landing pad

A sample list of environments built using the Box2D simulator

The tasks include training a bipedal robot to walk, navigating a lunar lander to its landing pad, and training a race car to drive around a race track. Exciting! In this book, we will train an AI agent using reinforcement learning to drive a race car around the track autonomously! Stay tuned.

- **Classic control**: This category has many tasks developed for it and was used widely in reinforcement learning literature in the past. These tasks formed the basis for some of the early development and benchmarking of reinforcement learning algorithms. For example, one of the environments available under the classic control category is the Mountain Car environment, which was first introduced in 1990 by Andrew Moore (Dean of the School of Computer Science at CMU, and Pittsburgh founder) in his PhD thesis. This environment is still used sometimes as a test bed for reinforcement learning algorithms. You will create your first OpenAI Gym environment from this category in just a few moments towards the end of this chapter!

- **Doom**: This category provides an environment interface for the popular first-person shooter game Doom. It is an unofficial, community-created Gym environment category and is based on ViZDoom, which is a Doom-based AI research platform providing an easy-to-use API suitable for developing intelligent agents from raw visual inputs. It enables the development of AI bots that can play several challenging rounds of the Doom game using only the screen buffer! If you have played this game, you know how thrilling and difficult it is to progress through some of the rounds without losing lives in the game! Although this is not a game with cool graphics like some of the new first-person shooter games, the visuals aside, it is a great game. In recent times, several studies in machine learning, especially in deep reinforcement learning, have utilized the ViZDoom platform and have developed new algorithms to tackle the goal-directed navigation problems encountered in the game. You can visit ViZDoom's research web page (http://vizdoom.cs.put.edu.pl/research) for a list of research studies that use this platform. The following screenshot lists some of the missions that are available as separate environments in the Gym for training your agents:

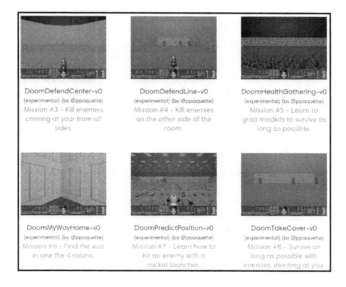

List of missions or rounds available in Doom environments

- **MineCraft**: This is another great platform. Game AI developers especially might be very much interested in this environment. MineCraft is a popular video game among hobbyists. The MineCraft Gym environment was built using Microsoft's Malmo project, which is a platform for artificial intelligence experimentation and research built on top of Minecraft. Some of the missions that are available as environments in the OpenAI Gym are shown in the following screenshot. These environments provide inspiration for developing solutions to challenging new problems presented by this unique environment:

CliffWalking1-v0   MinecraftDefaultFlat1-v0   MinecraftTrickyArena1-v0

Eating1-v0   MinecraftDefaultWorld1-v0   MinecraftBasic-v0

Environments in MineCraft available in OpenAI Gym

- **MuJoCo**: Are you interested in robotics? Do you dream of developing algorithms that can make a humanoid walk and run, or do a backflip like Boston Dynamic's Atlas Robot? You can! You will be able to apply the reinforcement learning methods you will learn in this book in the OpenAI Gym MuJoCo environment to develop your own algorithm that can make a 2D robot walk, run, swim, or hop, or make a 3D multi-legged robot walk or run! In the following screenshot, there are some cool, real-world, robot-like environments available under the MuJoCo environment:

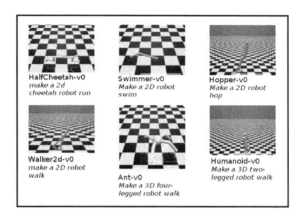

- **Soccer**: This an environment suitable for training multiple agents that can cooperate together. The soccer environments available through the Gym toolkit have continuous state and action spaces. Wondering what that means? You will learn all about it when we talk about reinforcement learning in the next chapter. For now, here is a simple explanation: a continuous state and action space means that the action that an agent can take and the input that the agent receives are both continuous values. This means that they can take any real number value between, say, *0* and *1* (*0.5, 0.005*, and so on), rather than being limited to a few discrete sets of values, such as {1, 2, 3}. There are three types of environment. The plain soccer environment initializes a single opponent on the field and gives a reward of *+1* for scoring a goal and *0* otherwise. In order for an agent to score a goal, it will need to learn to identify the ball, approach the ball, and kick the ball towards the goal. Sound simple enough? But it is really hard for a computer to figure that out on its own, especially when all you say is *+1* when it scores a goal and *0* in any other case. It does not have any other clues! You can develop agents that will learn all about soccer by themselves and learn to score goals using the methods that you will learn in this book.

- **Toy text**: OpenAI Gym also has some simple text-based environments under this category. These include some classic problems such as Frozen Lake, where the goal is to find a safe path to cross a grid of ice and water tiles. It is categorized under toy text because it uses a simpler environment representation—mostly through text.

With that, you have a very good overview of all the different categories and types of environment that are available as part of the OpenAI Gym toolkit. It is worth noting that the release of the OpenAI Gym toolkit was accompanied by an OpenAI Gym website (gym.openai.com), which maintained a scoreboard for every algorithm that was submitted for evaluation. It showcased the performance of user-submitted algorithms, and some submissions were also accompanied by detailed explanations and source code. Unfortunately, OpenAI decided to withdraw support for the evaluation website. The service went offline in September 2017.

Now you have a good picture of the various categories of environment available in OpenAI Gym and what each category provides you with. Next, we will look at the key features of OpenAI Gym that make it an indispensable component in many of today's advancements in intelligent agent development, especially those that use reinforcement learning or deep reinforcement learning.

Understanding the features of OpenAI Gym

In this section, we will take a look at the key features that have made the OpenAI Gym toolkit very popular in the reinforcement learning community and led to it becoming widely adopted.

Simple environment interface

OpenAI Gym provides a simple and common Python interface to environments. Specifically, it takes an action as input and provides *observation, reward, done* and an optional info object, based on the action as the output at each step. If this does not make perfect sense to you yet, do not worry. We will go over the interface again in a more detailed manner to help you understand. This paragraph is just to give you an overview of the interface to make it clear how simple it is. This provides great flexibility for users as they can design and develop their agent algorithms based on any paradigm they like, and not be constrained to use any particular paradigm because of this simple and convenient interface.

Comparability and reproducibility

We intuitively feel that we should be able to compare the performance of an agent or an algorithm in a particular task to the performance of another agent or algorithm in the same task. For example, if an agent gets a score of *1,000* on average in the Atari game of Space Invaders, we should be able to tell that this agent is performing worse than an agent that scores *5000* on average in the Space Invaders game in the same amount of training time. But what happens if the scoring system for the game is slightly changed? Or if the environment interface was modified to include additional information about the game states that will provide an advantage to the second agent? This would make the score-to-score comparison unfair, right?

To handle such changes in the environment, OpenAI Gym uses strict versioning for environments. The toolkit guarantees that if there is any change to an environment, it will be accompanied by a different version number. Therefore, if the original version of the Atari Space Invaders game environment was named `SpaceInvaders-v0` and there were some changes made to the environment to provide more information about the game states, then the environment's name would be changed to `SpaceInvaders-v1`. This simple versioning system makes sure we are always comparing performance measured on the exact same environment setup. This way, the results obtained are comparable and reproducible.

Ability to monitor progress

All the environments available as part of the Gym toolkit are equipped with a monitor. This monitor logs every time step of the simulation and every reset of the environment. What this means is that the environment automatically keeps track of how our agent is learning and adapting with every step. You can even configure the monitor to automatically record videos of the game while your agent is learning to play. How cool is that?

What can you do with the OpenAI Gym toolkit?

The Gym toolkit provides a standardized way of defining the interface for environments developed for problems that can be solved using reinforcement learning. If you are familiar with or have heard of the **ImageNet Large Scale Visual Recognition Challenge** (**ILSVRC**), you may realize how much of an impact a standard benchmarking platform can have on accelerating research and development. For those of you who are not familiar with ILSVRC, here is a brief summary: it is a competition where the participating teams evaluate the supervised learning algorithms they have developed for the given dataset and compete to achieve higher accuracy with several visual recognition tasks. This common platform, coupled with the success of deep neural network-based algorithms popularized by AlexNet (`https://papers.nips.cc/paper/4824-imagenet-classification-with-deep-convolutional-neural-networks.pdf`), paved the way for the deep learning era we are in at the moment.

In a similar way, the Gym toolkit provides a common platform to benchmark reinforcement learning algorithms and encourages researchers and engineers to develop algorithms that can achieve higher rewards for several challenging tasks. In short, the Gym toolkit is to reinforcement learning what ILSVRC is to supervised learning.

Creating your first OpenAI Gym environment

We will be going over the steps to set up the OpenAI Gym dependencies and other tools required for training your reinforcement learning agents in detail in Chapter 3, *Getting Started with OpenAI Gym and Deep Reinforcement Learning*. This section provides a quick way to get started with the OpenAI Gym Python API on Linux and macOS using `virtualenv` so that you can get a sneak peak into the Gym!

MacOS and Ubuntu Linux systems come with Python installed by default. You can check which version of Python is installed by running `python --version` from a terminal window. If this returns `python` followed by a version number, then you are good to proceed to the next steps! If you get an error saying the Python command was not found, then you have to install Python. Please refer to the detailed installation section in `Chapter 3`, *Getting Started with OpenAI Gym and Deep Reinforcement Learning* of this book:

1. Install `virtualenv`:

   $pip install virtualenv

 If **pip** is not installed on your system, you can install it by typing `sudo easy_install pip`.

2. Create a virtual environment named `openai-gym` using the virtualenv tool:

   $virtualenv openai-gym

3. Activate the `openai-gym` virtual environment:

   $source openai-gym/bin/activate

4. Install all the packages for the Gym toolkit from upstream:

   $pip install -U gym

 If you get **permission denied** or **failed with error code 1** when you run the `pip install` command, it is most likely because the permissions on the directory you are trying to install the package to (the `openai-gym` directory inside `virtualenv` in this case) needs special/root privileges. You can either run `sudo -H pip install -U gym[all]` to solve the issue or change permissions on the `openai-gym` directory by running `sudo chmod -R o+rw ~/openai-gym`.

5. Test to make sure the installation is successful:

   $python -c 'import gym; gym.make("CartPole-v0");'

Creating and visualizing a new Gym environment

In just a minute or two, you have created an instance of an OpenAI Gym environment to get started!

Let's open a new Python prompt and import the gym module:

```
>>import gym
```

Once the gym module is imported, we can use the gym.make method to create our new environment like this:

```
>>env = gym.make('CartPole-v0')
>>env.reset()
env.render()
```

This will bring up a window like this:

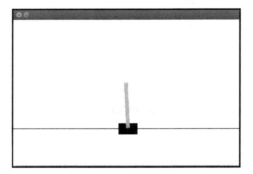

Hooray!

Summary

Congrats on completing the first chapter! Hope you had fun creating your own environment. In this chapter, you learned what OpenAI Gym is all about, what features it provides, and what you can do with the toolkit. You now have a very good idea about OpenAI Gym. In the next chapter, we will go over the basics of reinforcement learning to give you a good foundation, which will help you build your cool intelligent agents as you progress through the book. Excited? Move on to the next chapter!

2
Reinforcement Learning and Deep Reinforcement Learning

This chapter provides a concise explanation of the basic terminology and concepts in reinforcement learning. It will give you a good understanding of the basic reinforcement learning framework for developing artificial intelligent agents. This chapter will also introduce deep reinforcement learning and provide you with a flavor of the types of advanced problems the algorithms enable you to solve. You will find mathematical expressions and equations used in quite a few places in this chapter. Although there's enough theory behind reinforcement learning and deep reinforcement learning to fill a whole book, the key concepts that are useful for practical implementation are discussed in this chapter, so that when we actually implement the algorithms in Python to train our agents, you can clearly understand the logic behind them. It is perfectly alright if you are not able to grasp all of it in your first pass. You can always come back to this chapter and revise whenever you need a better understanding.

We will cover the following topics in this chapter:

- What is reinforcement learning?
- The Markov Decision Process
- The reinforcement learning framework
- What is deep reinforcement learning?
- How do deep reinforcement learning agents work in practice?

What is reinforcement learning?

If you are new to the field of **Artificial Intelligence** (**AI**) or machine learning, you might be wondering what reinforcement learning is all about. In simple terms, it is learning through reinforcement. *Reinforcement*, as you know from general English or psychology, is the act of increasing or strengthening the choice to take a particular action in response to something, because of the perceived benefit of receiving higher rewards for taking that action. We humans are good at learning through reinforcement from a very young age. Those who have kids may be utilizing this fact more often to teach good habits to them. Nevertheless, we will all be able to relate to this, because not so long ago we all went through that phase of life! Say parents reward their kid with chocolate if the kid completes their homework on time after school every day. The kid *learns* the fact that he/she will receive chocolate (*a reward*) if he/she completes their homework every day. Therefore, this strengthens their decision to finish their homework every day to receive the chocolate. This process of learning to strengthen a particular choice of action, motivated by the reward they will receive for taking such an action, is called learning by reinforcement or reinforcement learning.

You might be thinking, *"Oh yeah. That human psychology sounds very familiar to me. But what has that got to do with machine learning or AI?"* Good thought. The concept of reinforcement learning was in fact inspired by behavioral psychology. It is at the nexus of several fields of research, the most important being computer science, mathematics, neuroscience, and psychology, as shown in the following diagram:

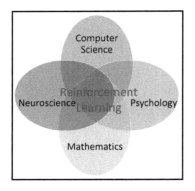

As we will soon realize, reinforcement learning is one of the most promising methods in machine learning leading towards AI. If all these terms are new to you, do not worry! Starting from the next paragraph, we will go over these terms and understand their relationship with each other to make you feel comfortable. If you already know these terms, it will be a refreshing read with a different perspective.

Understanding what AI means and what's in it in an intuitive way

The intelligence demonstrated by humans and animals is called *natural intelligence,* but the intelligence demonstrated by machines is called AI, for obvious reasons. We humans develop algorithms and technologies that provide intelligence to machines. Some of the greatest developments on this front are in the fields of machine learning, artificial neural networks, and deep learning. These fields collectively drive the development of AI. There are three main types of machine learning paradigms that have been developed to some reasonable level of maturity so far, and they are the following:

- Supervised learning
- Unsupervised learning
- Reinforcement learning

In the following diagram, you can get an intuitive picture of the field of AI. You can see that these learning paradigms are subsets of the field of machine learning, and machine learning itself is a subset/branch of AI:

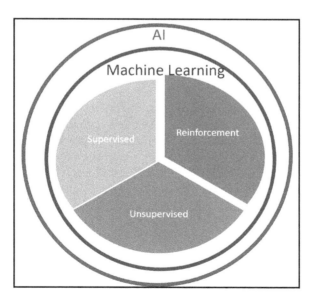

Supervised learning

Supervised learning is similar to how we would teach a kid to recognize someone or some object by name. We provide an input and a name/class label (*label* for short) associated with that input, and expect the machine to learn that input-to-label mapping. This might sound simple if we just want the machine to learn the input-to-label mapping for a few objects (like in object recognition-type tasks) or persons (like in face/voice/person recognition tasks), but what if we want a machine to learn about several thousand classes where each class may have several different variations in the input? For example, if the task is to recognize a person's face from image inputs, with a thousand other input images with faces to distinguish it from, the task might be complicated even for an adult. There might be several variations in the input images for the same person's face. The person may be wearing glasses in one of the input images, or wearing a hat in another, or sporting a different facial expression altogether. It is a much harder task for a machine to be able to see the input image, identify the face, and recognize it. With recent advancements in the field of deep learning, supervised classification tasks like these are no longer hard for machines. Machines can recognize faces, among several other things, at an unprecedented level of accuracy. For example, the DeepFace system (`https://research.fb.com/wp-content/uploads/2016/11/deepface-closing-the-gap-to-human-level-performance-in-face-verification.pdf`), developed by the Facebook AI research lab, reached an accuracy of 97.45% in face recognition on the Labelled Faces in the Wild dataset.

Unsupervised learning

Unsupervised learning is a form of learning in which there is no label provided to the learning algorithm along with the inputs, unlike the supervised learning paradigm. This class of learning algorithm is typically used to figure out patterns in the input data and cluster similar data together. A recent advancement in the field of deep learning introduced a new form of learning called Generative Adversarial Networks, which have gained massive popularity during the time this book was being written. If you are interested, you can learn a lot more about Generative Adversarial Networks from this video: `https://www.packtpub.com/big-data-and-business-intelligence/learning-generative-adversarial-networks-video`.

Reinforcement learning

Reinforcement learning is kind of a hybrid way of learning compared to supervised and unsupervised learning. As we learned at the start of this section, reinforcement learning is driven by a reward signal. In the case of the *kid with their homework* problem, the reward signal was the chocolate from their parents. In the machine learning world, a chocolate may not be enticing for a computer (well, we could program a computer to want chocolates, but why would we? Aren't kids enough?!), but a mere scalar value (a number) will do the trick! The reward signals are still human-specified in some way, signifying the intended goal of the task. For example, to train an agent to play Atari games using reinforcement learning, the scores from the games can be the reward signal. This makes reinforcement learning much easier (for humans and not for the machine!) because we don't have to label the button to be pressed at each point in the game to teach the machine how to play the game. Instead, we just ask the machine to learn on its own to maximize their score. Doesn't it sound fascinating that we could make a machine figure out how to play a game, or how to control a car, or how to do its homework all by itself, and all we have to do is just say how it did with a score? That is why we are learning about it in this chapter. You will develop some of those cool machines yourself in the upcoming chapters.

Practical reinforcement learning

Now that you have an intuitive understanding of what AI really means and the various classes of algorithm that drive its development, we will now focus on the practical aspects of building a reinforcement learning machine.

Here are the core concepts that you need to be aware of to develop reinforcement learning systems:

- Agent
- Rewards
- Environment
- State
- Value function
- Policy

Agent

In the reinforcement learning world, a machine is run or instructed by a (software) agent. The agent is the part of the machine that possesses intelligence and makes decisions on what to do next. You will come across the term "agent" several times as we dive deeper into reinforcement learning. Reinforcement learning is based on the reward hypothesis, which states that any goal can be described by the maximization of the expected cumulative reward. So, what is this reward exactly? That's what we'll discuss next.

Rewards

A reward, denoted by R_t, is usually a scalar quantity that is provided as feedback to the agent to drive its learning. The goal of the agent is to maximize the sum of the reward, and this signal indicates how well the agent is doing at time step t. The following examples of reward signals for different tasks may help you get a more intuitive understanding:

- For the Atari games we discussed before, or any computer games in general, the reward signal can be +1 for every increase in score and −1 for every decrease in score.
- For stock trading, the reward signal can be +1 for each dollar gained and −1 for each dollar lost by the agent.
- For driving a car in simulation, the reward signal can be +1 for every mile driven and −100 for every collision.
- Sometimes, the reward signal can be sparse. For example, for a game of chess or Go, the reward signal could be +1 if the agent wins the game and −1 if the agent loses the game. The reward is sparse because the agent receives the reward signal only after it completes one full game, not knowing how good each move it made was.

Environment

In the first chapter, we looked into the different environments provided by the OpenAI Gym toolkit. You might have been wondering why they were called environments instead of problems, or tasks, or something else. Now that you have progressed to this chapter, does it ring a bell in your head?

The environment is the platform that represents the problem or task that we are interested in, and with which the agent interacts. The following diagram shows the general reinforcement learning paradigm at the highest level of abstraction:

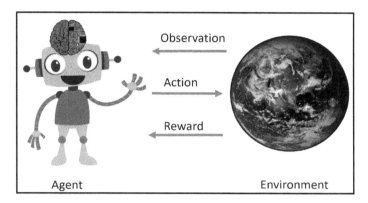

At each time step, denoted by t, the agent receives an observation O_t from the environment and then executes an action A_t, for which it receives a scalar reward R_t back from the environment, along with the next observation O_{t+1}, and then this process repeats until a terminal state is reached. What is an observation and what is a state? Let's look into that next.

State

As the agent interacts with an environment, the process results in a sequence of observations (O_i), actions (A_i), and rewards (R_i), as described previously. At some time step t, what the agent knows so far is the sequence of O_i, A_i, and R_i that it observed until time step t. It intuitively makes sense to call this the history:

$$H_t = \{O_1, A_1, R_1\}, \{O_2, A_2, R_2\}, \ldots \{O_t, A_t, R_t\}$$

What happens next at time step $t+1$ depends on the history. Formally, the information used to determine what happens next is called the *state*. Because it depends on the history up until that time step, it can be denoted as follows:

$$S_t = f(H_t),$$

Here, f denotes some function.

There is one subtle piece of information that is important for you to understand before we proceed. Let's have another look at the general representation of a reinforcement learning system:

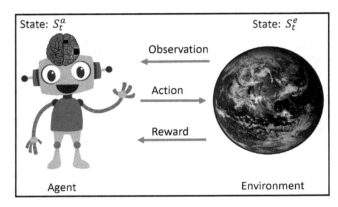

Now, you will notice that the two main entities in the system, the agent and the environment, each has its own representation of the state. The *environment state*, sometimes denoted by S_t^e, is the environment's own (private) representation, which the environment uses to pick the next observation and reward. This state is not usually visible/available to the agent. Likewise, the agent has its own internal representation of the state, sometimes denoted by S_t^a, which is the information used by the agent to base its actions on. Because this representation is internal to the agent, it is up to the agent to use any function to represent it. Typically, it is some function based on the history that the agent has observed so far. On a related note, a *Markov state* is a representation of the state using all the useful information from the history. By definition, using the Markov property, a state S_t is Markov or Markovian if, and only if, $\mathbb{P}[S_{t+1}|S_t] = \mathbb{P}[S_{t+1}|S_1, S_2, \ldots S_t]$, which means that *the future is independent of the past given the present*. In other words, such a state is a sufficient statistic of the future. Once the state is known, the history can be thrown away. Usually, the environment state, S_t^e, and the history, H_t, satisfy the Markov property.

In some cases, the environment may make its internal environmental state directly visible to the agent. Such environments are called *fully observable environments*. In cases where the agent cannot directly observe the environment state, the agent must construct its own state representation from what it observes. Such environments are called *partially observable environments*. For example, an agent playing poker can only observe the public cards and not the cards the other players possess. Therefore, it is a partially observed environment. Similarly, an autonomous car with just a camera does not know its absolute location in its environment, which makes the environment only partially observable.

In the next sections, we will learn about some of the key components of an agent.

Model

A model is an agent's representation of the environment. It is similar to the mental models we have about people and things around us. An agent uses its model of the environment to predict what will happen next. There are two key pieces to it:

- $\mathbb{P}$: The state transition model/probability
- $\mathbb{R}$: The reward model

The state transition model $\mathbb{P}$ is a probability distribution or a function that predicts the probability of ending up in a state S' in the next time step $t + 1$ given the state S and the action A at time step t. Mathematically, it is expressed as follows:

$$\mathbb{P}^A_{SS'} = \mathbb{P}[S_{t+1} = S' | S_t = S, A_t = A]$$

The agent uses the reward model $\mathbb{R}$ to predict the immediate next reward that it would get if it were to take action A while in state S at time step t. This expectation of the reward at the next time step $t + 1$ can be mathematically expressed as follows:

$$\mathbb{R}^A_S = \mathbb{E}[R_{t+1} | S_t = S, A_t = A]$$

Value function

A value function represents the agent's prediction of future rewards. There are two types of value function: state-value function and action-value function.

State-value function

A state-value function is a function that represents the agent's estimate of how good it is to be in a state s at time step t. It is denoted by $V(s)$ and is usually just called the *value function*. It represents the agent's prediction of the future reward it would get if it were to end up in state s at time step t. Mathematically, it can be represented as follows:

$$V_\pi(S) = \mathbb{E}[R_{t+1} + \gamma R_{t+2} + \gamma^2 R_{t+3} + \ldots | S_t = S]$$

What this expression means is that the value of state s under policy π is the expected sum of the discounted future rewards, where γ is the discount factor and is a real number in the range [0,1]. Practically, the discount factor is typically set to be in the range of [0.95,0.99]. The other new term is π, which is the policy of the agent.

Action-value function

The action-value function is a function that represents the agent's estimate of how good it is to take action a_t in state s_t. It is denoted by $Q(s_t, a_t)$. It is related to the state-value function by the following equation:

$$Q(S, A) = \mathbb{E}[r + \gamma V(S_{t+1})]$$

Policy

The policy denoted by π prescribes what action is to be taken given the state. It can be seen as a function that maps states to actions. There are two major types of policy: deterministic policies and stochastic policies.

A deterministic policy prescribes one action for a given state, that is, there is only one action, a, given s. Mathematically, it means $\pi(S) = A$.

A stochastic policy prescribes an action distribution given a state s at time step t, that is, there are multiple actions with a probability value for each action. Mathematically, it means $\pi(A|S) = \mathbb{P}[A_t = A | S_t = S]$.

Agents following different policies may exhibit different behaviors in the same environment.

Markov Decision Process

A **Markov Decision Process** (**MDP**) provides a formal framework for reinforcement learning. It is used to describe a fully observable environment where the outcomes are partly random and partly dependent on the actions taken by the agent or the decision maker. The following diagram is the progression of a Markov Process into a Markov Decision Process through the Markov Reward Process:

These stages can be described as follows:

- A **Markov Process** (or a *markov chain)* is a sequence of random states s1, s2,... that obeys the *Markov property.* In simple terms, it is a random process without any memory about its history.

- A **Markov Reward Process** (**MRP**) is a *Markov Process (*also called a *Markov chain)* with values.

- A **Markov Decision Process** is a *Markov Reward Process* with decisions.

Planning with dynamic programming

Dynamic programming is a very general method to efficiently solve problems that can be decomposed into overlapping sub-problems. If you have used any type of recursive function in your code, you might have already got some preliminary flavor of dynamic programming. Dynamic programming, in simple terms, tries to cache or store the results of sub-problems so that they can be used later if required, instead of computing the results again.

Okay, so how is that relevant here, you may ask. Well, they are pretty useful for solving a fully defined MDP, which means that an agent can find the most optimal way to act in an environment to achieve the highest reward using dynamic programming if it has full knowledge of the MDP! In the following table, you will find a concise summary of what the inputs and outputs are when we are interested in sequential prediction or control:

Task/objective	Input	Output
Prediction	MDP or MRP and policy π	Value function v
Control	MDP	Optimal value function v and optimal policy π

Monte Carlo learning and temporal difference learning

At this point, we understand that it is very useful for an agent to learn the state value function $V_\pi(S)$, which informs the agent about the long-term value of being in state s so that the agent can decide if it is a good state to be in or not. The **Monte Carlo** (**MC**) and **Temporal Difference** (**TD**) learning methods enable an agent to learn that!

The goal of MC and TD learning is to learn the value functions from the agent's experience as the agent follows its policy π.

The following table summarizes the value estimate's update equation for the MC and TD learning methods:

Learning method	State-value function
Monte Carlo	$V(S_t) = V(S_t) + \alpha(G_t - V(S_t))$
Temporal Difference	$V(S_t) = V(S_t) + \alpha(R_t + \gamma V(S_{t+1}) - V(S_t))$

MC learning updates the value towards the **actual return** G_t, which is the total discounted reward from time step t. This means that $G_t = R_{t+1} + \gamma R_{t+2} + \cdots$ until the end. It is important to note that we can calculate this value only after the end of the sequence, whereas TD learning (TD(0) to be precise), updates the value towards the *estimated return* given by $R_{t+1} + \gamma V(S_{t+1})$, which can be calculated after every step.

SARSA and Q-learning

It is also very useful for an agent to learn the action value function $Q_\pi(S, A)$, which informs the agent about the long-term value of taking action A in state S so that the agent can take those actions that will maximize its expected, discounted future reward. The SARSA and Q-learning algorithms enable an agent to learn that! The following table summarizes the update equation for the SARSA algorithm and the Q-learning algorithm:

Learning method	Action-value function
SARSA	$Q(S, A) = Q(S, A) + \alpha(R + \gamma Q(S', A') - Q(S, A))$
Q-learning	$Q(S, A) = Q(S, A) + \alpha(R + \gamma \max_{A' \in A} Q(S', A') - Q(S, A))$

SARSA is so named because of the sequence State->Action->Reward->State'->Action' that the algorithm's update step depends on. The description of the sequence goes like this: the agent, in state S, takes an action A and gets a reward R, and ends up in the next state S', after which the agent decides to take an action A' in the new state. Based on this experience, the agent can update its estimate of Q(S,A).

Q-learning is a popular off-policy learning algorithm, and it is similar to SARSA, except for one thing. Instead of using the Q value estimate for the new state and the action that the agent took in that new state, it uses the Q value estimate that corresponds to the action that leads to the *maximum* obtainable Q value from that new state, S'.

Deep reinforcement learning

With a basic understanding of reinforcement learning, you are now in a better state (hopefully you are not in a strictly Markov state where you have forgotten the history/things you have learned so far) to understand the basics of the cool new suite of algorithms that have been rocking the field of AI in recent times.

Deep reinforcement learning emerged naturally when people made advancements in the deep learning field and applied them to reinforcement learning. We learned about the state-value function, action-value function, and policy. Let's briefly look at how they can be represented mathematically or realized through computer code. The state-value function $V(S)$ is a real-value function that takes the current state S as the input and outputs a real-value number (such as 4.57). This number is the agent's prediction of how good it is to be in state S and the agent keeps updating the value function based on the new experiences it gains. Likewise, the action-value function $Q(S, A)$ is also a real-value function, which takes action A as an input in addition to state S, and outputs a real number. One way to represent these functions is using neural networks because neural networks are universal function approximators, which are capable of representing complex, non-linear functions. For an agent trying to play a game of Atari by just looking at the images on the screen (like we do), state S could be the pixel values of the image on the screen. In such cases, we could use a deep neural network with convolutional layers to extract the visual features from the state/image, and then a few fully connected layers to finally output $V(S)$ or $Q(S, A)$, depending on which function we want to approximate.

 Recall from the earlier sections of this chapter that $V(S)$ is the state-value function and provides an estimate of the value of being in state S, and $Q(S, A)$ is the action-value function, which provides an estimate of the value of each action given the state.

If we do this, then we are doing deep reinforcement learning! Easy enough to understand? I hope so. Let's look at some other ways in which we can use deep learning in reinforcement learning.

Recall that a policy is represented as $\pi(S) = A$ in the case of deterministic policies, and as $\pi(A|S) = \mathbb{P}[A_t = A | S_t = S]$ in the case of stochastic policies, where action A could be discrete (such as "move left," "move right," or "move straight ahead") or continuous values (such as "0.05" for acceleration, "0.67" for steering, and so on), and they can be single or multi-dimensional. Therefore, a policy can be a complicated function at times! It might have to take in a multi-dimensional state (such as an image) as input and output a multi-dimensional vector of probabilities as output (in the case of stochastic policies). So, this does look like it will be a monster function, doesn't it? Yes it does. That's where deep neural networks come to the rescue! We could approximate an agent's policy using a deep neural network and directly learn to update the policy (by updating the parameters of the deep neural network). This is called policy optimization-based deep reinforcement learning and it has been shown to be quite efficient in solving several challenging control problems, especially in robotics.

So in summary, deep reinforcement learning is the application of deep learning to reinforcement learning and so far, researchers have applied deep learning to reinforcement learning successfully in two ways. One way is using deep neural networks to approximate the value functions, and the other way is to use a deep neural network to represent the policy.

These ideas have been known from the early days, when researchers were trying to use neural networks as value function approximators, even back in 2005. But it rose to stardom only recently because although neural networks or other non-linear value function approximators can better represent the complex values of environment states and actions, they were prone to instability and often led to sub-optimal functions. Only recently have researchers such as Volodymyr Mnih and his colleagues at DeepMind (now part of Google) figured out the trick of stabilizing the learning and trained agents with deep, non-linear function approximators that converged to near-optimal value functions. In the later chapters of this book, we will in fact reproduce some of their then-groundbreaking results, which surpassed human Atari game playing capabilities!

Practical applications of reinforcement and deep reinforcement learning algorithms

Until recently, practical applications of reinforcement learning and deep reinforcement learning were limited, due to sample complexity and instability. But, these algorithms proved to be quite powerful in solving some really hard practical problems. Some of them are listed here to give you an idea:

- **Learning to play video games better than humans**: This news has probably reached you by now. Researchers at DeepMind and others developed a series of algorithms, starting with DeepMind's Deep-Q-Network, or DQN for short, which reached human-level performance in playing Atari games. We will actually be implementing this algorithm in a later chapter of this book! In essence, it is a deep variant of the Q-learning algorithm we briefly saw in this chapter, with a few changes that increased the speed of learning and the stability. It was able to reach human-level performance in terms of game scores after several games. What is more impressive is that the same algorithm achieved this level of play without any game-specific fine-tuning or changes!

- **Mastering the game of Go**: Go is a Chinese game that has challenged AI for several decades. It is played on a full-size 19 x 19 board and is orders of magnitude more complex than chess because of the large number (10^{172}) of possible board positions. Until recently, no AI algorithm or software was able to play anywhere close to the level of humans at this game. AlphaGo—the AI agent from DeepMind that uses deep reinforcement learning and Monte Carlo tree search—changed this all and beat the human world champions Lee Sedol (4-1) and Fan Hui (5-0). DeepMind released more advanced versions of their AI agent, named AlphaGO Zero (which uses zero human knowledge and learned to play all by itself!) and AlphaZero (which could play the games of Go, chess, and Shogi!), all of which used deep reinforcement learning as the core algorithm.
- **Helping AI win Jeopardy!**: IBM's Watson—an AI system developed by IBM, which came to fame by beating humans at Jeopardy!—used an extension of TD learning to create its *daily-double wagering* strategies that helped it to win against human champions.
- **Robot locomotion and manipulation:** Both reinforcement learning and deep reinforcement learning have enabled the control of complex robots, both for locomotion and navigation. Several recent works from the researchers at UC Berkeley have shown how, using deep reinforcement, they train policies that offer vision and control for robotic manipulation tasks and generate join actuations for making a complex bipedal humanoid walk and run.

Summary

In this chapter, we discussed how an agent interacts with an environment by taking an action based on the observation it receives from the environment, and the environment responds to the agent's action with an (optional) reward and the next observation.

With a concise understanding of the foundations of reinforcement learning, we went deeper to understand what deep reinforcement learning is, and uncovered the fact that we could use deep neural networks to represent value functions and policies. Although this chapter was a little heavy on notation and definitions, hopefully it laid a strong foundation for us to develop some cool agents in the upcoming chapters. In the next chapter, we will consolidate our learning in the first two chapters and put it to use by laying out the groundwork to train an agent to solve some interesting problems.

3
Getting Started with OpenAI Gym and Deep Reinforcement Learning

The introduction chapters gave you a good insight into the OpenAI Gym toolkit and reinforcement learning in general. In this chapter, we will jump right in and get you and your computer ready with all the required preparation, installations, and configurations to start developing your agents. More importantly, you will also find instructions to access the book's code repositories, which contain all the code you will need to follow this book in its entirety, along with several other code examples, useful instructions, and updates.

In this chapter, we will cover the following topics:

- Accessing the code repository for this book
- Creating an Anaconda environment for working through this book
- How to install and configure OpenAI Gym and dependencies on your system
- Installing tools, libraries, and dependencies for deep reinforcement learning

Code repository, setup, and configuration

First of all, let's make sure you have all the information to access the code repository for this book. The source code provides you with all the necessary code samples that we will discuss in this book and provides additional details on how to set up and run the training or testing scripts for each chapter specifically. To get started, head to the book's code repository on GitHub at the following link: `https://github.com/PacktPublishing/Hands-On-Intelligent-Agents-with-OpenAI-Gym`.

Create a GitHub account if you do not already have one and fork the repository so that it is added to your own GitHub account. This is recommended as it allows you to make any changes to the code you prefer while following along, and also allow you to send a pull request when you have something cool to show and be featured on the book's blog!

You can clone the repository to a folder named `HOIAWOG` in your home directory using the following command:

```
git clone
https://github.com/PacktPublishing/Hands-On-Intelligent-Agents-with-OpenAI-
Gym.git ~/HOIAWOG
```

Note that the book assumes that you have set up the code repository at this particular location: `~/HOIAWOG`. If you happen to change it for some reason, be sure to remember it and change some of the commands in the book accordingly.

If you are wondering why the directory name was chosen to be `HOIAWOG`, do not think anymore. It is an acronym for this book's title: **Hands On Intelligent Agents With OpenAI Gym (HOIAWOG)**!

The book's code repository will be kept up to date to take care of any changes in the external libraries or other software, so that the intelligent agent implementation code and other code samples are functional. Occasionally, new code and updates will also be added to help you explore developing intelligent agents further. To stay on top of the changes and be notified of updates, it is recommended you star the book's code repository from your GitHub account.

Toward the end of `Chapter 1`, *Introduction to Intelligent Agents and Learning Environments*, we did a quick install of OpenAI Gym to get a sneak peak into the Gym. That was a minimal install, to get us started quickly. In the next section, we will go over the installation step by step and make sure everything you need to develop agents using the Gym is installed and configured properly. We will go over the different levels and methods of installation here so that you are aware of the installation process in general. You may end up modifying your system, or using another system at home or work, or changing your computer altogether. This section will make sure that you can get everything set up in the right way. Feel free to pick the installation method that is suitable for your use cases.

Prerequisites

The only main prerequisite for using OpenAI Gym is Python 3.5+. To make further development easy and organized, we will use the Anaconda Python distribution. For those of you who are not familiar with Anaconda, it is a Python distribution (although a distribution for the R language is also available) that includes hundreds of popular machine learning and data science packages and comes with an easy-to-use package and virtual environment manager called *conda*. The good thing is that the Anaconda Python distribution is available for Linux, macOS, and Windows! Another main reason to use the Anaconda distribution is that it helps in easily creating, installing, managing, and upgrading an isolated Python virtual environment. This makes sure the code we learn about and develop in this book produces the same results, irrespective of the operating system we use. This will relieve you from solving dependency issues or library version mismatch issues that you would have had to handle manually if you were not using a Python distribution such as Anaconda. You will find that it just works, which is nice and cool. Let's get started and install the Anaconda Python distribution.

Open a command prompt or Terminal and enter the following:

```
praveen@ubuntu:~$wget
http://repo.continuum.io/archive/Anaconda3-4.3.0-Linux-x86_64.sh -O
~/anaconda.sh
```

This command uses the `wget` tool to fetch/download the installation script for Anaconda version 3-4.3 and saves it as `anaconda.sh` in your home directory. This command should work on macOS and Linux (Ubuntu, Kubuntu, and so on), which come with the `wget` tool pre-installed. Note that we are downloading a specific version of Anaconda (3-4.3). This will make sure we have the same configuration throughout this book. Do not worry if this is not the latest version available. You can always upgrade the distribution later using this command:

```
conda update conda
```

`anaconda.sh` is a shell script that has all the things that are needed to install Anaconda on your system! If you are interested, you can open it using your favorite text editor to see how cleverly the binaries, the installation process instructions, and the shell commands have been all lumped together into a single file.

Let's now install the Anaconda Python distribution under your home directory. The following installation process is carefully laid out to make sure it works both on Linux and macOS systems. Before you enter the command, you should be aware of one thing. The following command will run the installer in *silent mode*. This means that it will use the default installation parameters and go ahead with the installation, without asking you yes/no for each and every configuration. This also means that you agree to the Anaconda distribution's licensing terms. In case you want to manually go through the installation process step by step, run the following command without the arguments -b and -f:

```
praveen@ubuntu:~$bash ~/anaconda.sh -b -f -p $HOME/anaconda
```

Wait for the installation process to complete and then we are done!

To start using *conda* and the other goodness in the Anaconda Python distribution, we should make sure that your system knows where to find the Anaconda tools. Let's add the Anaconda binaries directory by appending its path to the PATH environment variable, as shown here:

```
praveen@ubuntu:~$export PATH=$HOME/anaconda/bin:$PATH
```

I strongly advise you to add this line to the end of your ~/.bashrc file so that whenever you open a new bash terminal, the Anaconda tools are accessible.

You can type the following command to make sure the installation was successful:

```
praveen@ubuntu:~$conda list
```

This command will just print the list of packages available in your default environment.

Creating the conda environment

Now that we have set up Anaconda, let's use conda to create a Python virtual environment, which we will use throughout this book.

 If you prefer a one-click install setup and do not want to go through the installation step by step, a greatly simplified way to create the environment with all the necessary packages installed is using the conda_env.yaml conda environment configuration file available in the book's code repository. You can simply run the following command from the book's code repository directory (HOIAWOG) which we created in the previous section:
```
praveen@ubuntu:~/HOIAWOG$ conda create -f conda_env.yaml
-n rl_gym_book
```

At this point, we will just create a new minimal environment to proceed. Enter the following command in a Terminal:

```
praveen@ubuntu:~$conda create --name rl_gym_book python=3.5
```

This will create a conda environment named `rl_gym_book` with a Python3 interpreter. It will print some information about what is going to be downloaded and the packages that will be installed. You may be prompted with a yes/no question as to whether you want to proceed. Type `y` and hit *Enter*. Once the environment creation process is complete, you can activate that environment using the following command:

```
praveen@ubuntu:~$source activate rl_gym_book
```

You will now see your command prompt's prefix changing to look something like this, to signify that you are inside the `rl_gym_book` virtual environment:

```
(rl_gym_book) praveen@ubuntu:~$
```

You can use this as an indicator as you progress through the chapters to know when commands have to be entered inside this environment and when commands can be entered outside the environment. To exit or deactivate the environment, you can simply type this:

```
praveen@ubuntu:~$source deactivate
```

Minimal install – the quick and easy way

The OpenAI Gym is a Python package and is available in the **Python Package Index (PyPI)** repository. You can use `easy_install` or `pip` to fetch and install packages from the PyPI repository. `Pip` is a package management tool for Python, which most of you might be familiar with if you have experience scripting in Python:

```
(rl_gym_book) praveen@ubuntu:~$pip install gym
```

That's it!

Let's quickly check the installation actually went fine by running the following code. Create a `gym_install_test.py` file under the `~/rl_gym_book` directory, type/copy the following code into it, and save it. You can also download the `gym_quick_install_test.py` file from the book's code repository:

```
#! /usr/bin/env python
import gym
env = gym.make("MountainCar-v0") # Create a MountainCar environment
env.reset()
```

```
for _ in range(2000): # Run for 2000 steps
    env.render()
    env.step(env.action_space.sample()) # Send a random action
```

Let's try running the script:

```
(rl_gym_book) praveen@ubuntu:~/HOIAWOG$python gym_quick_install_test.py
```

This should pop up a new window showing a car/carton and a v-shaped mountain, and you should see the car moving left and right randomly. The mountain car window should look something like this screenshot:

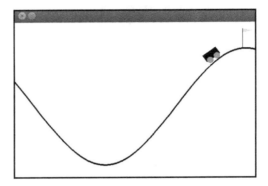

You will also see some values printed out to the console/Terminal that look like this:

```
(array([-0.53439364,  0.05070148]), -1.0, True, {})
(array([-0.48461121,  0.04978243]), -1.0, True, {})
(array([-0.43512052,  0.04949069]), -1.0, True, {})
(array([-0.38728565,  0.04783487]), -1.0, True, {})
(array([-0.33944487,  0.04784078]), -1.0, True, {})
(array([-0.29291606,  0.04652882]), -1.0, True, {})
(array([-0.24898253,  0.04393353]), -1.0, True, {})
(array([-0.20688342,  0.04209911]), -1.0, True, {})
(array([-0.16781806,  0.03906536]), -1.0, True, {})
(array([-0.1299425 ,  0.03787556]), -1.0, True, {})
(array([-0.09337938,  0.03656312]), -1.0, True, {})
(array([-0.05921881,  0.03416058]), -1.0, True, {})
(array([-0.02751888,  0.03169993]), -1.0, True, {})
(array([0.00068956, 0.02820844]), -1.0, True, {})
(array([0.02639801, 0.02570845]), -1.0, True, {})
(array([0.05061429, 0.02421628]), -1.0, True, {})
(array([0.07335933, 0.02274505]), -1.0, True, {})
(array([0.09466468, 0.02130535]), -1.0, True, {})
(array([0.11357016, 0.01890549]), -1.0, True, {})
(array([0.12911936, 0.01554919]), -1.0, True, {})
(array([0.14335377, 0.01423442]), -1.0, True, {})
(array([0.15631584, 0.01296207]), -1.0, True, {})
>>>
```

If you saw this happening, then rejoice! You now have a (minimal) setup of OpenAI Gym!

Complete install of OpenAI Gym learning environments

Not all environments are usable with the minimal installation. To be able to use most or all the environments available in the Gym, we will go through the installation of the dependencies and build OpenAI Gym from the latest source code on the master branch.

To get started, we will need to install the required system packages first. Next, you will find instructions for both Ubuntu and macOS. Choose the set of instructions based on your development platform.

Instructions for Ubuntu

The following commands were tested on Ubuntu 14.04 LTS and on Ubuntu 16.04 LTS, but should work in other/future Ubuntu releases as well.

Let's install the system packages needed by running the following command on the Terminal/console:

```
sudo apt-get update
```

```
sudo apt-get install -y build-essential cmake python-dev python-numpy
python-opengl libboost-all-dev zlib1g-dev libsdl2-dev libav-tools xorg-dev
libjpeg-dev swig
```

This command will install the prerequisite system packages. Note that the $-y$ flag will automatically say yes to confirm the installation of the package, without asking you to confirm manually. If you want to review the packages that are going to be installed for some reason, you may run the command without the flag.

Instructions for macOS

On macOS, the number of additional system packages that need to be installed is less than with Ubuntu systems.

Run the following commands from a Terminal:

```
brew install cmake boost sdl2 swig wget
```

```
brew install boost-python --with-python3
```

These commands will install the prerequisite system packages.

The robotics and control environment in OpenAI Gym make use of **Multi-Joint dynamics with Contact (MuJoCo)** as the physics engine to simulate the rigid body dynamics and other features. We briefly had a look at MuJoCo environments in `Chapter 1`, *Introduction to Intelligent Agents and Learning Environments* and learned that you can develop algorithms that can make a 2D robot walk, run, swim, or hop, or a 3D multi-legged robot walk or run using the MuJoCo environment. MuJoCo is a proprietary engine and therefore needs a license. Fortunately, we can get a free 30-day license!

Also, if you are a student, they offer a 1 year free MuJoCo Pro personal license, which is even better! For others, after the 30 days, sadly it costs a hefty sum (~$500 USD) for a 1 -year license. We will not be using the MuJoCo environments in this book because not everyone may be able to get hold of a license. You can always apply what you learn in this book regarding other environments to the MuJoCo environments if you have a license. If you plan to use these environments, you will have to follow the instructions in the MuJoCo installation section next. If not, you can skip it and go to the next section to set up OpenAI Gym.

MuJoCo installation

I hope you read the previous information box. MuJoCo is one odd library that we will encounter in this book because, unlike other libraries and software we use as part of this book, MuJoCo requires a license to use. The Python interface for MuJoCo, available in the Gym library, is compatible only with MuJoCo version 1.31 as of the time this chapter was written, even though the latest available MuJoCo version is higher (1.50 at the time of writing this chapter). Follow these two steps to set up MuJoCo for use with OpenAI Gym environments:

1. Download MuJoCo 1.31 for your platform (Linux/macOS) from this URL: `https://www.roboti.us/index.html`
2. Obtain a MuJoCo Pro license from this URL: `https://www.roboti.us/license.html`

Completing the OpenAI Gym setup

Let's update our version of pip first:

```
(rl_gym_book) praveen@ubuntu:~$ pip install --ignore-installed pip
```

Then, let's download the source code of OpenAI Gym from the GitHub repository into our home folder:

```
(rl_gym_book) praveen@ubuntu:~$cd ~
```

```
(rl_gym_book) praveen@ubuntu:~$git clone https://github.com/openai/gym.git
```

```
(rl_gym_book) praveen@ubuntu:~$cd gym
```

 If you get an error saying `git command not found` or something similar, you might have to install Git. On Ubuntu systems, you can install it by running this command, `sudo apt-get install git`. On macOS, if you don't have Git installed already, it will prompt you to install it when you run the `git clone` command.

We are now in the final stage of a complete Gym installation! If you got a MuJoCo license and followed the MuJoCo installation instructions successfully, then you can go ahead and complete a full installation by running the following command:

```
(rl_gym_book) praveen@ubuntu:~/gym$pip install -e '.[all]'
```

If you did not install MuJoCo, then this command will return errors. We will be installing the Gym environments that we will be using, other than MuJoCo (which requires a license to use). Make sure that you are still in the `gym` directory under your `home` folder, and also make sure that you are still inside the `rl_gym_book` conda environment. Your prompt should include the `rl_gym_book` prefix as follows, where `~/gym` means that the prompt is at the gym directory under the home folder:

(rl_gym_book) praveen@ubuntu:~/gym$

Here is a table summarizing the installation commands for installing the environments that have been discussed in `Chapter 1`, *Introduction to Intelligent Agents and Learning Environments*.

Environment	Installation command
Atari	`pip install -e '.[atari]'`

Box2D	`pip install -e '.[box2d]'`
	`conda install -c https://conda.anaconda.org/kne`
	`pybox2d`

Classic control	`pip install -e '.[classic_control]'`
MuJoCo (requires license)	`pip install -e '.[mujoco]'`
Robotics (requires license)	`pip install -e '.[robotics]'`

Let's go ahead and install the environments we do not need a license to use. Run the following commands to install Atarti, Box2D, and the classic control environments:

```
(rl_gym_book) praveen@ubuntu:~/gym$pip install -e '.[atari]'

(rl_gym_book) praveen@ubuntu:~/gym$pip install -e '.[box2d]'

(rl_gym_book) praveen@ubuntu:~/gym$conda install -c
https://conda.anaconda.org/kne pybox2d

(rl_gym_book) praveen@ubuntu:~/gym$pip install -e '.[classic_control]'
```

We are all set! We'll quickly run a check to make sure the installation went fine. Copy and paste the following code snippet into a file named `test_box2d.py` under the `~/rl_gym_book` directory:

```python
#!/usr/bin/env python
import gym
env = gym.make('BipedalWalker-v2')
env.reset()
for _ in range(1000):
    env.render()
    env.step(env.action_space.sample())
```

Run that code using the following commands:

```
(rl_gym_book) praveen@ubuntu:~/gym$cd ~/rl_gym_book

(rl_gym_book) praveen@ubuntu:~/rl_gym_book$python test_box2d.py
```

You will see a window pop up that shows the BipedalWalker-v2 environment and the walker trying to randomly perform some actions:

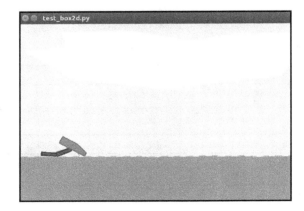

So, we have the Gym environment set up. What's next, you may ask. In the next section, we will set up the tools and libraries we need to develop deep reinforcement learning agents to train in these environments!

Installing tools and libraries needed for deep reinforcement learning

Chapter 2, *Reinforcement Learning and Deep Reinforcement Learning*, prepped you with the basics of reinforcement learning. With that theoretical background, we will be able to implement some cool algorithms. Before that, we will make sure we have the required tools and libraries at our disposal.

We can actually write cool reinforcement learning algorithms in Python without using any higher-level libraries. However, when we start to use function approximators for the value functions or the policy, and especially if we use deep neural networks as the function approximators, it is better to use highly optimized deep learning libraries instead of writing our own routines. A deep learning library is the major tool/library that we will need to install. There are different libraries out there today: PyTorch, TensorFlow, Caffe, Chainer, MxNet, and CNTK, to name a few. Each library has its own philosophy, merits, and demerits, depending on the use cases. We will be using PyTorch for developing the deep reinforcement learning algorithms in this book, due to its simplicity of use and dynamic graph definition. The algorithms we will discuss and the way we approach the implementation in this book will be explained in such a way that you can easily re-implement them using the framework of your choice.

If you do not have a GPU on your machine, or if you do not plan to use your GPU for training, you may skip the GPU driver installation steps and can install a CPU-only binary version of PyTorch using the following conda command:

```
(rl_gym_book) praveen@ubuntu:~$ conda install pytorch-cpu torchvision -c
pytorch
```

Note that you will *not* be able to accelerate the training of some of the agents we will develop as part of this book, which can utilize a GPU for faster training.

Installing prerequisite system packages

Let's begin by making sure we have the latest package versions from the Ubuntu upstream repositories. We can do that by running the following commands:

```
sudo apt-get update
```

```
sudo apt-get upgrade
```

Next, we will install the prerequisite packages. Note

hat some of these packages may already have been installed on your system, but it is good to make sure we have them all:

```
sudo apt-get install -y gfortran pkg-config software-properties-common
```

Installing Compute Unified Device Architecture (CUDA)

If you do not have an Nvidia GPU or if you have an older Nvidia GPU that does not support CUDA, you can skip this step and move on to the next section, where we go over the PyTorch installation:

1. Download the latest CUDA driver for your Nvidia GPU from the official Nvidia website here: https://developer.nvidia.com/cuda-downloads.
2. Choose **Linux** under the operating system and your architecture (mostly x86_64), and then choose your Linux OS distribution (Ubuntu) version 14.04, 16.04, or 18.04, depending on your version, and select **deb(local)** as the installer type. That will download the cuda local installation file, named something like cuda-repo-ubuntu1604-8-0-local_8.0.44-1_amd64. Note your cuda version (8.0 in this case). We will use this CUDA version later while installing PyTorch.
3. You can then follow the instructions or run the following command to install CUDA:

```
sudo dpkg -i cuda-repo-ubuntu*.deb
```

```
sudo apt-get update
```

```
sudo apt-get install -y cuda
```

If all goes well, you should now have Cuda successfully installed. To quickly check to see that everything went fine, run the following command:

```
nvcc -V
```

This will print out the Cuda version information, similar to the output shown in the following screenshot. Note that your output may be different, depending on the version of Cuda you installed:

If you got an output similar to this, it's good news!

You may go ahead and install the latest **CUDA Deep Neural Network (cuDNN)** on your system. We will not cover the installation steps in this book, but the installation steps are straightforward and listed on the Nvidia official CuDNN download page here: https:// developer.nvidia.com/rdp/form/cudnn-download-survey. Note that you need to register for a free Nvidia developer account to download it.

Installing PyTorch

We are now ready to install PyTorch! Fortunately, it is as simple as running the following command inside our rl_gym_book conda environment:

```
(rl_gym_book) praveen@ubuntu:~$ conda install pytorch torchvision -c pytorch
```

Note that this command will install PyTorch with CUDA 8.0. You noted the CUDA version that you installed before, and the command may change slightly depending on which CUDA version you installed. For example, if you installed CUDA 9.1, the command to install will be this:

```
conda install pytorch torchvision cuda91 -c pytorch
```

You can find the updated command to install at http://pytorch.org based on your OS, package manager (conda or pip or from source), Python version (we use 3.5), and CUDA version.

That's it! Let's quickly try importing the PyTorch library and make sure it works. Type or copy the following lines of code into a file named `pytorch_test.py` under the `~/rl_gym_book` directory:

```python
#!/usr/bin/env python
import torch
t = torch.Tensor(3,3) # Create a 3,3 Tensor
print(t)
```

Run this script inside the `rl_gym_book` conda environment. The following screenshot is provided as an example:

```
praveen@ubuntu: ~/rl_gym_book
(rl_gym_book) praveen@ubuntu:~/rl_gym_book$ python pytorch_test.py

1.00000e-36 *
  2.9928  0.0000  0.0000
  0.0000  0.1263  0.0000
  0.1326  0.0000  0.0000
[torch.FloatTensor of size 3x3]

(rl_gym_book) praveen@ubuntu:~/rl_gym_book$
```

Note that you may see different values for the tensor, and you may see different values when you run the script another time. It is because of the torch. The `Tensor()` function generates a random tensor of the given shape, (3, 3) in our case. PyTorch follows similar syntax to NumPy. If you are familiar with NumPy, you can pick up PyTorch easily. If you are not familiar with NumPy or PyTorch, it is advised that you follow the official PyTorch tutorial to get yourself acquainted with it.

You may notice that the folder name used in some of the sample console screenshots is `read rl_gym_book` rather than HOIAWOG. Both these directory names are interchangeable. In fact, they are symbolic links pointing to the same directory.

Summary

In this chapter, we went through the step-by-step setup process to install and configure our development environment using conda, OpenAI Gym, and Pytorch! This chapter helped us make sure that we have all the required tools and libraries installed to start developing our agents in Gym environments. In the next chapter, we will explore the features of Gym environments to understand how they work, and how we can use them to train our agents. In Chapter 5, *Implementing Your First Learning Agent – Solving the Mountain Car Problem*, we will jump right into developing our first reinforcement learning agent to solve the mountain car problem! We will then gradually move on and implement more sophisticated reinforcement learning algorithms in the subsequent chapters.

4
Exploring the Gym and its Features

Now that you have a working setup, we will start exploring the various features and options provided by the Gym toolkit. This chapter will walk you through some of the commonly used environments, the tasks they solve, and what it would take for your agent to master a task.

In this chapter, we will explore the following topics:

- Exploring the various types of Gym environment
- Understanding the structure of the reinforcement learning loop
- Understanding the different observation and action spaces

Exploring the list of environments and nomenclature

Let's start by picking an environment and understanding the Gym interface. You may already be familiar with the basic function calls to create a Gym environment from the previous chapters, where we used them to test our installations. Here, we will formally go through them.

Let's activate the `rl_gym_book` conda environment and open a Python prompt. The first step is to import the Gym Python module using the following line of code:

```
import gym
```

We can now use the `gym.make` method to create an environment from the available list of environments. You may be asking how to find the list of Gym environments available on your system. We will create a small utility script to generate the list of environments so that you can refer to it later when you need to. Let's create a script named `list_gym_envs.py` under the `~/rl_gym_book/ch4` directory with the following contents:

```python
#!/usr/bin/env python
from gym import envs
env_names = [spec.id for spec in envs.registry.all()]
for name in sorted(env_names):
 print(name)
```

This script will print the names of all the environments available through your Gym installation, sorted alphabetically. You can run this script using the following command to see the names of the environments installed and available in your system:

(rl_gym_book) praveen@ubntu:~/rl_gym_book/ch4$python list_gym_envs.py

You will get an output like this. Note that only the first few environment names are shown in it. They may be different, depending on the environments you installed on your system based on what we discussed in Chapter 3, *Getting Started with OpenAI Gym and Deep Reinforcement Learning*:

```
(rl_gym_book) praveen@ubuntu:~/rl_gym_book/ch4$ python list_gym_envs.py
Acrobot-v1
AirRaid-ram-v0
AirRaid-ram-v4
AirRaid-ramDeterministic-v0
AirRaid-ramDeterministic-v4
AirRaid-ramNoFrameskip-v0
AirRaid-ramNoFrameskip-v4
AirRaid-v0
AirRaid-v4
AirRaidDeterministic-v0
AirRaidDeterministic-v4
AirRaidNoFrameskip-v0
AirRaidNoFrameskip-v4
Alien-ram-v0
Alien-ram-v4
Alien-ramDeterministic-v0
Alien-ramDeterministic-v4
Alien-ramNoFrameskip-v0
Alien-ramNoFrameskip-v4
Alien-v0
Alien-v4
AlienDeterministic-v0
AlienDeterministic-v4
AlienNoFrameskip-v0
AlienNoFrameskip-v4
Amidar-ram-v0
Amidar-ram-v4
Amidar-ramDeterministic-v0
Amidar-ramDeterministic-v4
Amidar-ramNoFrameskip-v0
Amidar-ramNoFrameskip-v4
Amidar-v0
Amidar-v4
AmidarDeterministic-v0
```

From the list of environment names, you may note that there are similar names, with some variations. For example, there are eight different variations for the Alien environment. Let's try to understand the nomenclature before we pick one and start using it.

Nomenclature

The presence of the word *ram* in the environment name means that the observation returned by the environment is the contents of the **Random Access Memory (RAM)** of the Atari console on which the game was designed to run.

The presence of the word *deterministic* in the environment names means that the actions sent to the environment by the agent are performed repeatedly for a *deterministic/fixed* duration of four frames, and then the resulting state is returned.

The presence of the word *NoFrameskip* means that the actions sent to the environment by the agent are performed once and the resulting state is returned immediately, without skipping any frames in-between.

By default, if *deterministic* and *NoFrameskip* are not included in the environment name, the action sent to the environment is repeatedly performed for a duration of n frames, where n is uniformly sampled from {2,3,4}.

The letter v followed by a number in the environment name represents the version of the environment. This is to make sure that any change to the environment implementation is reflected in its name so that the results obtained by an algorithm/agent in an environment are comparable to the results obtained by another algorithm/agent without any discrepancies.

Let's understand this nomenclature by looking at the Atari Alien environment. The various options available are listed with a description as follows:

Version name	Description
Alien-ram-v0	Observation is the RAM contents of the Atari machine with a total size of 128 bytes and the action sent to the environment is repeatedly performed for a duration of n frames, where n is uniformly sampled from {2,3,4}.
Alien-ram-v4	Observation is the RAM contents of the Atari machine with a total size of 128 bytes and the action sent to the environment is repeatedly performed for a duration of n frames, where n is uniformly sampled from {2,3,4}. There's some modification in the environment compared to v0.

`Alien-ramDeterministic-v0`	Observation is the RAM contents of the Atari machine with a total size of 128 bytes and the action sent to the environment is repeatedly performed for a duration of four frames.
`Alien-ramDeterministic-v4`	Observation is the RAM contents of the Atari machine with a total size of 128 bytes and the action sent to the environment is repeatedly performed for a duration of four frames. There's some modification in the environment compared to v0.
`Alien-ramNoFrameskip-v0`	Observation is the RAM contents of the Atari machine with a total size of 128 bytes and the action sent to the environment is applied, and the resulting state is returned immediately without skipping any frames.
`Alien-v0`	Observation is an RGB image of the screen represented as an array of shape (210, 160, 3) and the action sent to the environment is repeatedly performed for a duration of n frames, where n is uniformly sampled from {2,3,4}.
`Alien-v4`	Observation is an RGB image of the screen represented as an array of shape (210, 160, 3) and the action sent to the environment is repeatedly performed for a duration of n frames, where n is uniformly sampled from {2,3,4}. There's some modification in the environment compared to v0.
`AlienDeterministic-v0`	Observation is an RGB image of the screen represented as an array of shape (210, 160, 3) and the action sent to the environment is repeatedly performed for a duration of four frames.
`AlienDeterministic-v4`	Observation is an RGB image of the screen represented as an array of shape (210, 160, 3) and the action sent to the environment is repeatedly performed for a duration of four frames. There's some modification in the environment compared to v0.
`AlienNoFrameskip-v0`	Observation is an RGB image of the screen represented as an array of shape (210, 160, 3) and the action sent to the environment is applied, and the resulting state is returned immediately without skipping any frames.
`AlienNoFrameskip-v4`	Observation is an RGB image of the screen represented as an array of shape (210, 160, 3) and the action sent to the environment is applied, and the resulting state is returned immediately without skipping any frames. any frames. There's some modification in the environment compared to v0.

This summary should help you understand the nomenclature of the environments, and it applies to all environments in general. The RAM may be specific to the Atari environments, but you now have an idea of what to expect when you see several related environment names.

Exploring the Gym environments

To make it easy for us to visualize what an environment looks like or what its task is, we will make use of a simple script that can launch any environment and step through it with some randomly sampled actions. You can download the script from this book's code repository under ch4 or create a file named run_gym_env.py under ~/rl_gym_book/ch4 with the following contents:

```python
#!/usr/bin/env python

import gym
import sys

def run_gym_env(argv):
    env = gym.make(argv[1]) # Name of the environment supplied as 1st
argument
    env.reset()
    for _ in range(int(argv[2])):
        env.render()
        env.step(env.action_space.sample())
    env.close()
if __name__ == "__main__":
    run_gym_env(sys.argv)
```

This script will take the name of the environment supplied as the first command-line argument and the number of steps to be run. For example, we can run the script like this:

(rl_gym_book) praveen@ubntu:~/rl_gym_book/ch4$python `run_gym_env.py` **Alien-ram-v0 2000**

This command will launch the Alien-ram-v0 environment and step through it 2,000 times using random actions sampled from the action space of the environment.

You will see a window pop up with the `Alien-ram-v0` environment, like this:

Understanding the Gym interface

Let's continue our Gym exploration by understanding the interface between the Gym environment and the agents that we will develop. To help us with that, let's have another look at the picture we saw in `Chapter 2`, *Reinforcement Learning and Deep Reinforcement Learning*, when we were discussing the basics of reinforcement learning:

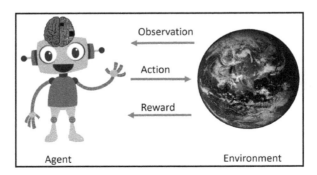

Did the picture give you an idea about the interface between the agent and the environment? We will make your understanding secure by going over the description of the interface.

After we `import gym`, we `make` an environment using the following line of code:

```
env = gym.make("ENVIRONMENT_NAME")
```

Here, `ENVIRONMENT_NAME` is the name of the environment we want, chosen from the list of the environments we found installed on our system. From the previous diagram, we can see that the first arrow comes from the environment to the agent, and is named **Observation**. From `Chapter 2`, *Reinforcement Learning and Deep Reinforcement Learning*, we understand the difference between partially observable environments and fully observable environments, and the difference between state and observation in each case. We get that first observation from the environment by calling `env.reset()`. Let's store the observation in a variable named `obs` using the following line of code:

```
obs = env.reset()
```

Now, the agent has received the observation (the end of the first arrow). It's time for the agent to take an action and send the action to the environment to see what happens. In essence, this is what the algorithms we develop for the agents should figure out! We'll be developing various state-of-the-art algorithms to develop agents in the next and subsequent chapters. Let's continue our journey towards understanding the Gym interface.

Once the action to be taken is decided, we send it to the environment (second arrow in the diagram) using the `env.step()` method, which will return four values in this order: `next_state`, `reward`, `done`, and `info`:

1. The `next_state` is the resulting state of the environment after the action was taken in the previous state.

 Some environments may internally run one or more steps using the same action before returning the `next_state`. We discussed *deterministic* and *NoFrameskip* types in the previous section, which are examples of such environments.

2. The `reward` (third arrow in the diagram) is returned by the environment.
3. The `done` variable is a Boolean (true or false), which gets a value of true if the episode has terminated/finished (therefore, it is time to reset the environment) and false otherwise. This will be useful for the agent to know when an episode has ended or when the environment is going to be reset to some initial state.

4. The `info` variable returned is an optional variable, which some environments may return with some additional information. Usually, this is not used by the agent to make its decision on which action to take.

Here is a consolidated summary of the four values returned by a Gym environment's `step()` method, together with their types and a concise description about them:

Returned value	Type	Description
`next_state` (or observation)	`Object`	Observation returned by the environment. The object could be the RGB pixel data from the screen/camera, RAM contents, join angles and join velocities of a robot, and so on, depending on the environment.
`reward`	`Float`	Reward for the previous action that was sent to the environment. The range of the `Float` value varies with each environment, but irrespective of the environment, a higher reward is always better and the goal of the agent should be to maximize the total reward.
`done`	`Boolean`	Indicates whether the environment is going to be reset in the next step. When the Boolean value is true, it most likely means that the episode has ended (due to loss of life of the agent, timeout, or some other episode termination criteria).
`info`	`Dict`	Some additional information that can optionally be sent out by an environment as a dictionary of arbitrary key-value pairs. The agent we develop should not rely on any of the information in this dictionary for taking action. It may be used (if available) for debugging purposes.

Note that the following code is provided to show the general structure and is not ready to be executed due to the ENVIRONMENT_NAME and the `agent.choose_action()` not being defined in this snippet.

Let's put all the pieces together and look at them in one place:

```
import gym
env = gym.make("ENVIRONMENT_NAME")
obs = env.reset() # The first arrow in the picture
# Inner loop (roll out)
action = agent.choose_action(obs) # The second arrow in the picture
next_state, reward, done, info = env.step(action) # The third arrow (and
more)
obs = next_state
# Repeat Inner loop (roll out)
```

I hope you got a good understanding of one cycle of the interaction between the environment and the agent. This process will repeat until we decide to terminate the cycle after a certain number of episodes or steps have passed. Let's now have a look at a complete example with the inner loop running for MAX_STEPS_PER_EPISODE and the outer loop running for MAX_NUM_EPISODES in a Qbert-v0 environment:

```
#!/usr/bin/env python
import gym
env = gym.make("Qbert-v0")
MAX_NUM_EPISODES = 10
MAX_STEPS_PER_EPISODE = 500
for episode in range(MAX_NUM_EPISODES):
    obs = env.reset()
    for step in range(MAX_STEPS_PER_EPISODE):
        env.render()
        action = env.action_space.sample()# Sample random action. This will
be replaced by our agent's action when we start developing the agent
algorithms
        next_state, reward, done, info = env.step(action) # Send the action
to the environment and receive the next_state, reward and whether done or
not
        obs = next_state

        if done is True:
            print("\n Episode #{} ended in {} steps.".format(episode,
step+1))
            break
```

When you run this script, you will notice a Qbert screen pop up and Qbert taking random actions and getting a score, as shown here:

You will also see print statements on the console like the following, depending on when the episode ended. Note that the step numbers you get might be different because the actions are random:

```
(rl_gym_book) praveen@ubuntu:~/rl_gym_book/ch4$ python rl_gym_boilerplate_code.py
Episode #0 ended in 375 steps.
Episode #1 ended in 363 steps.
Episode #3 ended in 495 steps.
Episode #4 ended in 437 steps.
Episode #5 ended in 355 steps.
Episode #6 ended in 443 steps.
Episode #7 ended in 407 steps.
Episode #8 ended in 400 steps.
Episode #9 ended in 376 steps.
```

The boilerplate code is available in this book's code repository under the `ch4` folder and is named `rl_gym_boilerplate_code.py`. It is indeed boilerplate code, because the overall structure of the program will remain the same. When we build our intelligent agents in subsequent chapters, we will extend this boilerplate code. It is worth taking a while and going through the script line by line to make sure you understand it well.

You may have noticed that in the example code snippets provided in this chapter and in *Chapter 3*, *Getting Started with OpenAI Gym and Deep Reinforcement Learning*, we used `env.action_space.sample()` in place of `action` in the previous code. `env.action_space` returns the type of the action space (`Discrete(18)`, for example, in the case of Alien-v0), and the `sample()` method randomly samples a value from that `action_space`. That's all it means!

We will now have a closer look at the spaces in the Gym to understand the state space and action spaces of environments.

Spaces in the Gym

We can see that each environment in the Gym is different. Every game environment under the Atari category is also different from the others. For example, in the case of the `VideoPinball-v0` environment, the goal is to keep bouncing a ball with two paddles to collect points based on where the ball hits, and to make sure that the ball never falls below the paddles, whereas in the case of `Alien-v0`, which is another Atari game environment, the goal is to move through a maze (the rooms in a ship) collecting *dots*, which are equivalent to destroying the eggs of the alien. Aliens can be killed by collecting a pulsar dot and the reward/score increases when that happens. Do you see the variations in the games/environments? How do we know what types of actions are valid in a game?

In the VideoPinball environment, naturally, the actions are to move the paddles up or down, whereas in the Alien environment, the actions are to command the player to move left, right, up, or down. Note that there is no "move left" or "move right" action in the case of VideoPinball. When we look at other categories of environment, the variations are even greater. For example, in the case of continuous control environments such as recently release robotics environments with the fetch robot arms, the action is to vary the continuous valued join positions and joint velocities to achieve the task. The same discussion can be had with respect to the values of the observations from the environment. We already saw the different observation object types in the case of Atari (RAM versus RGB images).

This is the motivation for why the *spaces* (as in mathematics) for the observation and actions are defined for each environment. At the time of the writing of this book, there are six spaces (plus one more called `prng` for random seed) that are supported by OpenAI Gym. They are listed in this table, with a brief description of each:

Space type	Description	Usage Example
Box	A box in the $\mathbb{R}^n$ space (an *n*-dimensional box) where each coordinate is bounded to lie in the interval defined by [low,high]. Values will be an array of *n* numbers. The shape defines the *n* for the space.	`gym.spaces.Box(low=-100, high=100, shape=(2,))`
Discrete	Discrete, integer-value space in the interval [0,n-1]. The argument for `Discrete()` defines *n*.	`gym.spaces.Discrete(4)`
Dict	A dictionary of sample space to create arbitrarily complex space. In the example, a Dict space is created, which consists of two discrete spaces for positions and velocities in three dimensions.	`gym.spaces.Dict({"position": gym.spaces.Discrete(3), "velocity": gym.spaces.Discrete(3)})`
MultiBinary	*n*-dimensional binary space. The argument to `MultiBinary()` defines *n*.	`gym.spaces.MultiBinary(5)`
MultiDiscrete	Multi-dimensional discrete space.	`gym.spaces.MultiDiscrete([-10,10], [0,1])`
Tuple	A product of simpler spaces.	`gym.spaces.Tuple((gym.spaces.Discrete(2), spaces.Discrete(2)))`

`Box` and `Discrete` are the most commonly used action spaces. We now have a basic understanding of the various space types available in the Gym. Let's look at how to find which observation and action spaces an environment uses.

The following script will print the observation and the action space of a given environment, and also optionally print the lower bound and upper bound of the values in the case of a `Box Space`. Additionally, it will also print a description/meaning of the possible action in the environment if it is provided by the environment:

```
#!/usr/bin/env python
import gym
from gym.spaces import *
import sys

def print_spaces(space):
    print(space)
    if isinstance(space, Box): # Print lower and upper bound if it's a Box
space
        print("\n space.low: ", space.low)
        print("\n space.high: ", space.high)

if __name__ == "__main__":
    env = gym.make(sys.argv[1])
    print("Observation Space:")
    print_spaces(env.observation_space)
    print("Action Space:")
    print_spaces(env.action_space)
    try:
        print("Action
description/meaning:",env.unwrapped.get_action_meanings())
    except AttributeError:
        pass
```

This script is also available for download in this book's code repository under `ch4`, named `get_observation_action_space.py`. You can run the script using the following command, where we supply the name of the environment as the first argument to the script:

```
(rl_gym_book) praveen@ubuntu:~/rl_gym_book/ch4$ python
get_observation_action_space.py CartPole-v0
```

The script will print an output like this:

```
(rl_gym_book) praveen@ubuntu:~/rl_gym_book/ch4$ python get_observation_action_space.py CartPole-v0
WARN: gym.spaces.Box autodetected dtype as <class 'numpy.float32'>. Please provide explicit dtype.
Observation Space:
Box(4,)

 space.low:  [ -4.80000019e+00  -3.40282347e+38  -4.18879032e-01  -3.40282347e+38]

 space.high:  [  4.80000019e+00   3.40282347e+38   4.18879032e-01   3.40282347e+38]
Action Space:
Discrete(2)
```

In this example, the script prints that the observation space for the `CartPole-v0` environment is `Box(4,)`, which corresponds to `cart position`, `cart velocity`, `pole angle`, and `pole velocity` at the tip for the four box values.

The action space is printed out to be `Discrete(2)`, which corresponds to *push cart to left* and *push cart to right* for the discrete values `0` and `1`, respectively.

Let's have a look at another example that has a few more complex spaces. This time, let's run the script with the `BipedalWalker-v2` environment:

> (rl_gym_book) praveen@ubuntu:~/rl_gym_book/ch4$ **python get_observation_action_space.py BipedalWalker-v2**

That produces an output like this:

```
(rl_gym_book) praveen@ubuntu:~/rl_gym_book/ch4$ python get_observation_action_space.py BipedalWalker-v2
WARN: gym.spaces.Box autodetected dtype as <class 'numpy.float32'>. Please provide explicit dtype.
WARN: gym.spaces.Box autodetected dtype as <class 'numpy.float32'>. Please provide explicit dtype.
Observation Space:
Box(24,)

 space.low:  [-inf -inf -inf -inf -inf -inf -inf -inf -inf -inf -inf -inf -inf -inf -inf
 -inf -inf -inf -inf -inf -inf -inf -inf -inf]

 space.high:  [ inf  inf  inf  inf  inf  inf  inf  inf  inf  inf  inf  inf  inf  inf  inf
  inf  inf  inf  inf  inf  inf  inf  inf  inf]
Action Space:
Box(4,)

 space.low:  [-1. -1. -1. -1.]

 space.high:  [ 1.  1.  1.  1.]
```

A detailed description of the state space of the Bipedal Walker (v2) environment is tabulated here for your quick and easy reference:

Index	Name/description	Min	Max
0	hull_angle	0	2*pi
1	hull_angularVelocity	-inf	+inf
2	vel_x	-1	+1
3	vel_y	-1	+1
4	hip_joint_1_angle	-inf	+inf
5	hip_joint_1_speed	-inf	+inf
6	knee_joint_1_angle	-inf	+inf
7	knee_joint_1_speed	-inf	+inf
8	leg_1_ground_contact_flag	0	1
9	hip_joint_2_angle	-inf	+inf
10	hip_joint_2_speed	-inf	+inf
11	knee_joint_2_angle	-inf	+inf
12	knee_joint_2_speed	-inf	+inf

| 13 | leg_2_ground_contact_flag | 0 | 1 |
| 14-23 | 10 lidar readings | -inf | +inf |

The state space, as you can see, is quite complicated, which is reasonable for a complex bipedal walking robot. It more or less resembles an actual bipedal robot system and sensor configuration that we can find in the real world, such as Boston Dynamics' (part of Alphabet) Atlas bipedal robot, who stole the limelight during the DARPA Robotics Challenge in 2015.

Next, we will look into and understand the action space. A detailed description of the action space for the Bipedal Walker (v2) environment is tabulated here for your quick and easy reference:

Index	Name/description	Min	Max
0	Hip_1 (torque/velocity)	-1	+1
1	Knee_1 (torque/velocity)	-1	+1
2	Hip_2 (torque/velocity)	-1	+1
3	Knee_2 (torque/velocity)	-1	+1

Action

The torque control is the default control method, which controls the amount of torque applied at the joints.

Summary

In this chapter, we explored the list of Gym environments available on your system, which you installed in the previous chapter, and then understood the naming conventions, or nomenclature, of the environments. We then revisited the agent-environment interaction (the RL loop) diagram and understood how the Gym environment provides the interfaces corresponding to each of the arrows we saw in the image. We then looked at a consolidated summary of the four values returned by the Gym environment's step() method in a tabulated, easy-to-understand format to *reinforce* your understanding of what they mean!

We also explored in detail the various types of spaces used in the Gym for the observation and action spaces, and we used a script to print out what spaces are used by an environment to understand the Gym environment interfaces better. In our next chapter, we will consolidate all our learning so far to develop our first artificially intelligent agent! Excited?! Flip the page to the next chapter now!

5
Implementing your First Learning Agent - Solving the Mountain Car problem

Well done on making it this far! In previous chapters, we got a good introduction to OpenAI Gym, its features, and how to install, configure, and use it in your own programs. We also discussed the basics of reinforcement learning and what deep reinforcement learning is, and we set up the PyTorch deep learning library to develop deep reinforcement learning applications. In this chapter, you will start developing your first learning agent! You will develop an intelligent agent that will learn how to solve the Mountain Car problem. Gradually in the following chapters, we will solve increasingly challenging problems as you get more comfortable developing reinforcement learning algorithms to solve problems in OpenAI Gym. We will start this chapter by understanding the Mountain Car problem, which has been a popular problem in the reinforcement learning and optimal control community. We will develop our learning agent from scratch and then train it to solve the Mountain Car problem using the Mountain Car environment in the Gym. We will finally see how the agent progresses and briefly look at ways we can improve the agent to use it for solving more complex problems. The topics we will be covering in this chapter are as follows:

- Understanding the Mountain Car problem
- Implementing a reinforcement learning-based agent to solve the Mountain Car problem
- Training a reinforcement learning agent at the Gym
- Testing the performance of the agent

Understanding the Mountain Car problem

For any reinforcement learning problem, two fundamental definitions concerning the problem are important, irrespective of the learning algorithm we use. They are the definitions of the state space and the action space. We mentioned earlier in this book that the state and action spaces could be discrete or continuous. Typically, in most problems, the state space consists of continuous values and is represented as a vector, matrix, or tensor (a multi-dimensional matrix). Problems and environments with discrete action spaces are relatively easy compared to continuous valued problems and environments. In this book, we will develop learning algorithms for a few problems and environments with a mix of state space and action space combinations so that you are comfortable dealing with any such variation when you start out on your own and develop intelligent agents and algorithms for your applications.

Let's start by understanding the Mountain Car problem with a high-level description, before moving on to look at the state and action spaces of the Mountain Car environment.

The Mountain Car problem and environment

In the Mountain Car Gym environment, a car is on a one-dimensional track, positioned between two mountains. The goal is to drive the car up the mountain on the right; however, the car's engine is not strong enough to drive up the mountain even at the maximum speed. Therefore, the only way to succeed is to drive back and forth to build up momentum. In short, the Mountain Car problem is to get an under-powered car to the top of a hill.

Before you implement your agent algorithm, it will help tremendously to understand the environment, the problem, and the state and action spaces. How do we find out the state and action spaces of the Mountain Car environment in the Gym? Well, we already know how to do that from Chapter 4, *Exploring the Gym and its Features*. We wrote a script named get_observation_action_space.py, which will print out the state and observation and action spaces of the environment whose name is passed as the first argument to the script. Let's ask it to print the spaces for the MountainCar-v0 environment with the following command:

```
(rl_gym_book) praveen@ubuntu:~/rl_gym_book/ch4$ python
get_observation_action_space.py 'MountainCar-v0'
```

Note that the command prompt has the `rl_gym_book` prefix, which signifies that we have activated the `rl_gym_book` conda Python virtual environment. Also, the current directory, `~/rl_gym_book/ch4`, signifies that the script is run from the `ch4` directory corresponding to the code for `Chapter 4`, *Exploring the Gym and its Features*, in the code repository for this book.

The preceding command will produce output like the following:

```
Observation Space:
Box(2,)

  space.low: [-1.20000005 -0.07 ]

  space.high: [ 0.60000002 0.07 ]
Action Space:
Discrete(3)
```

From this output, we can see that the state and observation space is a two-dimensional box and the action space is three-dimensional and discrete.

If you want a refresher on what **box** and **discrete** spaces mean, you can quickly flip to `Chapter 4`, *Exploring the Gym and its Features*, where we discussed these spaces and what they mean under the *Spaces in the Gym* section. It is important to understand them.

The state and action space type, description, and range of allowed values are summarized in the following table for your reference:

MountainCar-v0 environment	Type	Description	Range
State space	Box(2,)	(position, velocity)	Position: -1.2 to 0.6 Velocity: -0.07 to 0.07
Action space	Discrete(3)	0: Go left 1: Coast/do-nothing 2: Go right	0, 1, 2

So for example, the car starts at a random position between *-0.6* and *-0.4* with zero velocity, and the goal is to reach the top of the hill on the right side, which is at position *0.5*. (The car can technically go beyond *0.5*, up to *0.6*, which is also considered.) The environment will send *-1* as a reward every time step until the goal position (*0.5*) is reached. The environment will terminate the episode. The `done` variable will be equal to `True` if the car reaches the *0.5* position or the number of steps taken reaches 200.

Implementing a Q-learning agent from scratch

In this section, we will start implementing our intelligent agent step-by-step. We will be implementing the famous Q-learning algorithm using the `NumPy` library and the `MountainCar-V0` environment from the OpenAI Gym library.

Let's revisit the reinforcement learning Gym boiler plate code we used in Chapter 4, *Exploring the Gym and its Features*, as follows:

```python
#!/usr/bin/env python
import gym
env = gym.make("Qbert-v0")
MAX_NUM_EPISODES = 10
MAX_STEPS_PER_EPISODE = 500
for episode in range(MAX_NUM_EPISODES):
    obs = env.reset()
    for step in range(MAX_STEPS_PER_EPISODE):
        env.render()
        action = env.action_space.sample()# Sample random action. This will
be replaced by our agent's action when we start developing the agent
algorithms
        next_state, reward, done, info = env.step(action) # Send the action
to the environment and receive the next_state, reward and whether done or
not
        obs = next_state

        if done is True:
            print("\n Episode #{} ended in {} steps.".format(episode,
step+1))
            break
```

This code is a good starting point (aka boilerplate!) for developing our reinforcement learning agent. We will first start by changing the environment name from `Qbert-v0` to `MountainCar-v0`. Notice in the preceding script that we are setting `MAX_STEPS_PER_EPISODE`. This is the number of steps or actions that the agent can take before the episode ends. This may be useful in continuing, perpetual, or looping environments, where the environment itself does not end the episode. Here, we set a limit for the agent to avoid infinite loops. However, most of the environments defined in OpenAI Gym have an episode termination condition and once either of them is satisfied, the `done` variable returned by the `env.step(...)` function will be set to *True*. We saw in the previous section that for the Mountain Car problem we are interested in, the environment will terminate the episode if the car reaches the goal position (*0.5*) or if the number of steps taken reaches *200*. Therefore, we can further simplify the boilerplate code to look like the following for the Mountain Car environment:

```python
#!/usr/bin/env python
import gym
env = gym.make("MountainCar-v0")
MAX_NUM_EPISODES = 5000

for episode in range(MAX_NUM_EPISODES):
    done = False
    obs = env.reset()
    total_reward = 0.0 # To keep track of the total reward obtained in each episode
    step = 0
    while not done:
        env.render()
        action = env.action_space.sample()# Sample random action. This will be replaced by our agent's action when we start developing the agent algorithms
        next_state, reward, done, info = env.step(action) # Send the action to the environment and receive the next_state, reward and whether done or not
        total_reward += reward
        step += 1
        obs = next_state

    print("\n Episode #{} ended in {} steps. total_reward={}".format(episode, step+1, total_reward))
env.close()
```

If you run the preceding script, you will see the Mountain Car environment come up in a new window and the car moving left and right randomly for 1,000 episodes. You will also see the episode number, steps taken, and the total reward obtained printed at the end of every episode, as shown in the following screenshot:

The sample output should look similar to the following screenshot:

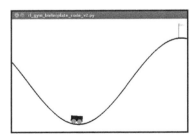

You should recall from our previous section that the agent gets a reward of *-1* for each step and that the `MountainCar-v0` environment will terminate the episode after *200* steps; this is why you the agent may sometimes get a total reward of *-200!* After all, the agent is taking random actions without thinking or learning from its previous actions. Ideally, we would want the agent to figure out how to reach the top of the mountain (near the flag, close to, at, or beyond position *0.5*) with the minimum number of steps. Don't worry - we will build such an intelligent agent by the end of this chapter!

Remember to always activate the `rl_gym_book` conda environment before running the scripts! Otherwise, you might run into **Module not found** errors unnecessarily. You can visually confirm whether you have activated the environment by looking at the shell prefix, which will show something like this: `(rl_gym_book)`
`praveen@ubuntu:~/rl_gym_book/ch5$`.

Let's move on by having a look at what Q-learning section.

Revisiting Q-learning

In `Chapter 2`, *Reinforcement Learning and Deep Reinforcement Learning*, we discussed the SARSA and Q-learning algorithms. Both of these algorithms provide a systematic way to update the estimate of the action-value function denoted by $Q_\pi(s, a)$. In particular, we saw that Q-learning is an off-policy learning algorithm, which updates the action-value estimate of the current state and action towards the maximum obtainable action-value in the subsequent state, s', which the agent will end up in according to its policy. We also saw that the Q-learning update is given by the following formula:

$$Q_\pi(s, a) = Q_\pi(s, a) + \alpha[r + \gamma \max_{a' in \mathbb{A}} Q(s', a') - Q_\pi(s, a)]$$

In the next section, we will implement a `Q_Learner` class in Python, which implements this learning update rule along with the other necessary functions and methods.

Implementing a Q-learning agent using Python and NumPy

Let's begin implementing our Q-learning agent by implementing the `Q_Learner` class. The main methods of this class are the following:

- __init__(self, env)
- discretize(self, obs)
- get_action(self, obs)
- learn(self, obs, action, reward, next_obs)

You will later find that the methods in here are common and exist in almost all the agents we will be implementing in this book. This makes it easy for you to grasp them, as these methods will be repeated (with some modifications) again and again.

The `discretize()` function is not necessary for agent implementations in general, but when the state space is large and continuous, it may be better to discretize the space into countable bins or ranges of values to simplify the representation. This also reduces the number of values that the Q-learning algorithm needs to learn, as it now only has to learn a finite set of values, which can be concisely represented in tabular formats or by using *n*-dimensional arrays instead of complex functions. Moreover, the Q-learning algorithm, used for optimal control, is guaranteed to converge for tabular representations of Q-values.

Defining the hyperparameters

Before our `Q_Learner` class declaration, we will initialize a few useful hyperparameters. Here are the hyperparameters that we will be using for our `Q_Learner` implementation:

- `EPSILON_MIN`: This is the minimum value of the epsilon value that we want the agent to use while following an epsilon-greedy policy.
- `MAX_NUM_EPISODES`: The maximum number of episodes that we want the agent to interact with the environment for.
- `STEPS_PER_EPISODE`: This is the number of steps in each episode. This could be the maximum number of steps that an environment will allow per episode or a custom value that we want to limit based on some time budget. Allowing a higher number of steps per episode means each episode might take longer to complete and in non-terminating environments, the environment won't be reset until this limit is reached, even if the agent is stuck at the same spot.

- ALPHA: This is the learning rate that we want the agent to use. This is the alpha in the Q-learning update equation listed in the previous section. Some algorithms vary the learning rate as the training progresses.

- GAMMA: This is the discount factor that the agent will use to factor in future rewards. This value corresponds to the gamma in the Q-learning update equation in the previous section.

- NUM_DISCRETE_BINS: This is the number of bins of values that the state space will be discretized into. For the Mountain Car environment, we will be discretizing the state space into *30* bins. You can play around with higher/lower values.

 Note that the MAX_NUM_EPISODES and STEPS_PER_EPISODE have been defined in the boilerplate code we went through in one of the previous sections of this chapter.

These hyperparameters are defined in the Python code like this, with some initial values:

```
EPSILON_MIN = 0.005
max_num_steps = MAX_NUM_EPISODES * STEPS_PER_EPISODE
EPSILON_DECAY = 500 * EPSILON_MIN / max_num_steps
ALPHA = 0.05  # Learning rate
GAMMA = 0.98  # Discount factor
NUM_DISCRETE_BINS = 30  # Number of bins to Discretize each observation dim
```

Implementing the Q_Learner class's __init__ method

Next, let us look into the Q_Learner class's member function definitions.

The __init__(self, env) function takes the environment instance, env, as an input argument and initializes the dimensions/shape of the observation space and the action space, and also determines the parameters to discretize the observation space based on the NUM_DISCRETE_BINS we set. The __init__(self, env) function also initializes the Q function as a NumPy array, based on the shape of the discretized observation space and the action space dimensions. The implementation of __init__(self, env) is straightforward as we are only initializing the necessary values for the agent. Here is our implementation:

```
class Q_Learner(object):
    def __init__(self, env):
        self.obs_shape = env.observation_space.shape
        self.obs_high = env.observation_space.high
        self.obs_low = env.observation_space.low
        self.obs_bins = NUM_DISCRETE_BINS  # Number of bins to Discretize
```

```
each observation dim
        self.bin_width = (self.obs_high - self.obs_low) / self.obs_bins
        self.action_shape = env.action_space.n
        # Create a multi-dimensional array (aka. Table) to represent the
        # Q-values
        self.Q = np.zeros((self.obs_bins + 1, self.obs_bins + 1,
                        self.action_shape))  # (51 x 51 x 3)
        self.alpha = ALPHA  # Learning rate
        self.gamma = GAMMA  # Discount factor
        self.epsilon = 1.0
```

Implementing the Q_Learner class's discretize method

Let's take a moment to understand how we are discretizing the observation space. The simplest, and yet an effective, way to discretize the observation space (and a metric space in general) is to divide the span of the range of values into a finite set of values called bins. The span/range of values is given by the difference between the maximum possible value and the minimum possible value in each dimension of the space. Once we calculate the span, we can divide it by the NUM_DISCRETE_BINS that we have decided on to get the width of the bin. We calculated the bin width in the __init__ function because it does not change with every new observation. The discretize(self, obs) function receives every new function and applies the discretization step to find the bin that the observation belongs to in the discretized space. It is as simple as doing this:

```
(obs - self.obs_low) / self.bin_width)
```

We want it to belong to any *one* of the bins (and not somewhere in between); therefore, we convert the previous code into an integer:

```
((obs - self.obs_low) / self.bin_width).astype(int)
```

Finally, we return this discretized observation as a tuple. All of this operation can be written in one line of Python code, like this:

```
def discretize(self, obs):
        return tuple(((obs - self.obs_low) / self.bin_width).astype(int))
```

Implementing the Q_Learner's get_action method

We want the agent to taken an action given an observation. `get_action(self, obs)` is the function we define to generate an action, given an observation in `obs`. The most widely used action selection policy is the epsilon-greedy policy, which takes the best action as per the agent's estimate with a (high) probability of *1-ϵ*, and takes a random action with a (small) probability given by epsilon *ϵ*. We implement the epsilon-greedy policy using the `random()` method from NumPy's random module, like this:

```
def get_action(self, obs):
    discretized_obs = self.discretize(obs)
    # Epsilon-Greedy action selection
    if self.epsilon > EPSILON_MIN:
        self.epsilon -= EPSILON_DECAY
    if np.random.random() > self.epsilon:
        return np.argmax(self.Q[discretized_obs])
    else:  # Choose a random action
        return np.random.choice([a for a in range(self.action_shape)])
```

Implementing the Q_learner class's learn method

As you might have guessed, this is the most important method of the `Q_Learner` class, which does the magic of learning the Q-values, which in turn enables the agent to take intelligent actions over time! The best part is that it is not that complicated to implement! It is merely the implementation of the Q-learning update equation that we saw earlier. Don't believe me when I say it is simple to implement?! Alright, here is the implementation of the learning function:

```
def learn(self, obs, action, reward, next_obs):
    discretized_obs = self.discretize(obs)
    discretized_next_obs = self.discretize(next_obs)
    td_target = reward + self.gamma *
np.max(self.Q[discretized_next_obs])
    td_error = td_target - self.Q[discretized_obs][action]
    self.Q[discretized_obs][action] += self.alpha * td_error
```

Now do you agree? :)

We could have written the Q learning update rule in one line of code, like this:

```
self.Q[discretized_obs][action] += self.alpha * (reward + self.gamma *
np.max(self.Q[discretized_next_obs] - self.Q[discretized_obs][action]
```

But, calculating each term on a separate line will make it easier to read and understand.

Full Q_Learner class implementation

If we put all the method implementations together, we will get a code snippet that looks like this:

```python
EPSILON_MIN = 0.005
max_num_steps = MAX_NUM_EPISODES * STEPS_PER_EPISODE
EPSILON_DECAY = 500 * EPSILON_MIN / max_num_steps
ALPHA = 0.05  # Learning rate
GAMMA = 0.98  # Discount factor
NUM_DISCRETE_BINS = 30  # Number of bins to Discretize each observation dim

class Q_Learner(object):
    def __init__(self, env):
        self.obs_shape = env.observation_space.shape
        self.obs_high = env.observation_space.high
        self.obs_low = env.observation_space.low
        self.obs_bins = NUM_DISCRETE_BINS  # Number of bins to Discretize
each observation dim
        self.bin_width = (self.obs_high - self.obs_low) / self.obs_bins
        self.action_shape = env.action_space.n
        # Create a multi-dimensional array (aka. Table) to represent the
        # Q-values
        self.Q = np.zeros((self.obs_bins + 1, self.obs_bins + 1,
                          self.action_shape))  # (51 x 51 x 3)
        self.alpha = ALPHA  # Learning rate
        self.gamma = GAMMA  # Discount factor
        self.epsilon = 1.0

    def discretize(self, obs):
        return tuple(((obs - self.obs_low) / self.bin_width).astype(int))

    def get_action(self, obs):
        discretized_obs = self.discretize(obs)
        # Epsilon-Greedy action selection
        if self.epsilon > EPSILON_MIN:
            self.epsilon -= EPSILON_DECAY
        if np.random.random() > self.epsilon:
            return np.argmax(self.Q[discretized_obs])
        else:  # Choose a random action
            return np.random.choice([a for a in range(self.action_shape)])

    def learn(self, obs, action, reward, next_obs):
        discretized_obs = self.discretize(obs)
        discretized_next_obs = self.discretize(next_obs)
```

```
        td_target = reward + self.gamma *
np.max(self.Q[discretized_next_obs])
        td_error = td_target - self.Q[discretized_obs][action]
        self.Q[discretized_obs][action] += self.alpha * td_error
```

So, we have the agent ready. What should we do next, you may ask. Well, we should train the agent in the Gym environment! In the next section, we will look at the training procedure.

Training the reinforcement learning agent at the Gym

The procedure to train the Q-learning agent may look familiar to you already, because it has many of the same lines of code as, and also a similar structure to, the boilerplate code that we used before. Instead of choosing a random action from the environment's actions space, we now get the action from the agent using the `agent.get_action(obs)` method. We also call the `agent.learn(obs, action, reward, next_obs)` method after sending the agent's action to the environment and receiving the feedback. The training function is listed here:

```
def train(agent, env):
    best_reward = -float('inf')
    for episode in range(MAX_NUM_EPISODES):
        done = False
        obs = env.reset()
        total_reward = 0.0
        while not done:
            action = agent.get_action(obs)
            next_obs, reward, done, info = env.step(action)
            agent.learn(obs, action, reward, next_obs)
            obs = next_obs
            total_reward += reward
        if total_reward > best_reward:
            best_reward = total_reward
        print("Episode#:{} reward:{} best_reward:{} eps:{}".format(episode,
                                total_reward, best_reward,
agent.epsilon))
    # Return the trained policy
    return np.argmax(agent.Q, axis=2)
```

Testing and recording the performance of the agent

Once we let the agent train at the Gym, we want to be able to measure how well it has learned. To do that, we let the agent go through a test. Just like in school! `test(agent, env, policy)` takes the agent object, the environment instance, and the agent's policy to test the performance of the agent in the environment, and returns the total reward for one full episode. It is similar to the `train(agent, env)` function we saw earlier, but it does not let the agent learn or update its Q-value estimates:

```
def test(agent, env, policy):
    done = False
    obs = env.reset()
    total_reward = 0.0
    while not done:
        action = policy[agent.discretize(obs)]
        next_obs, reward, done, info = env.step(action)
        obs = next_obs
        total_reward += reward
    return total_reward
```

Note that the `test(agent, env, policy)` function evaluates the agent's performance on one episode and returns the total reward obtained by the agent in that episode. We would want to measure how well the agent performs on several episodes to get a good measure of the agent's actual performance. Also, the Gym provides a handy wrapper function called *monitor* to record the progress of the agent in video files. The following code snippet illustrates how to test and record the agent's performance on *1,000* episodes and save the recorded agent's action in the environment as video files in the `gym_monitor_path` directory:

```
if __name__ == "__main__":
    env = gym.make('MountainCar-v0')
    agent = Q_Learner(env)
    learned_policy = train(agent, env)
    # Use the Gym Monitor wrapper to evalaute the agent and record video
    gym_monitor_path = "./gym_monitor_output"
    env = gym.wrappers.Monitor(env, gym_monitor_path, force=True)
    for _ in range(1000):
        test(agent, env, learned_policy)
    env.close()
```

A simple and complete Q-Learner implementation for solving the Mountain Car problem

In this section, we will put together the whole code into a single Python script to initialize the environment, launch the agent's training process, get the trained policy, test the performance of the agent, and also record how it acts in the environment!

```python
#!/usr/bin/env/ python
import gym
import numpy as np

MAX_NUM_EPISODES = 50000
STEPS_PER_EPISODE = 200 #  This is specific to MountainCar. May change with
env
EPSILON_MIN = 0.005
max_num_steps = MAX_NUM_EPISODES * STEPS_PER_EPISODE
EPSILON_DECAY = 500 * EPSILON_MIN / max_num_steps
ALPHA = 0.05  # Learning rate
GAMMA = 0.98  # Discount factor
NUM_DISCRETE_BINS = 30  # Number of bins to Discretize each observation dim

class Q_Learner(object):
    def __init__(self, env):
        self.obs_shape = env.observation_space.shape
        self.obs_high = env.observation_space.high
        self.obs_low = env.observation_space.low
        self.obs_bins = NUM_DISCRETE_BINS  # Number of bins to Discretize
each observation dim
        self.bin_width = (self.obs_high - self.obs_low) / self.obs_bins
        self.action_shape = env.action_space.n
        # Create a multi-dimensional array (aka. Table) to represent the
        # Q-values
        self.Q = np.zeros((self.obs_bins + 1, self.obs_bins + 1,
                        self.action_shape))  # (51 x 51 x 3)
        self.alpha = ALPHA  # Learning rate
        self.gamma = GAMMA  # Discount factor
        self.epsilon = 1.0

    def discretize(self, obs):
        return tuple(((obs - self.obs_low) / self.bin_width).astype(int))

    def get_action(self, obs):
        discretized_obs = self.discretize(obs)
        # Epsilon-Greedy action selection
```

```
        if self.epsilon > EPSILON_MIN:
            self.epsilon -= EPSILON_DECAY
        if np.random.random() > self.epsilon:
            return np.argmax(self.Q[discretized_obs])
        else:  # Choose a random action
            return np.random.choice([a for a in range(self.action_shape)])

    def learn(self, obs, action, reward, next_obs):
        discretized_obs = self.discretize(obs)
        discretized_next_obs = self.discretize(next_obs)
        td_target = reward + self.gamma *
np.max(self.Q[discretized_next_obs])
        td_error = td_target - self.Q[discretized_obs][action]
        self.Q[discretized_obs][action] += self.alpha * td_error

def train(agent, env):
    best_reward = -float('inf')
    for episode in range(MAX_NUM_EPISODES):
        done = False
        obs = env.reset()
        total_reward = 0.0
        while not done:
            action = agent.get_action(obs)
            next_obs, reward, done, info = env.step(action)
            agent.learn(obs, action, reward, next_obs)
            obs = next_obs
            total_reward += reward
        if total_reward > best_reward:
            best_reward = total_reward
        print("Episode#:{} reward:{} best_reward:{} eps:{}".format(episode,
                                    total_reward, best_reward,
agent.epsilon))
    # Return the trained policy
    return np.argmax(agent.Q, axis=2)

def test(agent, env, policy):
    done = False
    obs = env.reset()
    total_reward = 0.0
    while not done:
        action = policy[agent.discretize(obs)]
        next_obs, reward, done, info = env.step(action)
        obs = next_obs
        total_reward += reward
    return total_reward

if __name__ == "__main__":
    env = gym.make('MountainCar-v0')
```

```
agent = Q_Learner(env)
learned_policy = train(agent, env)
# Use the Gym Monitor wrapper to evalaute the agent and record video
gym_monitor_path = "./gym_monitor_output"
env = gym.wrappers.Monitor(env, gym_monitor_path, force=True)
for _ in range(1000):
    test(agent, env, learned_policy)
env.close()
```

This script is available in the code repository under the `ch5` folder,
named `Q_learner_MountainCar.py`.

Activate the `rl_gym_book` conda environment and launch the script to see it in
action! When you launch the script, you will see initial output like that shown in this
screenshot:

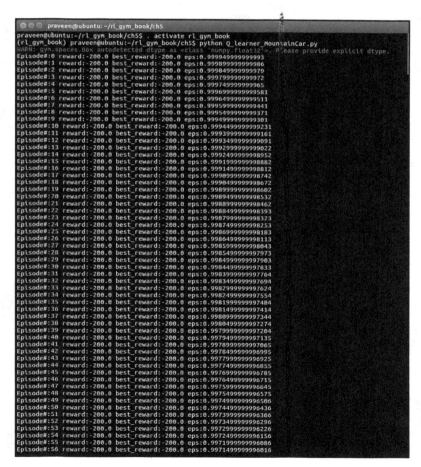

During the initial training episodes, when the agent is just getting started learning, you will see that it always ends up with a reward of *-200*. From your understanding of how the Gym's Mountain Car environment works, you can see that the agent does not reach the mountain top within the *200* time steps, and so the environment automatically resets the environment; thus, the agent only gets *-200*. You can also observe the ϵ (**eps**) exploration value decaying slowly.

If you let the agent learn for long enough, you will see the agent improving and learning to reach the top of the mountain in fewer and fewer steps. Here is a sample of its progress after *5* minutes of training on a typical laptop hardware:

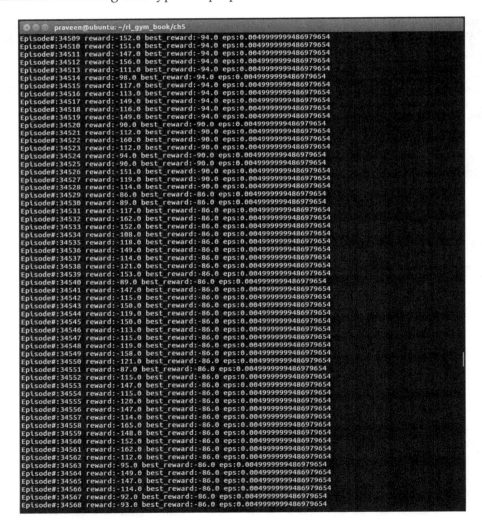

Once the script finishes running, you will see the recorded videos (along with some `.stats.json` and `.meta.json` files) of the agent's performance in the `gym_monitor_output` folder. You can watch the videos to see how your agent performed!

Here is a screenshot showing the agent successfully steering the car to the top of the mountain:

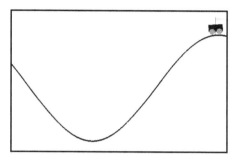

Hooray!

Summary

We learned a lot in this chapter. More importantly, we implemented an agent that learned to solve the Mountain Car problem smartly in 7 minutes or so!

We started by understanding the famous Mountain Car problem and looking at how the environment, the observation space, the state space, and rewards are designed in the Gym's `MountainCar-v0` environment. We revisited the reinforcement learning Gym boilerplate code we used in the previous chapter and made some improvements to it, which are also available in the code repository of this book.

We then defined the hyperparameters for our Q-learning agent and started implementing a Q-learning algorithm from scratch. We first implemented the agent's initialization function to initialize the agent's internal state variables, including the Q value representation, using a NumPy *n*-dimensional array. Then, we implemented the `discretize` method to discretize the `state space`; the `get_action(...)` method to select an action based on an epsilon-greedy policy; and then finally the `learn(...)` function, which implements the Q-learning update rule and forms the core of the agent. We saw how simple it was to implement them all! We also implemented functions to train, test, and evaluate the agent's performance.

I hope you had a lot of fun implementing the agent and watching it solve the Mountain Car problem at the Gym! We will get into advanced methods in the next chapter to solve a variety of more challenging problems.

6
Implementing an Intelligent Agent for Optimal Control using Deep Q-Learning

In the previous chapter, we implemented an intelligent agent that used Q-learning to solve the Mountain Car problem from scratch in about seven minutes on a dual-core laptop CPU. In this chapter, we will implement an advanced version of Q-learning called deep Q-learning, which can be used to solve several discrete control problems that are much more complex than the Mountain Car problem. Discrete control problems are (sequential) decision-making problems in which the action space is discretized into a finite number of values. In the previous chapter, the learning agent used a 2-dimensional state-space vector as the input, which contained the information about the position and velocity of the cart to take optimal control actions. In this chapter, we will see how we can implement a learning agent that takes (the on-screen) visual image as input and learns to take optimal control actions. This is close to how we would approach the problem, isn't it? We humans do not calculate the location and velocity of an object to decide what to do next. We simply observe what is going on and then learn to take actions that improve over time, eventually solving the problem completely.

This chapter will guide you in how to progressively build a better agent by improving upon our Q-learning agent implementation step-by-step using recently published methods for stable Q-learning with deep neural network function approximation. By the end of this chapter, you will have learnt how to implement and train a deep Q-learning agent that observes the pixels on the screen and plays Atari games using the Atari Gym environment and gets pretty good scores! We will also discuss how you can visualize and compare the performance of the agent as the learning progresses. You will see how the same agent algorithm can be trained on several different Atari games and that the agent is still able to learn to play the games well. If you cannot wait to see something in action or if you like to see and get a glimpse of what you will be developing before diving in, you can check out the code for this chapter under the `ch6` folder from the book's code repository and try out the pre-trained agents on several Atari games! Instructions on how to run the pre-trained agents are available in the `ch6/README.md` file.

This chapter has a lot of technical details to equip you with enough background and knowledge for you to understand the step-by-step process of improving the basic Q-learning algorithm and building a much more capable and intelligent agent based on deep Q-learning, along with several modules and tools needed to train and test the agent in a systematic manner. The following is an outline of the higher-level topics that will be covered in this chapter:

- Various methods to improve the Q-learning agent, including the following:
    - Neural network approximation of action-value functions
    - Experience replay
    - Exploration schedules
- Implementing deep convolutional neural networks using PyTorch for action-value function approximation
- Stabilizing deep Q-networks using target networks
- Logging and monitoring learning performance of PyTorch agents using TensorBoard
- Managing parameters and configurations
- Atari Gym environment
- Training deep Q-learners to play Atari games

Let's get started with the first topic and see how we can start from where we left off in the previous chapter and continue making progress toward a more capable and intelligent agent.

Improving the Q-learning agent

In the last chapter, we revisited the Q-learning algorithm and implemented the Q_Learner class. For the Mountain car environment, we used a multi-dimensional array of shape 51x51x3 to represent the action-value function, $Q_\pi(s, a)$. Note that we had discretized the state space to a fixed number of bins given by the NUM_DISCRETE_BINS configuration parameter (we used 50) . We essentially quantized or approximated the observation with a low-dimensional, discrete representation to reduce the number of possible elements in the n-dimensional array. With such a discretization of the observation/state space, we restricted the possible location of the car to a fixed set of 50 locations and the possible velocity of the car to a fixed set of 50 values. Any other location or velocity value would be approximated to one of those fixed set of values. Therefore, it is possible that the agent receives the same value for the position when the car was actually at different positions. For some environments, that can be an issue. The agent may not learn enough to distinguish between falling off a cliff versus standing just on the edge so as to leap forward. In the next section, we will look into how we can use a more powerful function approximator to represent the action-value function instead of a simple n-dimensional array/table that has its limitations.

Using neural networks to approximate Q-functions

Neural networks are shown to be effective as universal function approximators. In fact, there is a universal approximation theorem that states that a single hidden layer feed-forward neural network can approximate any continuous function that is closed and bounded in $\mathbb{R}^n$. It basically means that even simple (shallow) neural networks can approximate several functions. Doesn't it feel too good to be true that you can use a simple neural network with a fixed number of weights/parameters to approximate practically any function? It is actually true, except for one note that prevents it from being used practically anywhere and everywhere. Though a single hidden layer neural network can approximate any function with a finite set of parameters, we do not have a universally guaranteed way of *learning* those parameters that can best represent any function. You will see that researchers have been able to use neural networks to approximate several sophisticated and useful functions. Today, most of the intelligence that is built into the ubiquitous smartphones are powered by (heavily optimized) neural networks. Several best-performing systems that organize your photos into albums automatically based on people, places, and the context in the photos, systems that recognize your face and voice, or systems that automatically compose email replies for you are all powered by neural networks. Even the state-of-the-art techniques that generate human-like realistic voices that you hear from voice assistants such as Google Assistant, are powered by neural networks.

 Google Assistant currently uses WaveNet and WaveNet2 developed by Deepmind for **Text-To-Speech** (**TTS**) synthesis, which is shown to be much more realistic than any other TTS system that has been developed so far.

I hope that motivates you enough to use a neural network to approximate the Q-function! In this section, we will start by approximating the Q-function with a shallow (not deep) single-hidden layer neural network and use it to solve the famous Cart Pole problem. Though neural networks are powerful function approximators, we will see that it is not trivial to train even a single layer neural network to approximate Q-functions for reinforcement learning problems. We will look at some ways to improve Q-learning with neural network approximation and, in the later sections of this chapter, we will look at how we can use deep neural networks with much more representation power to approximate the Q-function.

Let's get started with the neural network approximation by first revisiting the Q_Learner class's __init__(...) method that we implemented in the previous chapter:

```
class Q_Learner(object):
    def __init__(self, env):
```

```
        self.obs_shape = env.observation_space.shape
        self.obs_high = env.observation_space.high
        self.obs_low = env.observation_space.low
        self.obs_bins = NUM_DISCRETE_BINS  # Number of bins to Discretize
each observation dim
        self.bin_width = (self.obs_high - self.obs_low) / self.obs_bins
        self.action_shape = env.action_space.n
        # Create a multi-dimensional array (aka. Table) to represent the
        # Q-values
        self.Q = np.zeros((self.obs_bins + 1, self.obs_bins + 1,
                           self.action_shape))  # (51 x 51 x 3)
        self.alpha = ALPHA  # Learning rate
        self.gamma = GAMMA  # Discount factor
        self.epsilon = 1.0
```

In the preceding code, the line in bold font is where we initialize the Q-function as a multi-dimensional NumPy array. In the following sections, we will see how we can replace the NumPy array representation with a more powerful neural network representation.

Implementing a shallow Q-network using PyTorch

In this section, we will start implementing a simple neural network using PyTorch's neural network module and then look at how we can use that to replace the multi-dimensional array-based Q action-value table-like function.

Let's start with the neural network implementation. The following code illustrates how you can implement a **Single Layer Perceptron (SLP)** using PyTorch:

```
import torch

class SLP(torch.nn.Module):
    """
    A Single Layer Perceptron (SLP) class to approximate functions
    """
    def __init__(self, input_shape, output_shape,
device=torch.device("cpu")):
        """
        :param input_shape: Shape/dimension of the input
        :param output_shape: Shape/dimension of the output
        :param device: The device (cpu or cuda) that the SLP should use to
store the inputs for the forward pass
        """
        super(SLP, self).__init__()
        self.device = device
        self.input_shape = input_shape[0]
        self.hidden_shape = 40
```

```
        self.linear1 = torch.nn.Linear(self.input_shape, self.hidden_shape)
        self.out = torch.nn.Linear(self.hidden_shape, output_shape)

    def forward(self, x):
        x = torch.from_numpy(x).float().to(self.device)
        x = torch.nn.functional.relu(self.linear1(x))
        x = self.out(x)
        return x
```

The SLP class implements a single layer neural network with 40 hidden units between the input and the output layer using the `torch.nn.Linear`class, and uses the **Rectified Linear Unit (ReLU** or **relu)** as the activation function. This code is available as `ch6/function_approximator/perceptron.py` in this book's code repository. The number 40 is nothing special, so feel free to vary the number of hidden units in the neural network.

Implementing the Shallow_Q_Learner

We can then modify the `Q_Learner` class to use this SLP to represent the Q-function. Note that we will have to modify the `Q_Learner` class `learn(...)` method as well to calculate the gradients of loss with respect to the weights of the SLP and backpropagate them so as to update and optimize the neural network's weights to improve its Q-value representation to be close to the actual values. We'll also slightly modify the `get_action(...)` method to get the Q-values with a forward pass through the neural network. The following code for the `Shallow_Q_Learner` class with the changes from the `Q_Learner` class implementation are shown in bold to make it easy for you to see the differences at a glance:

```
import torch
from function_approximator.perceptron import SLP

EPSILON_MIN = 0.005
max_num_steps = MAX_NUM_EPISODES * STEPS_PER_EPISODE
EPSILON_DECAY = 500 * EPSILON_MIN / max_num_steps
ALPHA = 0.05  # Learning rate
GAMMA = 0.98  # Discount factor
NUM_DISCRETE_BINS = 30  # Number of bins to Discretize each observation dim

class Shallow_Q_Learner(object):
    def __init__(self, env):
        self.obs_shape = env.observation_space.shape
        self.obs_high = env.observation_space.high
        self.obs_low = env.observation_space.low
        self.obs_bins = NUM_DISCRETE_BINS  # Number of bins to Discretize
each observation dim
        self.bin_width = (self.obs_high - self.obs_low) / self.obs_bins
```

```
            self.action_shape = env.action_space.n
            # Create a multi-dimensional array (aka. Table) to represent the
            # Q-values
            self.Q = SLP(self.obs_shape, self.action_shape)
            self.Q_optimizer = torch.optim.Adam(self.Q.parameters(), lr=1e-5)
            self.alpha = ALPHA  # Learning rate
            self.gamma = GAMMA  # Discount factor
            self.epsilon = 1.0

    def discretize(self, obs):
        return tuple(((obs - self.obs_low) / self.bin_width).astype(int))

    def get_action(self, obs):
        discretized_obs = self.discretize(obs)
        # Epsilon-Greedy action selection
        if self.epsilon > EPSILON_MIN:
            self.epsilon -= EPSILON_DECAY
        if np.random.random() > self.epsilon:
            return
np.argmax(self.Q(discretized_obs).data.to(torch.device('cpu')).numpy())
        else:  # Choose a random action
            return np.random.choice([a for a in range(self.action_shape)])

    def learn(self, obs, action, reward, next_obs):
        #discretized_obs = self.discretize(obs)
        #discretized_next_obs = self.discretize(next_obs)
        td_target = reward + self.gamma * torch.max(self.Q(next_obs))
        td_error = torch.nn.functional.mse_loss(self.Q(obs)[action],
td_target)
        #self.Q[discretized_obs][action] += self.alpha * td_error
        self.Q_optimizer.zero_grad()
        td_error.backward()
        self.Q_optimizer.step()
```

 The `Shallow_Q_Learner` class implementation is discussed here just to make it easy for you to understand how a neural network-based Q-function approximation can be implemented to replace the traditional tabular Q-learning implementations.

Solving the Cart Pole problem using a Shallow Q-Network

In this section, we will implement a full training script to solve the Cart Pole problem using the Shallow `Q_Learner` class that we developed in the previous section:

```
#!/usr/bin/env python import gym import random import torch from
torch.autograd import Variable import numpy as np from utils.decay_schedule
import LinearDecaySchedule from function_approximator.perceptron import SLP
```

```python
env = gym.make("CartPole-v0")
MAX_NUM_EPISODES = 100000
MAX_STEPS_PER_EPISODE = 300




class Shallow_Q_Learner(object):
    def __init__(self, state_shape, action_shape, learning_rate=0.005,
                 gamma=0.98):
        self.state_shape = state_shape
        self.action_shape = action_shape
        self.gamma = gamma # Agent's discount factor
        self.learning_rate = learning_rate # Agent's Q-learning rate
        # self.Q is the Action-Value function. This agent represents Q
using a
        # Neural Network.
        self.Q = SLP(state_shape, action_shape)
        self.Q_optimizer = torch.optim.Adam(self.Q.parameters(), lr=1e-3)
        # self.policy is the policy followed by the agent. This agents
follows
        # an epsilon-greedy policy w.r.t it's Q estimate.
        self.policy = self.epsilon_greedy_Q
        self.epsilon_max = 1.0
        self.epsilon_min = 0.05
        self.epsilon_decay =
LinearDecaySchedule(initial_value=self.epsilon_max,
                                final_value=self.epsilon_min,
                                max_steps= 0.5 * MAX_NUM_EPISODES *
MAX_STEPS_PER_EPISODE)
        self.step_num = 0

    def get_action(self, observation):
        return self.policy(observation)

    def epsilon_greedy_Q(self, observation):
        # Decay Epsilion/exploratin as per schedule
        if random.random() < self.epsilon_decay(self.step_num):
            action = random.choice([i for i in range(self.action_shape)])
        else:
            action = np.argmax(self.Q(observation).data.numpy())


        return action

    def learn(self, s, a, r, s_next):
        td_target = r + self.gamma * torch.max(self.Q(s_next))
        td_error = torch.nn.functional.mse_loss(self.Q(s)[a], td_target)
```

```
            # Update Q estimate
            #self.Q(s)[a] = self.Q(s)[a] + self.learning_rate * td_error
            self.Q_optimizer.zero_grad()
            td_error.backward()
            self.Q_optimizer.step()


if __name__ == "__main__":
    observation_shape = env.observation_space.shape
    action_shape = env.action_space.n
    agent = Shallow_Q_Learner(observation_shape, action_shape)
    first_episode = True
    episode_rewards = list()
    for episode in range(MAX_NUM_EPISODES):
        obs = env.reset()
        cum_reward = 0.0 # Cumulative reward
        for step in range(MAX_STEPS_PER_EPISODE):
            # env.render()
            action = agent.get_action(obs)
            next_obs, reward, done, info = env.step(action)
            agent.learn(obs, action, reward, next_obs)

            obs = next_obs
            cum_reward += reward

            if done is True:
                if first_episode: # Initialize max_reward at the end of
first episode
                    max_reward = cum_reward
                    first_episode = False
                episode_rewards.append(cum_reward)
                if cum_reward > max_reward:
                    max_reward = cum_reward
                print("\nEpisode#{} ended in {} steps. reward ={} ;
mean_reward={} best_reward={}".
                    format(episode, step+1, cum_reward,
np.mean(episode_rewards), max_reward))
                break
    env.close()
```

Create a script named `shallow_Q_Learner.py` with the preceding code in the `ch6` folder and run it like so:

```
(rl_gym_book) praveen@ubuntu:~/rl_gym_book/ch6$ python shallow_Q_Learner.py
```

You will see the agent learning to balance the Pole on the Cart in the Gym's `CartPole-v0` environment. You should see the episode number, the number of steps the agent took before the episode ended, the episode reward the agent received, the mean episode reward that the agent has received, and also the best episode reward that the agent has received so far printed on the console. You can uncomment the `env.render()` line if you want to visually see the Cart Pole environment and how the agent is trying to learn and balance it.

The `Shallow_Q_Learner` class implementation and the full training script shows how you can use a simple neural network to approximate the Q-function. It is not a good implementation to solve complex games like Atari. In the following subsequent sections, we will systematically improve their performance using new techniques. We will also implement a Deep Convolutional Q-Network that can take the raw screen image as the input and predict the Q-values that the agent can use to play various Atari games.

You may notice that it takes a very long time for the agent to improve and finally be able to solve the problem. In the next section, we will implement the concept of experience replay to improve the performance.

Experience replay

In most environments, the information received by the agent is not **independent and identically distributed (i.i.d)**. What this means is that the observation that the agent receives is strongly correlated with the previous observation it had received and the next observation it will receive. This is understandable because typically, the problems that the agent solves in typical reinforcement learning environments are sequential. Neural networks are shown to converge better if the samples are i.i.d.

Experience replay also enables the reuse of the past experience of the agent. Neural network updates, especially with lower learning rates, require several back-propagation and optimization steps to converge to good values. Reusing the past experience data, especially in mini-batches to update the neural network, greatly helps with the convergence of the Q-network which is close to the true action values.

Implementing the experience memory

Let's implement an experience memory class to store the experiences collected by the agent. Before that, let's cement our understanding of what we mean by *experience*. In reinforcement learning where the problems are represented using **Markov Decision Processes** (**MDP**), which we discussed in `Chapter 2`, *Reinforcement Learning and Deep Reinforcement Learning*, it is efficient to represent one experience as a data structure that consists of the observation at time step *t*, the action taken following that observation, the reward received for that action, and the next observation (or state) that the environment transitioned to due to the agent's action. It is useful to also include the "done" Boolean value that signifies whether this particular next observation marked the end of the episode or not. Let's use Python's `namedtuple` from the collections library to represent such a data structure, as shown in the following code snippet:

```
from collections import namedtuple
Experience = namedtuple("Experience", ['obs', 'action', 'reward',
'next_obs',
                                       'done'])
```

The `namedtuple` data structure makes it convenient to access the elements using a name attribute (like 'obs', 'action', and so on) instead of a numerical index (like 0, 1 and so on).

We can now move on to implement the experience memory class using the experience data structure we just created. To figure out what methods we need to implement in the experience memory class, let's think about how we will be using it later.

First, we want to be able to store new experiences in the experience memory that the agent collects. Then, we want to sample or retrieve experiences in batches from the experience memory when we want to replay to update the Q-function. So, essentially, we will need a method that can store new experiences and a method that can sample a single or a batch of experiences.

Let's dive into the experience memory implementation, starting with the initialization method where we initialize the memory with the desired capacity, as follows:

```
class ExperienceMemory(object):
    """
    A cyclic/ring buffer based Experience Memory implementation
    """
    def __init__(self, capacity=int(1e6)):
        """
        :param capacity: Total capacity (Max number of Experiences)
        :return:
        """
        self.capacity = capacity
```

```
self.mem_idx = 0 # Index of the current experience
self.memory = []
```

The `mem_idx` member variable will be used to point to the current writing head or the index location where we will be storing new experiences when they arrive.

 A "cyclic buffer" is also known by other names that you may have heard of: "circular buffer", "ring buffer", and "circular queue". They all represent the same underlying data structure that uses a ring-like fixed-size data representation.

Next, we'll look at the `store` method's implementation:

```
def store(self, experience):
    """
    :param experience: The Experience object to be stored into the
memory
    :return:
    """
    self.memory.insert(self.mem_idx % self.capacity, experience)
    self.mem_idx += 1
```

Simple enough, right? We are storing the experience at mem_idx, like we discussed.

The next code is our `sample` method implementation:

```
import random
    def sample(self, batch_size):
        """

        :param batch_size: Sample batch_size
        :return: A list of batch_size number of Experiences sampled at
random from mem
        """
        assert batch_size <= len(self.memory), "Sample batch_size is more
than available exp in mem"
        return random.sample(self.memory, batch_size)
```

In the preceding code, we make use of Python's random library to uniformly sample experiences from the experience memory at random. We will also implement a simple `get_size` helper method, which we will use to find out how many experiences are already stored in the experience memory:

```
def get_size(self):
    """

    :return: Number of Experiences stored in the memory
    """
    return len(self.memory)
```

The full implementation of the experience memory class is available at `ch6/utils/experience_memory.py`, in this book's code repository.

Next, we'll look at how we can replay experiences sampled from the experience memory to update the agent's Q-function.

Implementing the replay experience method for the Q-learner class

So, we have implemented a memory system for the agent to store its past experience using a neat cyclic buffer. In this section, we will look at how we can use the experience memory to replay experience in the Q-learner class.

The following code snippet implements the `replay_experience` method that shows how we sample from the experience memory and call a soon-to-be-implemented method that lets the agent learn from the sampled batch of experiences:

```
def replay_experience(self, batch_size=REPLAY_BATCH_SIZE):
    """
    Replays a mini-batch of experience sampled from the Experience
    Memory
    :param batch_size: mini-batch size to sample from the Experience
    Memory
    :return: None
    """
    experience_batch = self.memory.sample(batch_size)
    self.learn_from_batch_experience(experience_batch)
```

In the case of online learning methods like SARSA, the action value estimate was updated after every step of interaction between the agent and the environment. This way, the updates propagated information that the agent just experienced. If the agent does not experience something quite often, such updates may let the agent forget about those experiences and may result in bad performance when the agent encounters a similar situation in the future. This is undesirable, especially with neural networks which have many parameters (or weights) that needs to be adjusted to the right set of values. That is one of the main motivations behind using an experience memory and replaying the past experiences during updates to the Q action-value estimates. We will now implement the `learn_from_batch_experience` method that extends the `learn` method we implemented in the previous chapter to learn from a batch of experiences rather than from a single experience. The following is the method's implementation:

```python
device = torch.device("cuda" if torch.cuda.is_available() else "cpu")
def learn_from_batch_experience(self, experiences):
    """
    Updated the DQN based on the learning from a mini-batch of
experience.
    :param experiences: A mini-batch of experience
    :return: None
    """
    batch_xp = Experience(*zip(*experiences))
    obs_batch = np.array(batch_xp.obs)
    action_batch = np.array(batch_xp.action)
    reward_batch = np.array(batch_xp.reward)
    next_obs_batch = np.array(batch_xp.next_obs)
    done_batch = np.array(batch_xp.done)

    td_target = reward_batch + ~done_batch * \
            np.tile(self.gamma, len(next_obs_batch)) * \
            self.Q(next_obs_batch).detach().max(1)[0].data

    td_target = td_target.to(device)
    action_idx = torch.from_numpy(action_batch).to(device)
    td_error = torch.nn.functional.mse_loss(
        self.Q(obs_batch).gather(1, action_idx.view(-1, 1)),
        td_target.float().unsqueeze(1))

    self.Q_optimizer.zero_grad()
    td_error.mean().backward()
    self.Q_optimizer.step()
```

The method receives a batch (or a mini-batch) of experience and first extracts the observation batches, action batches, reward batches, and the next observation batches separately in order to use them individually in the subsequent steps.
The `done_batch` signifies for each experience whether or not the next observation is the end of an episode. We then calculate the **Temporal Difference** (**TD**) error with a max over action, which is the Q-learning target. Note that we multiply the second term in the `td_target` calculation with `~done_batch`.

This takes care of specifying a zero value for terminal states. So, if a particular `next_obs` in the `next_obs_batch` was terminal, the second term would become 0, resulting in just `td_target = rewards_batch`.

We then calculate a mean squared error between the `td_target` (target Q-value) and the Q-value predicted by the Q-network. We use this error as the guiding signal and back-propagate it to all the nodes in the neural network before making an optimization step to update the parameters/weights to minimize the error.

Revisiting the epsilon-greedy action policy

In the previous chapter, we discussed the ϵ-greedy action selection policy which takes the best action as per the agent's action-value estimate with a probability of 1-ϵ and takes a random action with a probability given by epsilon, ϵ. Epsilon is a hyperparameter that can be tuned based on the experiments to a good value. A higher value of ϵ means that the agent's actions will be random and a lower value of ϵ means that the agent's action will more likely exploit what it already knows about the environment and will not try to explore. Should I explore more by taking never/less tried actions? Or should I exploit what I already know and take the best action to my knowledge which may be limited? This is the exploration-exploitation dilemma that a reinforcement learning agent suffers from.

Intuitively, it is helpful to have a very high value (the maximum is 1.0) for ϵ during the initial stages of the agent's learning process so that the agent can explore the state space by taking mostly random actions. Once it has got enough experience and has gained a better understanding of the environment, lowering the ϵ value will let the agent take actions based on what it believes to be the best actions more often. It will be useful to have a utility function that takes care of varying the ϵ value, right? Let's implement such a function in the next section.

Implementing an epsilon decay schedule

We can decay (or decrease) the ϵ value linearly (in the following left-hand side graph), exponentially (in the following right-hand side graph) or using some other decay schedule. Linear and exponential schedules are the most commonly used decay schedules for the exploration parameter ϵ:

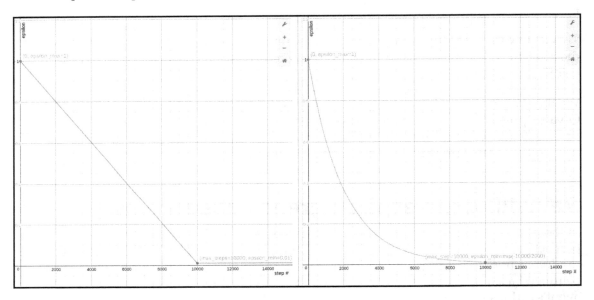

In the preceding graphs, you can see how the epsilon (exploration) value varies with the different schedule schemes (linear on the left graph, exponential on the right graph). The decay schedule shown in the preceding graphs use an epsilon_max (start) value of 1, epsilon_min (final) value of 0.01 in the linear case, and exp(-10000/2000) in the exponential case, with both of them maintaining a constant value of epsilon_min after 10,000 episodes.

The following code implements the LinearDecaySchedule, which we will use for our Deep_Q_Learning agent implementation to play Atari games:

```python
#!/usr/bin/env python

class LinearDecaySchedule(object):
    def __init__(self, initial_value, final_value, max_steps):
        assert initial_value > final_value, "initial_value should be <
final_value"
        self.initial_value = initial_value
        self.final_value = final_value
        self.decay_factor = (initial_value - final_value) / max_steps
```

```
    def __call__(self, step_num):
        current_value = self.initial_value - self.decay_factor * step_num
        if current_value < self.final_value:
            current_value = self.final_value
        return current_value

if __name__ == "__main__":
    import matplotlib.pyplot as plt
    epsilon_initial = 1.0
    epsilon_final = 0.05
    MAX_NUM_EPISODES = 10000
    MAX_STEPS_PER_EPISODE = 300
    linear_sched = LinearDecaySchedule(initial_value = epsilon_initial,
                            final_value = epsilon_final,
                            max_steps = MAX_NUM_EPISODES *
MAX_STEPS_PER_EPISODE)
    epsilon = [linear_sched(step) for step in range(MAX_NUM_EPISODES *
MAX_STEPS_PER_EPISODE)]
    plt.plot(epsilon)
    plt.show()
```

The preceding script is available at `ch6/utils/decay_schedule.py` in this book's code repository. If you run the script, you will see that the `main` function creates a linear decay schedule for epsilon and plots the value. You can experiment with different values of `MAX_NUM_EPISODES, MAX_STEPS_PER_EPISODE, epsilon_initial,` and `epsilon_final` to visually see how the epsilon values vary with the number of steps. In the next section, we will implement the `get_action(...)` method which implements the ϵ-greedy action selection policy.

Implementing a deep Q-learning agent

In this section, we will discuss how we can scale up our shallow Q-learner to a more sophisticated and powerful deep Q-learner-based agent that can learn to act based on raw visual image inputs, which we will use towards the end of this chapter to train agents that play Atari games well. Note that you can train this deep Q-learning agent in any learning environments with a discrete action space. The Atari game environments are one such interesting class of environments that we will use in this book.

We will start with a deep convolutional Q-network implementation and incorporate it into our Q-learner. Then, we will see how we can use the technique of target Q-networks to improve the stability of the deep Q-learner. We will then combine all the techniques we have discussed so far to put together the full implementation of our deep Q learning-based agent.

Implementing a deep convolutional Q-network in PyTorch

Let's implement a 3-layer deep **Convolutional Neural Network** (**CNN**) that takes the Atari game screen pixels as the input and outputs the action-values for each of the possible actions for that particular game, which is defined in the OpenAI Gym environment. The following code is for the CNN class:

```
import torch


class CNN(torch.nn.Module):
    """
    A Convolution Neural Network (CNN) class to approximate functions with
visual/image inputs
    """
    def __init__(self, input_shape, output_shape, device="cpu"):
        """
        :param input_shape: Shape/dimension of the input image. Assumed to
be resized to C x 84 x 84
        :param output_shape: Shape/dimension of the output.
        :param device: The device (cpu or cuda) that the CNN should use to
store the inputs for the forward pass
        """
        # input_shape: C x 84 x 84
        super(CNN, self).__init__()
        self.device = device
        self.layer1 = torch.nn.Sequential(
            torch.nn.Conv2d(input_shape[0], 64, kernel_size=4, stride=2,
padding=1),
            torch.nn.ReLU()
        )
        self.layer2 = torch.nn.Sequential(
            torch.nn.Conv2d(64, 32, kernel_size=4, stride=2, padding=0),
            torch.nn.ReLU()
        )
        self.layer3 = torch.nn.Sequential(
            torch.nn.Conv2d(32, 32, kernel_size=3, stride=1, padding=0),
            torch.nn.ReLU()
        )
        self.out = torch.nn.Linear(18 * 18 * 32, output_shape)

    def forward(self, x):
        x = torch.from_numpy(x).float().to(self.device)
        x = self.layer1(x)
        x = self.layer2(x)
```

```
x = self.layer3(x)
x = x.view(x.shape[0], -1)
x = self.out(x)
return x
```

 As you can see, it is easy to add more layers to the neural network. We could use a deeper network that has more than three layers, but it will come at the cost of requiring more compute power and time. In deep reinforcement learning, and especially in Q learning with function approximation, there are no proven convergence guarantees. We should therefore make sure that our agent's implementation is good enough to learn and make progress well before increasing the capacity of the Q/value-function representation by using a much deeper neural network.

Using the target Q-network to stabilize an agent's learning

A simple technique of freezing the Q-network for a fixed number of steps and then using that to generate the Q learning targets to update the parameters of the deep Q-network was shown to be considerably effective in reducing the oscillations and stabilize Q learning with neural network approximation. This technique is a relatively simpler one, but it turns out to be very helpful for stable learning.

The implementation is going to be straightforward and simple. We have to make two changes or updates to our existing deep Q-learner class:

1. Create a target Q-network and sync/update it with the original Q-network periodically
2. Use the target Q-network to generate the Q-learning targets

To compare how the agent performs with and without the target Q-network, you can use the parameter manager and the logging and visualization tools that we developed in the earlier sections of this chapter to visually verify the performance gain with the target Q-network enabled.

We will first add a new class member called `Q_target` that we can add to the `__init__` method of our deep Q-learner class. The following code snippet shows the lines of code where we add the new member right after our previous declaration of `self.DQN` in the `deep_Q_learner.py` script:

```
self.Q = self.DQN(state_shape, action_shape, device).to(device)
self.Q_optimizer = torch.optim.Adam(self.Q.parameters(),
```

```
                lr=self.learning_rate)
if self.params['use_target_network']:
    self.Q_target = self.DQN(state_shape, action_shape, device).to(device)
```

We can then modify the `learn_from_batch_experience` method that we implemented earlier to use the target Q-network to create the Q-learning target. The following code snippet shows the changes in bold font from our first implementation:

```
def learn_from_batch_experience(self, experiences):
        batch_xp = Experience(*zip(*experiences))
        obs_batch = np.array(batch_xp.obs)
        action_batch = np.array(batch_xp.action)
        reward_batch = np.array(batch_xp.reward)
        next_obs_batch = np.array(batch_xp.next_obs)
        done_batch = np.array(batch_xp.done)

        if self.params['use_target_network']:
            if self.step_num % self.params['target_network_update_freq'] ==
0:
                # The *update_freq is the Num steps after which target net
is updated.
                # A schedule can be used instead to vary the update freq.
                self.Q_target.load_state_dict(self.Q.state_dict())
            td_target = reward_batch + ~done_batch * \
                np.tile(self.gamma, len(next_obs_batch)) * \
                self.Q_target(next_obs_batch).max(1)[0].data
        else:
            td_target = reward_batch + ~done_batch * \
                np.tile(self.gamma, len(next_obs_batch)) * \
                self.Q(next_obs_batch).detach().max(1)[0].data

        td_target = td_target.to(device)
        action_idx = torch.from_numpy(action_batch).to(device)
        td_error = torch.nn.functional.mse_loss(
self.Q(obs_batch).gather(1, action_idx.view(-1, 1)),
td_target.float().unsqueeze(1))

        self.Q_optimizer.zero_grad()
        td_error.mean().backward()
        writer.add_scalar("DQL/td_error", td_error.mean(), self.step_num)
        self.Q_optimizer.step()
```

This completes our target Q-network implementation.

How do we know if the agent is benefiting from the target Q-network and other improvements we discussed in the previous sections? In the next section, we will look at ways to log and visualize the agent's performance so that we can monitor and figure out whether or not the improvements we discussed actually lead to better performances.

Logging and visualizing an agent's learning process

We now have a learning agent that uses a neural network to learn Q-values and update itself to perform better at the task. The agent takes a while to learn before it starts acting wisely. How do we know what is going on with the agent at a given time? How do we know if the agent is making progress or simply acting dumb? How do we see and measure the progress of the agent with time? Should we just sit and wait for the training to end? No. There should be some better way, don't you think?

Yes, and there is! It is actually important for us, the developers of the agents, to be able to observe how the agent is performing in order to figure out if there is an issue with the implementation or if some of the hyperparameters are too bad for the agent to learn anything. We have had the preliminary version of logging and seen how the agent's learning was progressing with the console outputs generated using the print statements. That gave us a first-hand look into the episode number, episode reward, the maximum reward, and so on, but it was more like a single snapshot at a given time. We want to be able to see the history of the progress to see if the agent's learning is converging with the learning error decreasing or not, and so on. This will enable us to think in the right direction to update our implementation or tweak the parameters to improve the learning performance of the agent.

The TensorFlow deep learning library offers a tool called TensorBoard. It is a powerful tool to visualize the neural network graphs, plot quantitative metrics like learning errors, rewards, and so on as the training progresses. It can even be used to visualize images and a few other useful data types. It makes it easier to understand, identify, and debug our deep learning algorithm implementations. In the next section, we will see how we can use TensorBoard to log and visualize our agent's progress.

Using TensorBoard for logging and visualizing a PyTorch RL agent's progress

Though TensorBoard is a tool that was released for the TensorFlow deep learning library, it is a flexible tool in itself, which can be used with other deep learning libraries like PyTorch. Basically, the TensorBoard tool reads the TensorFlow events summary data from log files and updates the visualizations and plots periodically. Fortunately, we have a library called `tensorboardX` that provides a convenient interface to create the events that TensorBoard can work with. This way, we can easily generate the appropriate events from our agent training code to log and visualize how our agent's learning process is progressing. The use of this library is pretty straightforward and simple. We import `tensorboardX` and create a `SummaryWriter` object with the desired log file name. We can then add new scalars (and also other supported data) using the `SummaryWriter` object to add new data points to the plot which will be updated periodically. The following screenshot is an example of what the TensorBoard's output will look like with the kind of information we will be logging in our agent training script to visualize its progress:

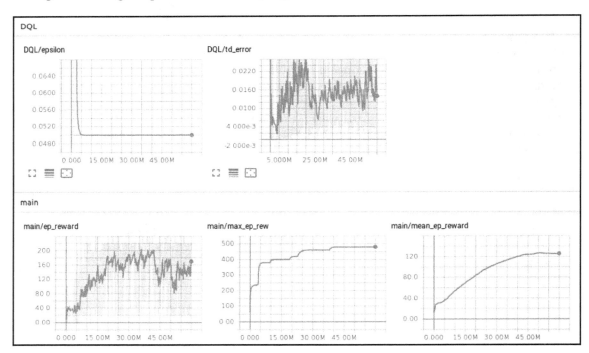

In the preceding screenshot, the bottom-right most plot titled **main/mean_ep_reward** shows how the agent has been learning to progressively get higher and higher rewards over time steps. In all the plots in the preceding screenshot, the x-axis shows the number of training steps and the y-axis has the value of the data that was logged, as signified by the titles of each of the plots.

Now, we know how to log and visualize the performance of the agent as it is training. But still, a question remains as to how we can compare the agent with and without one or more of the improvements we discussed in the earlier sections in this chapter. We discussed several improvements, and each adds new hyperparameters. In order to manage the various hyperparameters and to easily turn on and off the improvements and configurations, in the next section, we will discuss a way to achieve this by building a simple parameter management class.

Managing hyperparameters and configuration parameters

As you may have noticed, our agent has several hyperparameters like the learning rate, gamma, epsilon start/minimum value, and so on. There are also several configuration parameters for both the agent and the environment that we would want to be able to modify easily and run instead of searching through the code to find where that parameter was defined. Having a simple and good way to manage these parameters also helps when we want to automate the training process or run parameter sweeps or other methods to tune and find the best set of parameters that work for the agent.

In the following two subsections, we will look at how we can use a JSON file to specify the parameters and hyperparameters in an easy to use way and implement a parameter manager class to handle these externally configurable parameters to update the agent and the environment configuration.

Using a JSON file to easily configure parameters

Before we implement our parameter manager, let's get an idea of what our parameter configuration JSON file will look like. The following is a snippet of the `parameters.json` file that we will use to configure the parameters of the agent and the environment. The **JavaScript Object Notation (JSON)** file is a convenient and human-readable format for such data representation. We will discuss what each of these parameters mean in the later sections of this chapter. For now, we will concentrate on how we can use such a file to specify or change the parameters used by the agent and the environment:

```
{
  "agent": {
    "max_num_episodes": 70000,
    "max_steps_per_episode": 300,
    "replay_batch_size": 2000,
    "use_target_network": true,
    "target_network_update_freq": 2000,
    "lr": 5e-3,
    "gamma": 0.98,
    "epsilon_max": 1.0,
    "epsilon_min": 0.05,
    "seed": 555,
    "use_cuda": true,
    "summary_filename_prefix": "logs/DQL_"
  },
  "env": {
    "type": "Atari",
    "episodic_life": "True",
    "clip_reward": "True",
    "useful_region": {
        "Default":{
                "crop1": 34,
                "crop2": 34,
                "dimension2": 80
        }
    }
  }
}
```

The parameters manager

Did you like the parameter configuration file example that you just saw? I hope you did. In this section, we will implement a parameter manger that will help us load, get, and set these parameters as necessary.

We will start by creating a Python class named `ParamsManger` that initializes the `params` member variable with the dictionary of parameters read from the `params_file` using the JSON Python library, as follows:

```
#!/usr/bin/env python
import JSON

class ParamsManager(object):
    def __init__(self, params_file):
        """

        A class to manage the Parameters. Parameters include configuration
parameters and Hyper-parameters
        :param params_file: Path to the parameters JSON file
        """
        self.params = JSON.load(open(params_file, 'r'))
```

We will then implement a few methods that will be convenient for us. We will start with the `get_params` method that returns the whole dictionary of parameters that we read from the JSON file:

```
    def get_params(self):
        """

        Returns all the parameters
        :return: The whole parameter dictionary
        """

        return self.params
```

Sometimes, we may just want to get the parameters that correspond to the agent or those that correspond to the environment which we can pass in while we initialize the agent or the environment. Since we had neatly separated the agent and the environment parameters in the `parameters.json` file that we saw in the previous section, the implementation is straightforward, as follows:

```
    def get_env_params(self):
        """

        Returns the environment configuration parameters
        :return: A dictionary of configuration parameters used for the
environment
        """

        return self.params['env']
    def get_agent_params(self):
        """

        Returns the hyper-parameters and configuration parameters used by
the agent
        :return: A dictionary of parameters used by the agent
        """

        return self.params['agent']
```

We will also implement another simple method to update the agent parameters so that we can also supply/read the agent parameters from the command line when we launch our training script:

```
def update_agent_params(self, **kwargs):
    """
    Update the hyper-parameters (and configuration parameters) used by
the agent
    :param kwargs: Comma-separated, hyper-parameter-key=value pairs.
Eg.: lr=0.005, gamma=0.98
    :return: None
    """
    for key, value in kwargs.items():
        if key in self.params['agent'].keys():
            self.params['agent'][key] = value
```

The preceding parameter manager implementation, along with a simple test procedure, is available at ch6/utils/params_manager.py, in this book's code repository. In the next section, we will consolidate all the techniques we have discussed and implemented so far to put together a complete deep Q learning-based agent.

A complete deep Q-learner to solve complex problems with raw pixel input

From the beginning of this chapter, we have implemented several additional techniques and utility tools to improve the agent. In this section, we will consolidate all the improvements and the utility tools we have discussed so far into a unified deep_Q_Learner.py script. We will be using this unified agent script to train on the Atari Gym environment in the next section and watch the agent improving its performance and fetching more and more scores over time.

The following code is the unified version that utilizes the following features that we developed in the previous sections of this chapter:

- Experience memory
- Experience replay to learn from (mini) batches of experience
- Linear epsilon decay schedule
- Target network for stable learning

- Parameter management using JSON files
- Performance visualization and logging using TensorBoard:

```python
#!/usr/bin/env python

import gym
import torch
import random
import numpy as np

import environment.atari as Atari
from utils.params_manager import ParamsManager
from utils.decay_schedule import LinearDecaySchedule
from utils.experience_memory import Experience, ExperienceMemory
from function_approximator.perceptron import SLP
from function_approximator.cnn import CNN
from tensorboardX import SummaryWriter
from datetime import datetime
from argparse import ArgumentParser

args = ArgumentParser("deep_Q_learner")
args.add_argument("--params-file",
                  help="Path to the parameters JSON file. Default is
parameters.JSON",
                  default="parameters.JSON",
                  type=str,
                  metavar="PFILE")
args.add_argument("--env-name",
                  help="ID of the Atari environment available in OpenAI
Gym. Default is Pong-v0",
                  default="Pong-v0",
                  type=str,
                  metavar="ENV")
args = args.parse_args()

params_manager= ParamsManager(args.params_file)
seed = params_manager.get_agent_params()['seed']
summary_file_path_prefix =
params_manager.get_agent_params()['summary_file_path_prefix']
summary_file_name = summary_file_path_prefix + args.env_name + "_" +
datetime.now().strftime("%y-%m-%d-%H-%M")
writer = SummaryWriter(summary_file_name)
global_step_num = 0
use_cuda = params_manager.get_agent_params()['use_cuda']
# new in PyTorch 0.4
device = torch.device("cuda" if torch.cuda.is_available() and use_cuda else
"cpu")
torch.manual_seed(seed)
```

```python
np.random.seed(seed)
if torch.cuda.is_available() and use_cuda:
    torch.cuda.manual_seed_all(seed)


class Deep_Q_Learner(object):
    def __init__(self, state_shape, action_shape, params):
        """
        self.Q is the Action-Value function. This agent represents Q using
a Neural Network
        If the input is a single dimensional vector, uses a Single-Layer-
Perceptron else if the input is 3 dimensional
        image, use a Convolutional-Neural-Network

        :param state_shape: Shape (tuple) of the observation/state
        :param action_shape: Shape (number) of the discrete action space
        :param params: A dictionary containing various Agent configuration
parameters and hyper-parameters
        """
        self.state_shape = state_shape
        self.action_shape = action_shape
        self.params = params
        self.gamma = self.params['gamma'] # Agent's discount factor
        self.learning_rate = self.params['lr'] # Agent's Q-learning rate

        if len(self.state_shape) == 1: # Single dimensional
observation/state space
            self.DQN = SLP
        elif len(self.state_shape) == 3: # 3D/image observation/state
            self.DQN = CNN

        self.Q = self.DQN(state_shape, action_shape, device).to(device)
        self.Q_optimizer = torch.optim.Adam(self.Q.parameters(),
lr=self.learning_rate)
        if self.params['use_target_network']:
            self.Q_target = self.DQN(state_shape, action_shape,
device).to(device)
        # self.policy is the policy followed by the agent. This agents
follows
        # an epsilon-greedy policy w.r.t it's Q estimate.
        self.policy = self.epsilon_greedy_Q
        self.epsilon_max = 1.0
        self.epsilon_min = 0.05
        self.epsilon_decay = \
LinearDecaySchedule(initial_value=self.epsilon_max,
                                    final_value=self.epsilon_min,
                                    max_steps=
self.params['epsilon_decay_final_step'])
```

```
        self.step_num = 0
        self.memory =
ExperienceMemory(capacity=int(self.params['experience_memory_capacity'])) #
Initialize an Experience memory with 1M capacity

    def get_action(self, observation):
        if len(observation.shape) == 3: # Single image (not a batch)
            if observation.shape[2] < observation.shape[0]: # Probably
observation is in W x H x C format
                # Reshape to C x H x W format as per PyTorch's convention
                observation = observation.reshape(observation.shape[2],
observation.shape[1], observation.shape[0])
            observation = np.expand_dims(observation, 0) # Create a batch
dimension
        return self.policy(observation)

    def epsilon_greedy_Q(self, observation):
        # Decay Epsilon/exploration as per schedule
        writer.add_scalar("DQL/epsilon", self.epsilon_decay(self.step_num),
self.step_num)
        self.step_num +=1
        if random.random() < self.epsilon_decay(self.step_num):
            action = random.choice([i for i in range(self.action_shape)])
        else:
            action =
np.argmax(self.Q(observation).data.to(torch.device('cpu')).numpy())


        return action

    def learn(self, s, a, r, s_next, done):
        # TD(0) Q-learning
        if done: # End of episode
            td_target = reward + 0.0 # Set the value of terminal state to
zero
        else:
            td_target = r + self.gamma * torch.max(self.Q(s_next))
        td_error = td_target - self.Q(s)[a]
        # Update Q estimate
        #self.Q(s)[a] = self.Q(s)[a] + self.learning_rate * td_error
        self.Q_optimizer.zero_grad()
        td_error.backward()
        self.Q_optimizer.step()

    def learn_from_batch_experience(self, experiences):
        batch_xp = Experience(*zip(*experiences))
        obs_batch = np.array(batch_xp.obs)
        action_batch = np.array(batch_xp.action)
```

```python
        reward_batch = np.array(batch_xp.reward)
        next_obs_batch = np.array(batch_xp.next_obs)
        done_batch = np.array(batch_xp.done)

        if self.params['use_target_network']:
            if self.step_num % self.params['target_network_update_freq'] ==
0:
                # The *update_freq is the Num steps after which target net
is updated.
                # A schedule can be used instead to vary the update freq.
                self.Q_target.load_state_dict(self.Q.state_dict())
            td_target = reward_batch + ~done_batch * \
                np.tile(self.gamma, len(next_obs_batch)) * \
                self.Q_target(next_obs_batch).max(1)[0].data
        else:
            td_target = reward_batch + ~done_batch * \
                np.tile(self.gamma, len(next_obs_batch)) * \
                self.Q(next_obs_batch).detach().max(1)[0].data

        td_target = td_target.to(device)
        action_idx = torch.from_numpy(action_batch).to(device)
        td_error = torch.nn.functional.mse_loss(
self.Q(obs_batch).gather(1, action_idx.view(-1, 1)),
td_target.float().unsqueeze(1))

        self.Q_optimizer.zero_grad()
        td_error.mean().backward()
        writer.add_scalar("DQL/td_error", td_error.mean(), self.step_num)
        self.Q_optimizer.step()

    def replay_experience(self, batch_size = None):
        batch_size = batch_size if batch_size is not None else
self.params['replay_batch_size']
        experience_batch = self.memory.sample(batch_size)
        self.learn_from_batch_experience(experience_batch)

    def save(self, env_name):
        file_name = self.params['save_dir'] + "DQL_" + env_name + ".ptm"
        torch.save(self.Q.state_dict(), file_name)
        print("Agent's Q model state saved to ", file_name)

    def load(self, env_name):
        file_name = self.params['load_dir'] + "DQL_" + env_name + ".ptm"
        self.Q.load_state_dict(torch.load(file_name))
        print("Loaded Q model state from", file_name)


if __name__ == "__main__":
```

```
    env_conf = params_manager.get_env_params()
    env_conf["env_name"] = args.env_name
    # If a custom useful_region configuration for this environment ID is
available, use it if not use the Default
    custom_region_available = False
    for key, value in env_conf['useful_region'].items():
        if key in args.env_name:
            env_conf['useful_region'] = value
            custom_region_available = True
            break
    if custom_region_available is not True:
        env_conf['useful_region'] = env_conf['useful_region']['Default']
    print("Using env_conf:", env_conf)
    env = Atari.make_env(args.env_name, env_conf)
    observation_shape = env.observation_space.shape
    action_shape = env.action_space.n
    agent_params = params_manager.get_agent_params()
    agent = Deep_Q_Learner(observation_shape, action_shape, agent_params)
    if agent_params['load_trained_model']:
        try:
            agent.load(env_conf["env_name"])
        except FileNotFoundError:
            print("WARNING: No trained model found for this environment.
Training from scratch.")
    first_episode = True
    episode_rewards = list()
    for episode in range(agent_params['max_num_episodes']):
        obs = env.reset()
        cum_reward = 0.0 # Cumulative reward
        done = False
        step = 0
        #for step in range(agent_params['max_steps_per_episode']):
        while not done:
            if env_conf['render']:
                env.render()
            action = agent.get_action(obs)
            next_obs, reward, done, info = env.step(action)
            #agent.learn(obs, action, reward, next_obs, done)
            agent.memory.store(Experience(obs, action, reward, next_obs,
done))

            obs = next_obs
            cum_reward += reward
            step += 1
            global_step_num +=1

            if done is True:
                if first_episode: # Initialize max_reward at the end of
```

```
first episode
                    max_reward = cum_reward
                    first_episode = False
                episode_rewards.append(cum_reward)
                if cum_reward > max_reward:
                    max_reward = cum_reward
                    agent.save(env_conf['env_name'])
                print("\nEpisode#{} ended in {} steps. reward ={} ;
mean_reward={:.3f} best_reward={}".
                        format(episode, step+1, cum_reward,
np.mean(episode_rewards), max_reward))
                writer.add_scalar("main/ep_reward", cum_reward,
global_step_num)
                writer.add_scalar("main/mean_ep_reward",
np.mean(episode_rewards), global_step_num)
                writer.add_scalar("main/max_ep_rew", max_reward,
global_step_num)
                if agent.memory.get_size() >= 2 *
agent_params['replay_batch_size']:
                    agent.replay_experience()

                break
        env.close()
        writer.close()
```

The preceding code, along with some additional changes required for using the Atari wrappers that we will be discussing in the next section, are available at ch6/deep_Q_Learner.py, in this book's code repository. After we complete the next section on *The Atari Gym environment*, we will use the agent implementation in deep_Q_Learner.py to train the agents on the Atari games and see their performance in the end.

This book's code repository will have the latest and up-to-date code implementations with improvements and bug fixes that will be committed after this book is printed. So, it is a good idea to star and watch the book's code repository on GitHub to get automatic updates about these changes and improvements.

The Atari Gym environment

In Chapter 4, *Exploring the Gym and its Features*, we looked at the various list of environments available in the Gym, including the Atari games category, and used a script to list all the Gym environments available on your computer. We also looked at the nomenclature of the environment names, especially for the Atari games. In this section, we will use the Atari environments and see how we can customize the environments with Gym environment wrappers. The following is a collage of 9 screenshots from 9 different Atari environments:

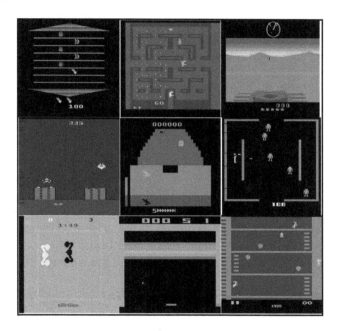

Customizing the Atari Gym environment

Sometimes, we may want to change the way the observations are sent back by the environment or change the scale of the rewards so that our agents can learn better or filter out some information before the agent receives them or change the way the environment is rendered on the screen. So far, we have been developing and customizing our agent to make it act well in the environment. Wouldn't it be nice to have some flexibility around how and what the environment sends back to the agent so that we can customize how the agent learns to act? Fortunately, the Gym library makes it easy to extend or customize the information sent by the environment with the help of Gym environment wrappers. The wrapper interface allows us to subclass and add routines as layers on top of the previous routines. We can add custom processing statements to one or more of the following methods of the Gym environment class:

- `__init__(self, env)__`
- `_seed`
- `_reset`
- `_step`
- `_render`
- `_close`

Depending on the customization we would like to do to the environment, we can decide which methods we want to extend. For example, if we want to change the shape/size of the observation, we can extend the `_step` and `_reset` methods. In the next subsection, we will see how we can make use of the wrapper interface to customize the Atari Gym environments.

Implementing custom Gym environment wrappers

In this section, we will look at a few Gym environment wrappers that are especially very useful for the Gym Atari environments. Most of the wrappers we will implement in this section can be used with other environments as well to improve the learning performance of the agents.

The following table mentions a list of the wrappers will be implementing in the following section with a brief description for each of the wrappers to give you an overview:

Wrapper	Brief description of the purpose
`ClipRewardEnv`	To implement reward clipping
`AtariRescale`	To rescale the screen pixels to a 84x84x1 gray scale image

NormalizedEnv	To normalize the images based on the mean and variance observed in the environment
NoopResetEnv	To perform a random number of noop (empty) actions on reset to sample different initial states
FireResetEnv	To perform a fire action on reset
EpisodicLifeEnv	To mark end of life as end of episode and reset when game is over
MaxAndSkipEnv	Repeats the action for a fixed number (specified using the skip argument; the default is 4) of steps

Reward clipping

Different problems or environments provide different ranges of reward values. For example, we saw in the previous chapter that in the Mountain Car v0 environment, the agent receives a reward of -1 for every time step until episode termination, no matter which way the agent moves the car. In the Cart Pole v0 environment, the agent receives a reward of +1 for every time step until episode termination. In Atari game environments like MS Pac-Man, if the agent eats a single ghost, it will receive a reward of up to +1,600. We can start to see how the magnitudes of the reward as well as the occasion of the reward varies widely across different environments and learning problems. If our deep Q-learner agent algorithm has to solve this variety of problems without us trying to fine-tune the hyperparameters to work well for each of the environments independently, we have to do something about the varying scales of reward. This is exactly the intuition behind reward clipping, in which we clip the reward to be either -1, 0, or +1, depending on the sign of the actual reward received from the environment. This way, we limit the magnitude of the reward which can vary widely across the different environments. We can implement this simple reward clipping technique and apply it to our environments by inheriting from the gym.RewardWrapper class and modifying the reward(...) function, as shown in the following code snippet:

```
class ClipRewardEnv(gym.RewardWrapper):
    def __init__(self, env):
        gym.RewardWrapper.__init__(self, env)

    def reward(self, reward):
        """ Clip rewards to be either -1, 0 or +1 based on the sign"""
        return np.sign(reward)
```

The technique of clipping the reward to (-1, 0, 1) works well for Atari games. But, it is good to know that this may not be the the best technique to universally handle environments with varying reward magnitudes and frequency. Clipping the reward value modifies the learning objective of the agent and may sometimes lead to qualitatively different policies being learned by the agent than what is desired.

Preprocessing Atari screen image frames

The Atari Gym environment produces observations which typically have a shape of 210x160x3, which represents a RGB (color) image of a width of 210 pixels and a height of 160 pixels. While the color image at the original resolution of 210x160x3 has more pixels and therefore more information, it turns out that often, better performance is possible with reduced resolution. Lower resolution means less data to be processed by the agent at every step, which translates to faster training time, especially on consumer grade computing hardware that you and I own.

Let's create a preprocessing pipeline that would take the original observation image (of the Atari screen) and perform the following operations:

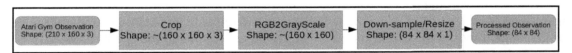

We can crop out the region on the screen that does not have any useful information regarding the environment for the agent.

Finally, we resize the image to a dimension of 84x84. We can choose a different number, other than 84, as long as it contains a reasonable amount of pixels. However, it is efficient to have a square matrix (like 84x84 or 80x80) as the convolution operations (for example, with CUDA) are optimized for such square input:

```python
def process_frame_84(frame, conf):
    frame = frame[conf["crop1"]:conf["crop2"] + 160, :160]
    frame = frame.mean(2)
    frame = frame.astype(np.float32)
    frame *= (1.0 / 255.0)
    frame = cv2.resize(frame, (84, conf["dimension2"]))
    frame = cv2.resize(frame, (84, 84))
    frame = np.reshape(frame, [1, 84, 84])
    return frame


class AtariRescale(gym.ObservationWrapper):
    def __init__(self, env, env_conf):
        gym.ObservationWrapper.__init__(self, env)
        self.observation_space = Box(0.0, 1.0, [1, 84, 84])
        self.conf = env_conf

    def observation(self, observation):
        return process_frame_84(observation, self.conf)
```

Note that with a resolution of 84x84 pixels for one observation frame with a data type of `numpy.float32` which takes 4 bytes, we need about 4x84x84 = 28,224 bytes. As you may recall from the *Experience memory* section, one experience object contains two frames (one for the observation and the other for the next observation), which means we'll need 2x 28,224 = 56,448 bytes (+ 2 bytes for *action* + 4 bytes for *reward*). The 56,448 bytes (or 0.056448 MB) may not seem much, but if you consider the fact that it is typical to be using an experience memory capacity in the order of 1e6 (million), you may realize that we need about 1e6 x 0.056448 MB = 56,448 MB or 56.448 GB! This means that we will need 56.448 GB of RAM just for the experience memory with a capacity of 1 million experiences!

You can do a couple of memory optimizations to reduce the required RAM for training the agent. Using a smaller experience memory is a straightforward way to reduce the memory footprint in some games. In some environments, having a larger experience memory will help the agent to learn faster. One way to reduce the memory footprint it by not scaling the frames (by dividing by 255) while storing, which requires a floating point representation (`numpy.float32`) and rather storing the frames as numpy.uint8 so that we only need 1 byte instead of 4 bytes per pixels, which will help in reducing the memory requirement by a factor of 4. Then, when we want to use the stored experiences in our forward pass to the network to the deep Q-network to get the Q-value predictions, we can scale the images to be in the range 0.0 to 1.0.

Normalizing observations

In some cases, normalizing the observations can help with convergence speed. The most commonly used normalization process involves two steps:

1. Zero-centering using mean subtraction
2. Scaling using the standard deviation

In essence, the following is the normalization process:

```
(x - numpy.mean(x)) / numpy.std(x)
```

In the previous process, x is the observation. Note that other normalization processes are also used, depending on the range of the normalized value that is desired. For example, if we wanted the values after the normalization to lie between 0 and 1, we could use the following:

```
(x - numpy.min(x)) / (numpy.max(x) - numpy.min(x))
```

In the previous process, instead of subtracting the mean, we subtract the minimum value and divide by the difference between the maximum and the minimum value. This way, the minimum value in the observation/x gets normalized to 0 and the maximum value gets normalized to a value of 1.

Alternatively, if we wanted the values after the normalization to lie between -1 and +1, then the following can be used:

```
2 * (x - numpy.min(x)) / (numpy.max(x) - numpy.min(x)) - 1
```

In our environment normalization wrapper implementation, we will use the first method where we zero-center the observation data using mean subtraction and scale using the standard deviation of the data in the observation. In fact, we will go one step further and calculate the running mean and standard deviation of all the observations we have received so far to normalize the observations based on the distribution of the observation data the agent has observed so far. This is more appropriate as there can be high variance between different observations from the same environment. The following is the implementation code for the normalization wrapper that we discussed:

```python
class NormalizedEnv(gym.ObservationWrapper):
    def __init__(self, env=None):
        gym.ObservationWrapper.__init__(self, env)
        self.state_mean = 0
        self.state_std = 0
        self.alpha = 0.9999
        self.num_steps = 0

    def observation(self, observation):
        self.num_steps += 1
        self.state_mean = self.state_mean * self.alpha + \
            observation.mean() * (1 - self.alpha)
        self.state_std = self.state_std * self.alpha + \
            observation.std() * (1 - self.alpha)

        unbiased_mean = self.state_mean / (1 - pow(self.alpha,
self.num_steps))
        unbiased_std = self.state_std / (1 - pow(self.alpha,
self.num_steps))
```

```
return (observation - unbiased_mean) / (unbiased_std + 1e-8)
```

 The image frames that we get as observation from the environment (even after our preprocessing wrapper) is already on the same scale (0-255 or 0.0 to 1.0). The scaling step in the normalization procedure may not be very helpful in this case. This wrapper in general could be useful for other environment types and was also not observed to be detrimental to the performance for already scaled image observations from Gym environments like Atari.

Random no-ops on reset

When the environment is reset, the agent usually starts from the same initial state and therefore receives the same observation on reset. The agent may memorize or get used to the starting state in one game level so much that they might start performing poorly they start in a slightly different position or game level. Sometimes, it was found to be helpful to randomize the initial state, such as sampling different initial states from which the agent starts the episode. To make that happen, we can add a Gym wrapper that performs a random number of "no-ops" before sending out the first observation after the reset. The Arcade Learning Environment for the Atari 2600 that the Gym library uses for the Atari environment supports a "NOOP" or no-operation action, which in the Gym library is coded as an action with a value of 0. So, we will step the environment with a random number of *action*=0 before returning the observation to the agent, as shown in the following code snippet:

```python
class NoopResetEnv(gym.Wrapper):
    def __init__(self, env, noop_max=30):
        """Sample initial states by taking random number of no-ops on
reset.
        No-op is assumed to be action 0.
        """
        gym.Wrapper.__init__(self, env)
        self.noop_max = noop_max
        self.noop_action = 0
        assert env.unwrapped.get_action_meanings()[0] == 'NOOP'

    def reset(self):
        """ Do no-op action for a number of steps in [1, noop_max]."""
        self.env.reset()
        noops = random.randrange(1, self.noop_max + 1) # pylint:
disable=E1101
        assert noops > 0
        obs = None
        for _ in range(noops):
            obs, _, done, _ = self.env.step(self.noop_action)
```

```
            return obs

    def step(self, ac):
        return self.env.step(ac)
```

Fire on reset

Some Atari games require the player to press the **Fire** button to start the game. Some games require the **Fire** button to be pressed after every life is lost. More often that not, this is the only use for the **Fire** button! Although it might look trivial for us to realize that, it may be difficult for the reinforcement learning agents to figure that out on their own sometimes. It is not the case that they are incapable of learning that. In fact, they are capable of figuring out lots of hidden glitches or modes in the game that no human has ever figured out! For example, in the game of Qbert, an agent trained using Evolutionary Strategies (which is a black-box type learning strategy inspired by genetic algorithms) figured out a peculiar way with which it can keep receiving scores and never let the game end! You know how much the agent was able to score? ~1,000,000! They could only get that much because the game was reset artificially due to a time limit. Can you try scoring that much in the game of Qbert? You can see that agent scoring in action here: https://www.youtube.com/watch?v=meE5aaRJ0Zs.

The point is not that the agents are so smart to figure all these things out. They definitely can, but most of the time, this harms the progress the agent can make in a reasonable amount of time. This is especially true when we want a single agent to tackle several different varieties of games (one at a time). We are better off starting with simpler assumptions and making them more complicated after we have been able to train the agents to play well using the simpler assumptions.

Therefore, we will implement a `FireResetEnv` Gym wrapper that will press the Fire button on every reset and get the environment started for the agent. The code's implementation is as follows:

```
    class FireResetEnv(gym.Wrapper):
        def __init__(self, env):
            """Take action on reset for environments that are fixed until
    firing."""
            gym.Wrapper.__init__(self, env)
            assert env.unwrapped.get_action_meanings()[1] == 'FIRE'
            assert len(env.unwrapped.get_action_meanings()) >= 3

        def reset(self):
            self.env.reset()
            obs, _, done, _ = self.env.step(1)
            if done:
```

```
        self.env.reset()
    obs, _, done, _ = self.env.step(2)
    if done:
        self.env.reset()
    return obs

def step(self, ac):
    return self.env.step(ac)
```

Episodic life

In many games, including Atari games, the player gets to play with more than one life.

It was observed, used, and reported by Deepmind that terminating an episode when a life is lost helps the agent learn better. It has to be noted that the intention is to signify to the agent that losing a life is a bad thing to do. In this case, when the episode terminates, we will not reset the environment and rather continue until the game is actually over, after which we reset the environment. If we reset the game after every loss of life, we would be limiting the agent's exposure to observations and experiences that can be collected with just one life, which is usually bad for the agent's learning performance.

To implement what we just discussed, we will use the `EpisodicLifeEnv` class that marks the end of an episode when a life is lost, and reset the environment when the game is over, as shown in the following code snippet:

```
class EpisodicLifeEnv(gym.Wrapper):
    def __init__(self, env):
        """Make end-of-life == end-of-episode, but only reset on true game
over.
        Done by DeepMind for the DQN and co. since it helps value
estimation.
        """
        gym.Wrapper.__init__(self, env)
        self.lives = 0
        self.was_real_done = True

    def step(self, action):
        obs, reward, done, info = self.env.step(action)
        self.was_real_done = True
        # check current lives, make loss of life terminal,
        # then update lives to handle bonus lives
        lives = info['ale.lives']
        if lives < self.lives and lives > 0:
            # for Qbert sometimes we stay in lives == 0 condition for a few
frames
            # so its important to keep lives > 0, so that we only reset
```

```
once
            # the environment advertises done.
            done = True
            self.was_real_done = False
        self.lives = lives
        return obs, reward, done, info

    def reset(self):
        """Reset only when lives are exhausted.
        This way all states are still reachable even though lives are
episodic,
        and the learner need not know about any of this behind-the-scenes.
        """
        if self.was_real_done:
            obs = self.env.reset()
            self.lives = 0
        else:
            # no-op step to advance from terminal/lost life state
            obs, _, _, info = self.env.step(0)
            self.lives = info['ale.lives']
        return obs
```

Max and skip-frame

The Gym library provides environments that have NoFrameskip in their ID, which we discussed in Chapter 4, *Exploring the Gym and its Features*, where we discussed the nomenclature of the Gym environments. As you may recall from our discussion in Chapter 4, *Exploring the Gym and its Features*, by default, if there is no presence of Deterministic or NoFrameskip in the environment name, the action sent to the environment is repeatedly performed for a duration of *n* frames, where *n* is uniformly sampled from (2, 3, 4). If we want to step through the environment at a specific rate, we can use the Gym Atari environments with NoFrameskip in their ID, which will step through the underlying environment without any alteration to the step duration. The step rate, in this case, is of $\frac{1}{60}^{th}$ a second, which is 60 frames per second. We can then customize the environment to skip at our choice to skip the rate (*k*) to step at a specific rate. The implementation for such a custom step/skip rate is as follows:

```
class MaxAndSkipEnv(gym.Wrapper):
    def __init__(self, env=None, skip=4):
        """Return only every `skip`-th frame"""
        gym.Wrapper.__init__(self, env)
        # most recent raw observations (for max pooling across time steps)
        self._obs_buffer = deque(maxlen=2)
        self._skip = skip
```

```
def step(self, action):
    total_reward = 0.0
    done = None
    for _ in range(self._skip):
        obs, reward, done, info = self.env.step(action)
        self._obs_buffer.append(obs)
        total_reward += reward
        if done:
            break

    max_frame = np.max(np.stack(self._obs_buffer), axis=0)
    return max_frame, total_reward, done, info

def reset(self):
    """Clear past frame buffer and init. to first obs. from inner
env."""
    self._obs_buffer.clear()
    obs = self.env.reset()
    self._obs_buffer.append(obs)
    return obs
```

Notice that we are also taking the maximum of the pixel values over the frames that were skipped and sending that as the observation instead of totally ignoring all the intermediate image frames that were skipped.

Wrapping the Gym environment

Finally, we will apply the preceding wrappers that we developed based on the environment configuration we specify using the `parameters.JSON` file:

```
def make_env(env_id, env_conf):
    env = gym.make(env_id)
    if 'NoFrameskip' in env_id:
        assert 'NoFrameskip' in env.spec.id
        env = NoopResetEnv(env, noop_max=30)
        env = MaxAndSkipEnv(env, skip=env_conf['skip_rate'])

    if env_conf['episodic_life']:
        env = EpisodicLifeEnv(env)

    if 'FIRE' in env.unwrapped.get_action_meanings():
        env = FireResetEnv(env)

    env = AtariRescale(env, env_conf['useful_region'])
    env = NormalizedEnv(env)
```

```
    if env_conf['clip_reward']:
        env = ClipRewardEnv(env)
    return env
```

All of the environment wrappers that we discussed previously are implemented and available in the `ch6/environment/atari.py` in this book's code repository.

Training the deep Q-learner to play Atari games

We have gone through several new techniques in this chapter. You deserve a pat on your back for making it this far! Now starts the fun part where you can let your agents train by themselves to play several Atari games and see how they are progressing. What is great about our deep Q-learner is the fact that we can use the same agent to train and play any of the Atari games!

By the end of this section, you should be able to use our deep Q learning agent to observe the pixels on the screen and take actions by sending the joystick commands to the Atari Gym environment, just like what is shown in the following screenshot:

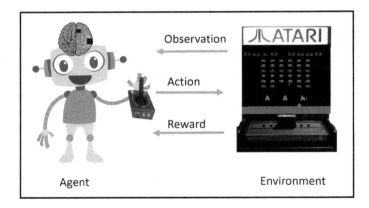

Putting together a comprehensive deep Q-learner

It is time to combine all the techniques we have discussed into a comprehensive implementation that makes use of all of those techniques to get maximum performance. We will use the `environment.atari` module that we created in the previous section with several useful Gym environment wrappers. Let's look at the code outline to understand the code's structure:

 You will notice that some sections of the code are removed for brevity and replaced with. . ., signifying that the code in that section has been folded/hidden. You can find the latest version of the complete code in this book's code repository at `ch6/deep_Q_Learner.py`.

```python
#!/usr/bin/env python
#!/usr/bin/env python

import gym
import torch
import random
import numpy as np

import environment.atari as Atari
import environment.utils as env_utils
from utils.params_manager import ParamsManager
from utils.decay_schedule import LinearDecaySchedule
from utils.experience_memory import Experience, ExperienceMemory
from function_approximator.perceptron import SLP
from function_approximator.cnn import CNN
from tensorboardX import SummaryWriter
from datetime import datetime
from argparse import ArgumentParser

args = ArgumentParser("deep_Q_learner")
args.add_argument("--params-file", help="Path to the parameters json file.
Default is parameters.json",
                  default="parameters.json", metavar="PFILE")
args.add_argument("--env-name", help="ID of the Atari environment available
in OpenAI Gym. Default is Seaquest-v0",
                  default="Seaquest-v0", metavar="ENV")
args.add_argument("--gpu-id", help="GPU device ID to use. Default=0",
default=0, type=int, metavar="GPU_ID")
args.add_argument("--render", help="Render environment to Screen. Off by
default", action="store_true", default=False)
args.add_argument("--test", help="Test mode. Used for playing without
learning. Off by default", action="store_true",
                  default=False)
```

```
args = args.parse_args()

params_manager= ParamsManager(args.params_file)
seed = params_manager.get_agent_params()['seed']
summary_file_path_prefix =
params_manager.get_agent_params()['summary_file_path_prefix']
summary_file_path= summary_file_path_prefix + args.env_name + "_" +
datetime.now().strftime("%y-%m-%d-%H-%M")
writer = SummaryWriter(summary_file_path)
# Export the parameters as json files to the log directory to keep track of
the parameters used in each experiment
params_manager.export_env_params(summary_file_path + "/" +
"env_params.json")
params_manager.export_agent_params(summary_file_path + "/" +
"agent_params.json")
global_step_num = 0
use_cuda = params_manager.get_agent_params()['use_cuda']
# new in PyTorch 0.4
device = torch.device("cuda:" + str(args.gpu_id) if
torch.cuda.is_available() and use_cuda else "cpu")
torch.manual_seed(seed)
np.random.seed(seed)
if torch.cuda.is_available() and use_cuda:
    torch.cuda.manual_seed_all(seed)


class Deep_Q_Learner(object):
    def __init__(self, state_shape, action_shape, params):
        ...
    def get_action(self, observation):
        ...

    def epsilon_greedy_Q(self, observation):
        ...

    def learn(self, s, a, r, s_next, done):
        ...

    def learn_from_batch_experience(self, experiences):
        ...

    def replay_experience(self, batch_size = None):
        ...

    def load(self, env_name):
        ...
```

```
if __name__ == "__main__":
    env_conf = params_manager.get_env_params()
    env_conf["env_name"] = args.env_name
    # If a custom useful_region configuration for this environment ID is
available, use it if not use the Default
    ...
    # If a saved (pre-trained) agent's brain model is available load it as
per the configuration
    if agent_params['load_trained_model']:
    ...

    # Start the training process
    episode = 0
    while global_step_num <= agent_params['max_training_steps']:
        obs = env.reset()
        cum_reward = 0.0 # Cumulative reward
        done = False
        step = 0
        #for step in range(agent_params['max_steps_per_episode']):
        while not done:
            if env_conf['render'] or args.render:
                env.render()
            action = agent.get_action(obs)
            next_obs, reward, done, info = env.step(action)
            #agent.learn(obs, action, reward, next_obs, done)
            agent.memory.store(Experience(obs, action, reward, next_obs,
done))

            obs = next_obs
            cum_reward += reward
            step += 1
            global_step_num +=1

            if done is True:
                episode += 1
                episode_rewards.append(cum_reward)
                if cum_reward > agent.best_reward:
                    agent.best_reward = cum_reward
                if np.mean(episode_rewards) > prev_checkpoint_mean_ep_rew:
                    num_improved_episodes_before_checkpoint += 1
                if num_improved_episodes_before_checkpoint >=
agent_params["save_freq_when_perf_improves"]:
                    prev_checkpoint_mean_ep_rew = np.mean(episode_rewards)
                    agent.best_mean_reward = np.mean(episode_rewards)
                    agent.save(env_conf['env_name'])
                    num_improved_episodes_before_checkpoint = 0
                print("\nEpisode#{} ended in {} steps. reward ={} ;
mean_reward={:.3f} best_reward={}".
```

```
                      format(episode, step+1, cum_reward,
    np.mean(episode_rewards), agent.best_reward))
                    writer.add_scalar("main/ep_reward", cum_reward,
    global_step_num)
                    writer.add_scalar("main/mean_ep_reward",
    np.mean(episode_rewards), global_step_num)
                    writer.add_scalar("main/max_ep_rew", agent.best_reward,
    global_step_num)
                    # Learn from batches of experience once a certain amount of
    xp is available unless in test only mode
                    if agent.memory.get_size() >= 2 *
    agent_params['replay_start_size'] and not args.test:
                        agent.replay_experience()

                    break
        env.close()
        writer.close()
```

Hyperparameters

The following is a list of hyperparameters that our deep Q-learner uses, with a brief description of what they are and the types of values they take:

Hyperparameter	Brief description	Value type
max_num_episodes	Maximum number of episodes to run the agent.	Integer (for example, 100,000)
replay_memory_capacity	Total capacity of the experience memory capacity.	Integer or exponential notation (for example, 1e6)
replay_batch_size	Number of transitions used in a (mini) batch to update the Q-function in each update iteration during experience replay.	Integer (for example, 2,000)
use_target_network	Whether a target Q-network is to be used or not.	Boolean (true/false)
target_network_update_freq	The number of steps after which the target Q-network is updated using the main Q-network.	Integer (for example, 1,000)
lr	The learning rate for the deep Q-network.	float (for example, 1e-4)
gamma	The discount factor for the MDP.	float (for example, 0.98)

epsilon_max	The maximum value of the epsilon from which the decay starts.	float (for example, 1.0)
epsilon_min	The minimum value for epsilon to which the decay will finally settle to.	float (for example, :0.05)
seed	The seed used to seed numpy and torch (and `torch.cuda`) to be able to reproduce (to some extent) the randomness introduced by those libraries.	Integer (for example, :555)
use_cuda	Whether or not to use CUDA based GPU if a GPU is available.	Boolean (for example, : true)
load_trained_model	Whether or not to load a trained model if one exists for this environment/problem. If this parameter is set to true but no trained model is available, the model will be trained from scratch.	Boolean (for example, : true)
load_dir	The path to the directory (including the forward slash) from where the trained model should be loaded from to resume training.	String (for example, : "trained_models/")
save_dir	The path to a directory where the models should be saved. New models are saved every time the agent achieves a new best score/reward.	string (for example, : trained_models/")

Please refer to the `ch6/parameters.JSON` file in this book's code repository for the updated list of parameters used by the agent.

Launching the training process

We have now put together all the pieces for the deep Q-learner and are ready to train the agent! Be sure to check out/pull/download the latest code from this book's code repository.

You can pick any environment from the list of Atari environments and train the agent we developed using the following command:

```
(rl_gym_book) praveen@ubuntu:~/HOIAWOG/ch6$ python deep_Q_learner.py --env "ENV_ID"
```

In the previous command, `ENV_ID` is the name/ID of the Atari Gym environment. For example, if you want to train the agent on the `pong` environment with no frame skip, you would run the following command:

```
(rl_gym_book) praveen@ubuntu:~/HOIAWOG/ch6$ python deep_Q_learner.py --env
"PongNoFrameskip-v4"
```

By default, the training logs will be saved to `./logs/DQL_{ENV}_{T}`, where `{ENV}` is the name of the environment and `{T}` is the time stamp obtained when you run the agent. If you start a TensorBoard instance using the following command:

```
(rl_gym_book) praveen@ubuntu:~/HOIAWOG/ch6$ tensorboard --logdir=logs/
```

By default, our `deep_Q_learner.py` script will use the `parameters.JSON` file located in the same directory as the script for reading the configurable parameter values. You can override with a different parameter configuration file using the command-line `--params-file` argument.

If the `load_trained_model` parameter is set to `true` in the `parameters.JSON` file and if a saved model for the chosen environment is available, our script will try to initialize the agent with the model that it learned previously so that it can resume from where it left off rather than train from scratch.

Testing performance of your deep Q-learner in Atari games

It feels great, doesn't it? You have now developed an agent that can learn to play any Atari game and get better at it by itself! Once you have your agent trained on any Atari game, you can use the test mode of the script to test the agent's performance based on its learning so far. You can enable the test mode by using the `--test` argument in the `deep_q_learner.py` script. It is useful to enable rendering of the environment, too, so that you can visually see (apart from the rewards printed on the console) how the agent is performing. As an example, you can test the agent in the `Seaquest` Atari game using the following command:

```
(rl_gym_book) praveen@ubuntu:~/HOIAWOG/ch6$ python deep_Q_learner.py --env
"Seaquest-v0" --test --render
```

You will see the Seaquest game window come up and the agent showing of its skills!

A couple of points to note regarding the `test` mode are the following:

- The test mode will turn off the agent's learning routine. Therefore, the agent will not learn or update itself in the test mode. This mode is only used to test how a trained agent is performing. If you want to see how the agent is performing while it is learning, you can just use the `--render` option without the `--test` option.
- The test mode assumes that a trained model for the environment you choose exists in the `trained_models` folder. Otherwise, a newborn agent, without any prior knowledge, will start playing the game from scratch. Also, since learning is disabled, you will not see the agent improving!

Now, it's your turn to go out, experiment, review, and compare the performance of the agent we implemented in different Atari Gym environments and see how much the agent can score! If you train an agent to play well in a game, you can show and share it to other fellow readers by opening a pull request on this book's code repository from your fork. You will be featured on the page!

Once you get comfortable using the code base we developed, you can do several experiments with it. For example, you can turn off the target Q-network or increase/decrease the experience memory/replay batch size by simply changing the `parameters.JSON` file and comparing the performance using the very convenient TensorBoard dashboard.

Summary

We started this chapter with the grand goal of developing intelligent learning agents that can achieve great scores in Atari games. We made incremental progress towards it by implementing several techniques to improve upon the Q-learner that we developed in the previous chapter. We first started with learning how we can use a neural network to approximate the Q action-value function and made our learning concrete by practically implementing a shallow neural network to solve the famous Cart Pole problem. We then implemented experience memory and experience replay that enables the agent to learn from (mini) randomly sampled batches of experiences that helped in improving the performance by breaking the correlations between the agent's interactions and increasing the sample efficiency with the batch replay of the agent's prior experience. We then revisited the epsilon-greedy action selection policy and implemented a decay schedule to decrease the exploration based on a schedule to let the agent rely more on its learning.

We then looked at how to use TensorBoard's logging and visualization capabilities with our PyTorch-based learning agent so that we can watch the agent's training progress in a simple and intuitive way. We also implemented a neat little parameter manager class that enabled us to configure the hyperparameters of the agent and other configuration parameters using an external easy-to-read JSON file.

After we got a good baseline and the helpful utility tools implemented, we started our implementation of the deep Q-learner. We started that section by implementing a deep convolutional neural network in PyTorch which we then used to represent our agent's Q (action-value) function. We then saw how easy it was to implement the idea of using a target Q-network which is known to stabilize the agent's Q learning process. We then put together our deep Q learning-based agent that can learn to act based on just the raw pixel observations from a Gym environment.

We then laid our eyes and hands on the Atari Gym environments and looked at several ways to customize the Gym environments using Gym environment wrappers. We also discussed several useful wrappers for the Atari environment and specifically implemented wrappers to clip the reward, preprocess the observation image frames, normalize the observations over all the entire sampled observation distribution, send random noop actions on reset to sample different start states, press the Fire button on resets, and to step at a custom rate by frame skipping. We finally saw how we can consolidate this all together into a comprehensive agent training code base and train the agent on any Atari game and see the progress summary on TensorBoard. We also looked at how we could save the state and resume the training of the agent from a previous saved state instead of rerunning the training from scratch. Towards the end, we saw the improving performance of the agent we implemented and trained.

We hope that you had a lot of fun throughout this whole chapter. We will be looking at and implementing a different algorithm in the next chapter, which can be used for taking much more complex actions rather than a discrete set of button presses and how we can use it to train an agent to autonomously control a car in simulation!

7
Creating Custom OpenAI Gym Environments - CARLA Driving Simulator

In the first chapter, we looked at the various categories of learning environments available in the OpenAI Gym environment catalog. We then explored the list of environments and their nomenclature in `Chapter 5`, *Implementing your First Learning Agent – Solving the Mountain Car problem*, as well as a sneak peek into some of them. We also developed our agents to solve the Mountain Car and Cart Pole problems, and a few Atari game environments. By now, then, you should have a good understanding of the various environment types and flavors that are available with OpenAI Gym. Most often, once we learn how to develop our own intelligent agents, we want to use that knowledge and skill to develop intelligent agents to solve new problems, problems that we already face, or even problems that are of interest to us. For instance, you might be a game developer wanting to add intelligent behaviors to your game characters or a robotics engineer wanting to instill artificial intelligence to your robot, or you could be an autonomous driving engineer wanting to apply reinforcement learning to autonomous driving. You might be a tinkerer wanting to turn a gadget into an intelligent **Internet of Things** (**IoT**) device, or you might even be a healthcare professional wanting to improve your lab's diagnostic capabilities using machine learning. The potential for application is almost limitless.

One of the reasons we have chosen OpenAI Gym as our learning environment is because of its simple yet standard interface that decouples the type and nature of the environment from the environment-agent interface. In this chapter, we will look at how you can create your own environment based on your own personal or professional needs. This will enable you to use agent implementations, training and testing scripts, the parameter manager, and the logging and visualization routines that we developed in earlier chapters with your own design or problem.

Understanding the anatomy of Gym environments

Any Gym-compatible environment should subclass the `gym.Env` class and implement the `reset` and `step` methods and the `observation_space` and `action_space` properties and attributes. There is also the opportunity to implement other, optional methods that can add additional functionality to our custom environments. The following table lists and describes the other methods available:

Method	Functionality description
observation_space	The shape and type of the observations returned by the environment.
action_space	The shape and type of the actions accepted by the environment.
reset()	Routines to reset the environment at the start or end of an episode.
step(...)	Routines that calculate the necessary information to advance the environment, simulation, or game to the next step. The routine includes applying the chosen action in the environment, calculating the reward, producing the next observation, and determining if an episode has ended.
_render()	(Optional) This renders the state or observation of the Gym environment.
_close()	(Optional) This closes the Gym environment.
_seed	(Optional) This seeds the random functions in the Gym environment with a custom seed that makes the environment behave in a reproducible way for a given seed.
_configure	(Optional) This enables additional environment configuration.

Creating a template for custom Gym environment implementations

Based on the anatomy of the Gym environment we have already discussed, we will now lay out a basic version of a custom environment class implementation named `CustomEnv`, which will be a subclass of `gym.Env` and implement the essential methods and arguments required to make it a Gym-compatible environment. A template for a minimal implementation is as follows:

```python
import gym

class CustomEnv(gym.Env):
    """
    A template to implement custom OpenAI Gym environments

    """

    metadata = {'render.modes': ['human']}
    def __init__(self):
        self.__version__ = "0.0.1"
        # Modify the observation space, low, high and shape values
        according to your custom environment's needs
        self.observation_space = gym.spaces.Box(low=0.0, high=1.0,
        shape=(3,))
        # Modify the action space, and dimension according to your custom
        environment's needs
        self.action_space = gym.spaces.Box(4)

    def step(self, action):
        """
        Runs one time-step of the environment's dynamics. The reset()
        method is called at the end of every episode
        :param action: The action to be executed in the environment
        :return: (observation, reward, done, info)
            observation (object):
                Observation from the environment at the current time-step
            reward (float):
                Reward from the environment due to the previous action
        performed
            done (bool):
                a boolean, indicating whether the episode has ended
            info (dict):
                a dictionary containing additional information about the
        previous action
        """
```

```
            # Implement your step method here
            #    - Calculate reward based on the action
            #    - Calculate next observation
            #    - Set done to True if end of episode else set done to False
            #    - Optionally, set values to the info dict
            # return (observation, reward, done, info)

    def reset(self):
        """
        Reset the environment state and returns an initial observation

        Returns
        -------
        observation (object): The initial observation for the new episode
    after reset
        :return:
        """

        # Implement your reset method here
        # return observation

    def render(self, mode='human', close=False):
        """

        :param mode:
        :return:
        """
        return
```

After we have finished our environment class implementation, we should register it with the OpenAI Gym registry so that we can use `gym.make(ENV_NAME)` to create an instance of the environment, as we have previously with Gym environments.

Registering custom environments with OpenAI Gym

The registration of a custom Gym environment is easy with the use of the `gym.envs.registration.register` module; this provides the `register` method, which in turn takes as an argument `id`, which is the name of the environment we want to use when calling `gym.make(...)` and `entry_point`, the class name for the custom environment implementation we discussed earlier. The code snippet to register the `CustomEnv` class we implemented is as follows:

```
from gym.envs.registration import register

register(
    id='CustomEnv-v0',
    entry_point='custom_environments.envs:CustomEnv',
)
```

We will make use of this template later on in this chapter to create a custom Gym environment that uses a very sophisticated driving simulator.

Creating an OpenAI Gym-compatible CARLA driving simulator environment

CARLA is a driving simulator environment built on top of the UnrealEngine4 game engine with more realistic rendering compared to some of its competitors. You can read more about the CARLA simulator on their official website at `https://carla.org`. In this section, we will look into how we can create a custom OpenAI Gym-compatible car driving environment to train our learning agents. This is a fairly complex environment and requires a GPU to run—which is unlike other Gym environments we have seen so far. Once you understand how to create a custom environment interface that is Gym-compatible for CARLA, you may well have enough information to develop interfaces for any of your own custom environments, no matter how complex they might be.

The latest version of CARLA is CARLA 0.8.2. While most (if not all) of the core environment interfaces, especially the `PythonClient` library, might stay the same, there is a chance of future changes that necessitate tweaks in this custom environment implementation. If that happens, the code repository of this book will be updated accordingly to support newer versions of CARLA. You may want to make sure you use the latest version of the code from the book's code repository when you work on this chapter (which is yet another reason to subscribe to notifications in GitHub). Nevertheless, the custom environment implementation building blocks discussed in this chapter will stay generally applicable, and will walk you through defining your own custom environments that are compatible with the OpenAI Gym interface. The complete code for the custom CARLA environment interface is available in the book's code repository under `ch7/carla-gym`.

Before we start a Gym-compatible CARLA environment, let's first take a look at the CARLA simulator. So, let's go ahead and download the CARLA release binaries. In the following section, we will use VER_NUM to denote the version number, so be sure to replace the VER_NUM text with the version number you are using before running the following commands:

1. First, create a folder named `software` in your home directory using the following bash command:

```
mkdir ~/software && cd ~/software
```

2. Download the CARLA binary release version for Linux (`CARLA_VER_NUM.tar.gz`) using the link on the official release page at `https://github.com/carla-simulator/carla/releases/tag/VER_NUM`. (The direct link to version 0.8.2 is: `https://drive.google.com/open?id=1ZtVt1AqdyGxgyTm69nzuwrOYoPUn_Dsm`.) Then, extract it into `~/software`. You should now have a file named `CarlaUE4.sh` in the `~/software/CARLA_VER_NUM` folder.

3. Set the `CARLA_SERVER` environment variable to point to `CarlaUE4.sh` on your computer using the following command:

```
export CARLA_SERVER=~/software/CARLA_VER_NUM/CarlaUE4.sh
```

Now you are ready to test-run the CARLA driving simulator! Just execute $CARLA_SERVER or, directly, `~/software/CARLA_VER_NUM/CarlaUE4.sh`. For CARLA version 0.8.2, this command will be `~/software/CARLA_0.8.2/CarlaUE4.sh`. You should now see a CARLA simulator screen, as shown in the following screenshot:

The previous screenshot shows the vehicle (the agent) in one of CARLA's starting positions. The following screenshot shows the vehicle in another starting position in the CARLA environment:

Once the vehicle is initialized, you should be able to control the vehicle using the *w*, *a*, *s*, *d* keys on your keyboard. The *w* key will move the car forwards, the *a* key will turn the car to the left, and... you can probably figure out the rest!

Let's now move on and start our Gym-compatible CARLA environment implementation with configuration and initialization.

Configuration and initialization

We will first define some environment-specific configuration parameters, as well as briefly look at scenario configurations, as well. We will then start the initialization process for the CarlaEnv class implementation, which will inherit from the Gym.Env class.

Configuration

Let's first define a list of configuration parameters for the environment using a dictionary, shown as follows:

```
# Default environment configuration
ENV_CONFIG = {
    "enable_planner": True,
    "use_depth_camera": False,
    "discrete_actions": True,
    "server_map": "/Game/Maps/" + city,
    "scenarios": [scenario_config["Lane_Keep_Town2"]],
    "framestack": 2, # note: only [1, 2] currently supported
    "early_terminate_on_collision": True,
    "verbose": False,
    "render_x_res": 800,
    "render_y_res": 600,
    "x_res": 80,
    "y_res": 80
}
```

`scenario_config` defines several parameters that are useful for creating a variety of driving scenarios. The scenario configuration is described in the `scenarios.json` file, which can be found in the book's code repository at `ch7/carla-gym/carla_gym /envs/scenarios.json`.

Initialization

In the `__init__` method, we define the initialization parameters along with the action and state spaces, which, as we saw in the previous section, are necessary. The implementation is straight-forward, as follows:

```
def __init__(self, config=ENV_CONFIG):
        self.config = config
        self.city = self.config["server_map"].split("/")[-1]
        if self.config["enable_planner"]:
            self.planner = Planner(self.city)

        if config["discrete_actions"]:
            self.action_space = Discrete(len(DISCRETE_ACTIONS))
        else:
            self.action_space = Box(-1.0, 1.0, shape=(2,))
        if config["use_depth_camera"]:
            image_space = Box(
                -1.0, 1.0, shape=(
```

```
                    config["y_res"], config["x_res"],
                    1 * config["framestack"]))
        else:
            image_space = Box(
                0.0, 255.0, shape=(
                    config["y_res"], config["x_res"],
                    3 * config["framestack"]))
        self.observation_space = Tuple(
            [image_space,
             Discrete(len(COMMANDS_ENUM)),  # next_command
             Box(-128.0, 128.0, shape=(2,))])  # forward_speed, dist to
    goal

        self._spec = lambda: None
        self._spec.id = "Carla-v0"

        self.server_port = None
        self.server_process = None
        self.client = None
        self.num_steps = 0
        self.total_reward = 0
        self.prev_measurement = None
        self.prev_image = None
        self.episode_id = None
        self.measurements_file = None
        self.weather = None
        self.scenario = None
        self.start_pos = None
        self.end_pos = None
        self.start_coord = None
        self.end_coord = None
        self.last_obs = None
```

Implementing the reset method

As you may have noticed, at the beginning of every episode, we call the `reset` method of the Gym environment. For the CARLA environment, we want to update the CARLA server to restart the level through the CARLA client.

So, let's get on with starting our implementation of the `reset` method.

Customizing the CARLA simulation using the CarlaSettings object

When we start a new episode, we want to be able to configure the start state (where the agent or vehicle starts), the goal state (the agent or vehicle's intended destination), the complexity of the episode (measured by the number of vehicles or pedestrians in the episode), the type and sources of observations (the sensors configured on the vehicle), and so on.

The CARLA project manages the interface between the UE4 environment and the external configuration and control using a server-client architecture, for which there are two servers.

For the CARLA environment, we can configure the environment's start state, goal state, complexity level, and the sensor sources using the `CarlaSettings` object or the `CarlaSettings.ini` file.

Let's now create a `CarlaSettings` object and configure some of the settings, as follows:

```
settings = CarlaSettings()  # Initialize a CarlaSettings object with
default values
settings.set(
        SynchronousMode=True,
        SendNonPlayerAgentsInfo=True,  # To receive info about all
other objs
        NumberOfVehicles=self.scenario["num_vehicles"],
        NumberOfPedestrians=self.scenario["num_pedestrians"],
        WeatherId=self.weather)
```

In the previous code snippet, we are setting `SynchronousMode` to `True` to enable the synchronous mode, in which the CARLA server halts the execution of each frame until a control message is received. Control messages are based on the actions the agent takes and are sent through the CARLA client.

Adding cameras and sensors to a vehicle in CARLA

To add an RGB color camera in the CARLA environment, use the following code:

```
# Create a RGB Camera Object
camera1 = Camera('CameraRGB')
# Set the RGB camera image resolution in pixels
camera1.set_image_size(640, 480)
# Set the camera/sensor position relative to the car in meters
camera1.set_positions(0.25, 0, 1.30)
# Add the sensor to the Carla Settings object
settings.add_sensor(camera1)
```

You can also add a depth measuring sensor or camera using the following code snippet:

```
# Create a depth camera object that can provide us the ground-truth depth
of the driving scene
camera2 = Camera("CameraDepth",PostProcessing="Depth")
# Set the depth camera image resolution in pixels
camera2.set_image_size(640, 480)
# Set the camera/sensor position relative to the car in meters
camera2.set_position(0.30, 0, 1.30)
# Add the sensor to the Carla settings object
settings.add_sensor(camera) Setting up the start and end positions in the
scene for the Carla Simulation
```

To add LIDAR to the CARLA environment, use the following code:

```
# Create a LIDAR object. The default LIDAR supports 32 beams
lidar = Lidar('Lidar32')
# Set the LIDAR sensor's specifications
lidar.set(
    Channels=32,   # Number of beams/channels
    Range=50,      # Range of the sensor in meters
    PointsPerSecond=1000000,   # Sample rate
    RotationFrequency=10,   # Frequency of rotation
    UpperFovLimit=10,   # Vertical field of view upper limit angle
    LowerFovLimit=-30) # Vertical field of view lower limit angle
# Set the LIDAR position & rotation relative to the car in meters
lidar.set_position(0, 0, 2.5)
lidar.set_rotation(0, 0, 0)
# Add the sensor to the Carla settings object
settings.add_sensor(lidar)
```

Once we have created a CARLA settings object based on our desired driving simulation configuration, we can send it to the CARLA server to set up the environment and start the simulation.

Once we have sent the CARLA settings object to the CARLA server, it responds with a scene description object that contains the available start positions for the ego vehicle, as follows:

```
scene = self.client.load_settings(settings)
available_start_spots = scene.player_start_spots
```

We can now choose a particular starting position for the host or ego vehicle, or even choose a starting spot at random, as shown in the following code snippet:

```
start_spot = random.randint(0, max(0, available_start_spots))
```

We can also send this start spot preference to the server and request the start of a new episode using the following code snippet:

```
self.client.start_episode(start_spot)
```

Note that the previous line is a blocking function call that will block action until the CARLA server actually starts the episode.

We can now step through the episode from this starting position until the end. In the next section, we will see what we need to implement the CARLA environment's `step()` method, which is used to step through the environment to the end of an episode:

```
def _reset(self):
        self.num_steps = 0
        self.total_reward = 0
        self.prev_measurement = None
        self.prev_image = None
        self.episode_id = datetime.today().strftime("%Y-%m-%d_%H-%M-%S_%f")
        self.measurements_file = None

        # Create a CarlaSettings object. This object is a wrapper around
        # the CarlaSettings.ini file. Here we set the configuration we
        # want for the new episode.
        settings = CarlaSettings()
        # If config["scenarios"] is a single scenario, then use it if it's
an array of scenarios, randomly choose one and init
        self.config = update_scenarios_parameter(self.config)

        if isinstance(self.config["scenarios"],dict):
            self.scenario = self.config["scenarios"]
        else: #ininstance array of dict
            self.scenario = random.choice(self.config["scenarios"])
        assert self.scenario["city"] == self.city, (self.scenario,
self.city)
        self.weather = random.choice(self.scenario["weather_distribution"])
        settings.set(
            SynchronousMode=True,
            SendNonPlayerAgentsInfo=True,
            NumberOfVehicles=self.scenario["num_vehicles"],
            NumberOfPedestrians=self.scenario["num_pedestrians"],
            WeatherId=self.weather)
        settings.randomize_seeds()

        if self.config["use_depth_camera"]:
            camera1 = Camera("CameraDepth", PostProcessing="Depth")
            camera1.set_image_size(
                self.config["render_x_res"], self.config["render_y_res"])
```

```
        camera1.set_position(30, 0, 130)
        settings.add_sensor(camera1)

    camera2 = Camera("CameraRGB")
    camera2.set_image_size(
        self.config["render_x_res"], self.config["render_y_res"])
    camera2.set_position(30, 0, 130)
    settings.add_sensor(camera2)

    # Setup start and end positions
    scene = self.client.load_settings(settings)
    positions = scene.player_start_spots
    self.start_pos = positions[self.scenario["start_pos_id"]]
    self.end_pos = positions[self.scenario["end_pos_id"]]
    self.start_coord = [
        self.start_pos.location.x // 100, self.start_pos.location.y //
100]
    self.end_coord = [
        self.end_pos.location.x // 100, self.end_pos.location.y // 100]
    print(
        "Start pos {} ({}), end {} ({})".format(
            self.scenario["start_pos_id"], self.start_coord,
            self.scenario["end_pos_id"], self.end_coord))

    # Notify the server that we want to start the episode at the
    # player_start index. This function blocks until the server is
ready
    # to start the episode.
    print("Starting new episode...")
    self.client.start_episode(self.scenario["start_pos_id"])

    image, py_measurements = self._read_observation()
    self.prev_measurement = py_measurements
    return self.encode_obs(self.preprocess_image(image),
py_measurements)
```

Implementing the step function for the CARLA environment

Once we have initialized the CARLA simulator by sending the CARLA settings object to the CARLA server and calling `client.start_episode(start_spot)`, the driving simulation will begin. We can then use the `client.read_data()` method to get the data produced by the simulation at a given step. We can do this using the following line of code:

```
measurements, sensor_data = client.read_data()
```

Accessing camera or sensor data

We can retrieve the sensor data at any given time step using the returned `sensor_data` object's `data` property. To retrieve the RGB camera frames, input the following code:

```
rgb_image = sensor_data['CameraRGB'].data
```

`rgb_image` is a NumPy n-d array, which you can access and manipulate as you would usually access and manipulate a NumPy n-d array.

For example, to access the pixel value of the RGB camera image at the (x, y) image plane coordinates, you can do so using the following line:

```
pixel_value_at_x_y = rgb_image[X, Y]
```

To retrieve the depth camera frames, input the following code:

```
depth_image = sensor_data['CameraDepth'].data
```

Sending actions to control agents in CARLA

We can control the car in CARLA by sending the desired steer, throttle, brake, hand-brake, and reverse (gear) commands to the CARLA server through a TCP client. The following table displays the value, range, and a description of the commands that a car in CARLA will obey:

Command/action name	Value type, range	Description
Steer	Float, [-1.0, +1.0]	Normalized steering angle
Throttle	Float, [0.0, 1.0]	Normalized throttle input
Brake	Float, [0.0, 1.0]	Normalized brake input
Hand Brake	Boolean, True/False	This tells the car whether to engage the hand brake (True) or not (False)
Reverse	Boolean, True/False	This tells the car whether to be in reverse gear (True) or not (False)

As noted in the CARLA documentation, the actual steering angle will depend on the vehicle. For example, the default Mustang vehicle has a maximum steering angle of 70 degrees, as defined in the vehicle's front wheel UE4 blueprint file. Those are the five different commands that are needed to control a car in CARLA. Among the five commands, three of them (steer, throttle, and brake) are real-value floating-point numbers. Though their range is limited between -1 and +1 or 0 and 1, the number of (unique) possible values is enormous. For example, if we use single precision floating point representation for throttle values that lie between 0 and 1, there are $126 * 2^{23}$, which means there are 1,056,964,608 different possible values for that throttle command. The same holds true for the brake command, as it also lies between 0 and 1. There are about twice as many possible float values for the steering command, as it lies between -1 and +1. Since a single control message is composed of a set of values for each of the five commands, the number of distinct actions (or control messages) is the product of the unique values for each of the commands, which are roughly in the order that follows:

$$\underbrace{(252*2^{23})}_{steering}*\underbrace{(126*2^{23})}_{throttle}*\underbrace{(126*2^{23})}_{brake} \quad \underbrace{*2}_{handbrake} \quad \underbrace{*2}_{reverse} \approx 5.63055788 \times 10^{20}$$

This generates a huge action space as you can see, and it might prove to be a very hard problem for a deep learning agent to regress onto such a huge action space. So, let's simplify the action space and define the action space in two flavors – one for continuous space and the other for discrete space, which is useful for applying different reinforcement learning algorithms. For example, the deep Q-learning based algorithms (without the naturalized advantage function) can only work on discrete action spaces.

Continuous action space in CARLA

While driving, we don't usually accelerate and brake at the same time; because the action space in CARLA is continuous, and the agent will apply an action at every step, it may be enough to have one command for accelerating and decelerating. Let's now combine the throttle and brake commands into one with a value range of -1 to +1, using the value range between -1 and 0 for the brake command and the value range between 0 and 1 for the throttle or acceleration command. We can define this using the following command:

```
action_space = gym.space.Box(-1.0, 1.0, shape=2(,))
```

`action[0]` signifies the command for steering, while `action[1]` signifies the value for our combined throttle and brake commands. For now, we will set both `hand_brake` and `reverse` to False. Next, we will look at how we can define a discrete action space so we choose what we want for our agent.

Discrete action space in CARLA

We've already seen that the full action space is quite large (in the order of 10^{20}). You may have played video games where you only used a joystick with four arrow buttons or the arrow keys on a keyboard to control the speed and heading (the direction in which the car is pointed) to drive, so why can't we ask the agent to control the car in a similar way here? Well, that is the idea behind discretizing the action space. Although we won't be able to have precise control over the car, we can make sure that the discretized space gives us good control in a simulation environment.

Let's begin by using the similar convention we used in the continuous action space case – where we used one floating point value to represent the throttle (acceleration) and brake (deceleration) actions, thereby using a two-dimensional bounded space internally. This means the action space, in this case, can be defined as follows:

```
action_space = gym.spaces.Discrete(NUM_DISCRETE_ACTIONS)
```

As you can see here, `NUM_DISCRETE_ACTONS` is equal to the number of different actions available, which we will define later on in this section.

We will then discretize the space using two-dimensional bounded space and exposing this as the discrete action space to the agent. To keep the number of possible actions to a minimum while still allowing control over the car, we use the following list of actions:

Action index	Action description	Action array value
0	Coast	[0.0, 0.0]
1	Turn Left	[0.0, -0.5]
2	Turn Right	[0.0, 0.5]
3	Forward	[1.0, 0.0]
4	Brake	[-0.5, 0.0]
5	Bear Left & Accelerate	[1.0, -0.5]
6	Bear Right & Accelerate	[1.0, 0.5]
7	Bear Left & Decelerate	[-0.5, -0.5]
8	Bear Right & Decelerate	[-0.5, 0.5]

Let's now define the previous set of discrete actions in a DISCRETE_ACTIONS dictionary in our carla_env implementation script, shown as follows:

```
DISCRETE_ACTIONS = {
    0: [0.0, 0.0],      # Coast
    1: [0.0, -0.5],     # Turn Left
    2: [0.0, 0.5],      # Turn Right
    3: [1.0, 0.0],      # Forward
    4: [-0.5, 0.0],     # Brake
    5: [1.0, -0.5],     # Bear Left & accelerate
    6: [1.0, 0.5],      # Bear Right & accelerate
    7: [-0.5, -0.5],    # Bear Left & decelerate
    8: [-0.5, 0.5],     # Bear Right & decelerate
}
```

Sending actions to the CARLA simulation server

Now that we have the action space of the CARLA Gym environment defined, we can look at how to convert the continuous or discrete actions we have defined into values the CARLA simulation server will accept.

Since we have followed the same convention for two-dimensional bounded action values in both the continuous and discrete action spaces, we can simply convert the actions into steer, throttle, and brake commands using the following code snippet:

```
throttle = float(np.clip(action[0], 0, 1))
brake = float(np.abs(np.cllip(action[0], -1, 0))
steer = float(p.clip(action[1], -1, 1))
hand_brake = False
reverse = False
```

As you can see, this is where action[0] is for throttle and brake, and action[1] is for the steering angle.

We will make use of the CarlaClient class implementation in the CARLA PythonClient library to handle the communication with the CARLA server. You can look at the implementation of the CarlaClient class in ch7/carla-gym/carla_gym/envs/carla/client.py, if you want to understand how communication with the server is handled using protocol buffers.

To implement a reward function for the CARLA environment, input the following code:

```
def calculate_reward(self, current_measurement):
    """
    Calculate the reward based on the effect of the action taken using
    the previous and the current measurements
    :param current_measurement: The measurement obtained from the Carla
    engine after executing the current action
    :return: The scalar reward
    """
    reward = 0.0

    cur_dist = current_measurement["distance_to_goal"]

    prev_dist = self.prev_measurement["distance_to_goal"]

    if env.config["verbose"]:
        print("Cur dist {}, prev dist {}".format(cur_dist, prev_dist))

    # Distance travelled toward the goal in m
    reward += np.clip(prev_dist - cur_dist, -10.0, 10.0)

    # Change in speed (km/hr)
    reward += 0.05 * (current_measurement["forward_speed"] -
    self.prev_measurement["forward_speed"])

    # New collision damage
    reward -= .00002 * (
        current_measurement["collision_vehicles"] +
    current_measurement["collision_pedestrians"] +
        current_measurement["collision_other"] -
    self.prev_measurement["collision_vehicles"] -
        self.prev_measurement["collision_pedestrians"] -
    self.prev_measurement["collision_other"])

    # New sidewalk intersection
    reward -= 2 * (
        current_measurement["intersection_offroad"] -
    self.prev_measurement["intersection_offroad"])

    # New opposite lane intersection
    reward -= 2 * (
        current_measurement["intersection_otherlane"] -
    self.prev_measurement["intersection_otherlane"])

    return reward
```

Determining the end of episodes in the CARLA environment

We have implemented `meta hod` to calculate the reward and defined the permitted actions, observations, and the reset method for the custom CARLA environment. According to our custom Gym environment creation template, those are the required methods we need to implement for creating a custom environment that is compatible with the OpenAI Gym interface.

While this is true, there is one more thing we need to take care of so that the agent can interact with our environment continuously. Remember when we were developing our Q-learning agent in `Chapter 5`, *Implementing your First Learning Agent – Solving the Mountain Car problem*, for the mountain car environment, the environment that always resets itself after 200 steps? Or in the cart pole environment, where the environment resets itself if the pole falls below a certain threshold value? Or how about in Atari games, where the environment is reset automatically if an agent loses their final life? Yes, we need to look at the routine that determines when to reset the environment, which is currently missing in our custom CARLA Gym environment implementation.

While we could pick any criteria to reset the CARLA Gym environment, there are three things to consider, as follows:

- When the host or ego car the agent is controlling collides with a car, pedestrian, building, or other roadside object, that can be fatal (similar to losing a life in Atari games)
- When the host or ego car reaches its destination or end goal
- When a time limit has been exceeded (similar to the 200 time step limit we have in the mountain car Gym environment)

We can use these conditions to form the criteria that will determine the end of an episode. The pseudo-code to determine the value of the `done` variable that `.step(...)` will return is as follows (note that the complete code can be found in the book's code repository in `ch7/carla-gym/carla_gym/envs/`):

```
# 1. Check if a collision has occured
m = measurements_from_carla_server
collided = m["collision_vehicles"] > 0 or m["collision_pedestrians"] > 0 or
m["collision_other"] > 0

# 2. Check if the ego/host car has reached the destination/goal
planner = carla_planner
goal_reached = planner["next_command"] == "REACHED_GOAL"
```

```
# 3. Check if the time-limit has been exceeded
time_limit = scenario_max_steps_config
time_limit_exceeded = num_steps > time_limit

# Set "done" to True if either of the above 3 criteria becomes true
done = collided or goal_reached or time_limit_exceeded
```

We have now gone through all the required components for creating our own custom Gym-compatible environment based on the CARLA driving simulator! In the next section, we will test the environment and finally see it in action.

Testing the CARLA Gym environment

To make it easy to test the basics of our environment implementation, we will implement a simple main() routine so we can run the environment as a script. This will show us if the basic interfaces have been set up correctly, as well as how the environment actually looks!

The main routine of the carla_env.py file is shown in the following snippet. This file creates an instance of the default CarlaEnv and runs five episodes with a fixed action of going forward. The ENV_CONFIG action, which we created during initialization, can be changed to use discrete or continuous action spaces, as follows:

```
# Part of https://github.com/PacktPublishing/Hands-On-Intelligent-Agents-
with-OpenAI-Gym/ch7/carla-gym/carla_gym/envs/carla_env.py
if __name__ == "__main__":
    for _ in range(5):
        env = CarlaEnv()
        obs = env.reset()
        done = False
        t = 0
        total_reward = 0.0
        while not done:
            t += 1
            if ENV_CONFIG["discrete_actions"]:
                obs, reward, done, info = env.step(3) # Go Forward
            else:
                obs, reward, done, info = env.step([1.0, 0.0]) # Full
throttle, zero steering angle
            total_reward += reward
            print("step#:", t, "reward:", round(reward, 4),
"total_reward:", round(total_reward, 4), "done:", done)
```

Now, go ahead and test the environment we just created! Keep in mind that CARLA requires a GPU to run smoothly, and the system environment CARLA_SERVER variable to be defined and pointing to the CarlaUE4.sh file on your system. Once you are ready, you can test the environment we created by running the following command inside the rl_gym_book conda environment:

```
(rl_gym_book) praveen@ubuntu:~/rl_gym_book/ch7$ python carla-gym/carla_gym/envs/carla_env.py
```

The previous command should open a small CARLA simulator window and initialize the vehicle for the scenario configuration used in the carla_env.py script. This should look similar to the following screenshots:

As you can see, by default, the vehicle is scripted to drive straight. Note that the carla_env.py script will also produce a console output to show the current time step in the environment, the calculated instantaneous reward, the total reward in the episode, and the value of done (True or False), which is all useful for testing our environment. As the vehicle starts moving forward, you should see the reward value increasing!

The console output is as follows:

So, you now have your custom CARLA Gym environment working! You can create several different driving scenarios using the definitions in the ch7/carla-gym/carla_gym/envs/scenarios.json file. You can then create new custom CARLA environments for each of those scenarios, which you can use with the usual gym.make(...) command after you have registered the custom environment, for example, gym.make("Carla-v0").

The code in the book's code repository takes care of the environment registration with the OpenAI Gym registry using the method we discussed earlier in this chapter. You can now use OpenAI Gym to create an instance of the custom environment we built.

The following screenshot shows the Python commands you can use to test the custom Gym environment:

And that's it! The rest is similar to any other Gym environment.

Summary

In this chapter, we went through a custom Gym environment implementation step-by-step, starting with a template that laid out the bare-bones structure of an OpenAI Gym environment that provided all of the necessary interfaces to the agents. We also looked at how to register a custom environment implementation in the Gym registry so that we can use the familiar `gym.make(ENV_NAME)` command to create an instance of an existing environment. We then looked at how to create a Gym-compatible environment implementation for the UnrealEngine based on the open-source driving simulator, CARLA. We then quickly walked through the steps required to install and run CARLA and then started implementing the `CarlaEnv` class piece-by-piece, carefully covering all the important details involved in implementing custom environments compatible with OpenAI Gym.

In the next chapter, we will build an advanced agent from the ground up with hands-on examples, before eventually using the custom CARLA environment we created in this chapter to train an intelligent agent that can learn to drive the car around all by itself!

8
Implementing an Intelligent - Autonomous Car Driving Agent using Deep Actor-Critic Algorithm

In `Chapter 6`, Implementing an Intelligent Agent for Optimal Control using Deep Q-Learning, we implemented agents using deep Q-learning to solve discrete control tasks that involve discrete actions or decisions to be made. We saw how they can be trained to play video games such as Atari, just like we do: by looking at the game screen and pressing the buttons on the game pad/joystick. We can use such agents to pick the best choice given a finite set of choices, make decisions, or perform actions where the number of possible decisions or actions is finite and typically small. There are numerous real-world problems that can be solved with an agent that can learn to take optimal through to discrete actions. We saw some examples in `Chapter 6`, *Implementing an Intelligent Agent for Optimal Discrete Control using Deep Q-Learning*.

In the real world, there are other classes of problems and tasks that require lower-level actions to be performed that are continuous values and not discrete. For example, an intelligent temperature control system or a thermostat needs to be capable of making fine adjustments to the internal control circuits to maintain a room at the specified temperature. The control action signal may include a continuous valued real number (such as *1.456*) to control **heating, ventilation, and air conditioning** (**HVAC**) systems. Consider another example in which we want to develop an intelligent agent to drive a car autonomously. Humans drive a car by shifting gears, pressing the accelerator or brake pedal, and steering the car. While the current gear is going to be one of a possible set of five to six values, depending on the transmission system of the car, if an intelligent software agent has to perform all of those actions, it has to be able to produce continuous valued real numbers for the throttle (accelerator), braking (brake), and steering.

In cases like these examples, where we need the agent to take continuous valued actions, we can use policy gradient-based actor-critic methods to directly learn and update the agent's policy in the policy space, rather than through a state and/or action value function like in the deep Q-learning agent we saw in Chapter 6, *Implementing an Intelligent Agent for Optimal Discrete Control using Deep Q-Learning*. In this chapter, we will start from the basics of an actor-critic algorithm and build our agent gradually, while training it to solve various classic control problems using OpenAI Gym environments along the way. We will build our agent all the way up to being able to drive a car in the CARLA driving simulation environment using the custom Gym interface that we implemented in the previous chapter.

The deep n-step advantage actor-critic algorithm

In our deep Q-learner-based intelligent agent implementation, we used a deep neural network as the function approximator to represent the action-value function. The agent then used the action-value function to come up with a policy based on the value function. In particular, we used the ϵ-greedy algorithm in our implementation. So, we understand that ultimately the agent has to know what actions are good to take given an observation/state. Instead of parametrizing or approximating a state/action action function and then deriving a policy based on that function, can we not parametrize the policy directly? Yes we can! That is the exact idea behind policy gradient methods.

In the following subsections, we will briefly look at policy gradient-based learning methods and then transition to actor-critic methods that combine and make use of both value-based and policy-based learning. We will then look at some of the extensions to the actor-critic method that have been shown to improve learning performance.

Policy gradients

In policy gradientbased methods, the policy is represented, for example, by using a neural network with parameters θ, and the goal is to find the best set of parameters θ. This can be intuitively seen as an optimization problem where we are trying to optimize the objective of the policy to find the best-performing policy. What is the objective of the agent's policy ? We know that the agent should achieve maximum rewards in the long term, in order to complete the task or achieve the goal. If we can formulate that objective mathematically, we can use optimization techniques to find the best policy for the agent to follow for the given task.

We know that the state value function $V^{\pi_\theta}(s)$ tells us the expected return starting from state s and following policy π_θ until the end of the episode. It tells us how good it is to be in state s. So ideally, a good policy will have a higher value for the starting state in the environment as it represents the expected/mean/average value of being in that state and taking actions according to policy π_θ until the end of the episode. The higher the value in the starting state, the higher the total long-term reward an agent following the policy can achieve. Therefore, in an episodic environment—where the environment is an episode; that is, it has a terminal state—we can measure how good a policy is based on the value of the start state. Mathematically, such an objective function can be written as follows:

$$J_{start}(\theta) = V^{\pi_\theta}(s_1) = \mathbb{E}_{\pi_\theta}[v_1]$$

But what if the environment is not episodic? This means it doesn't have a terminal state and keeps on going. In such as environment, we can use the average value of the states that are visited while following the current policy, π_θ. Mathematically, the average value objective function can be written as follows:

$$J_{avgV}(\theta) = \sum_s d^{\pi_\theta}(s) V^{\pi_\theta}(s)$$

Here, $d^{\pi_\theta}(s)$ is the stationary distribution of the Markov chain for π_θ, which gives the probability of visiting state s while following policy π_θ.

We can also use the average reward obtained per time step in such environments, which can be expressed mathematically using the following equation:

$$J_{avgR}(\theta) = \sum_s d^{\pi_\theta}(s) \sum_a \pi_\theta(s, a) R_s^a$$

This is essentially the expected value of rewards that can be obtained when the agent takes actions based on policy π_θ, which can be written in short form like this:

$$J(\theta) = \mathbb{E}_{\pi_\theta}[R_s^a]$$

To optimize this policy objective function using gradient descent, we would take the derivative of the equation with respect to θ, find the gradients, back-propagate, and perform the gradient descent step. From the previous equations, we can write the following:

$$J(\theta) = \mathbb{E}_{\pi_\theta}[R_s^a] = \sum_s d^{\pi_\theta}(s) \sum_a \pi_\theta(s, a) R_s^a$$

Let's differentiate the previous equation with respect to θ by expanding the terms and then simplifying it further. Follow the following equations from left to right to understand the series of steps involved in arriving at the result:

$$\nabla_\theta J(\theta) = \nabla_\theta \mathbb{E}_{\pi_\theta}[R_s^a] = \sum_s d^{\pi_\theta} \sum_a \underbrace{\nabla_\theta \pi_\theta(s,a)}_{policy\ gradient} R_s^a = \sum_s d^{\pi_\theta} \sum_a \pi_\theta(s,a) \underbrace{\nabla_\theta \log(\pi_\theta(s,a))}_{score\ function} R_s^a = \mathbb{E}_{\pi_\theta(s,a)}[\nabla_\theta \log(\pi_\theta(s,a)) R_s^a]$$

$$\underbrace{}_{Likelihood\ ratios\ trick}$$

To understand these equations and how the policy gradient, $\nabla_\theta \pi_\theta(s,a)$, is equal to the likelihood ratio, $\pi_\theta \nabla_\theta \log(\pi_\theta(s,a))$, let's take a step back and revisit what our goal is. Our goals is to find the optimal set of parameters θ for the policy so that the agent following the policy will reap the maximum rewards in expectation (i.e on an average average). To achieve that goal, we start with a set of parameters and then keep updating the parameters until we reach the optimal set of parameters. To figure out which direction in the parameter space the policy parameters have to be updated, we make use of the direction indicated by the gradient of policy π_θ with respect to parameters θ. Let's start with the second term in the previous equation, $\nabla_\theta \mathbb{E}_{\pi_\theta(s,a)} R_s^a$, (which was a result of the first term, $\nabla_\theta J(\theta)$, by definition):

$\nabla_\theta \mathbb{E}_{\pi_\theta(s,a)} R_s^a$ is the gradient of the expected value, under policy π_θ, of the step reward that resulted from taking action a in state s. This, by the definition of expectation, can be written as the following sum:

$$\sum_s d^{\pi_\theta} \sum_a \nabla_\theta \pi_\theta(s,a) R_s^a$$

We'll look at the likelihood ratio trick, which is used in this context to transform this equation into a form that makes the computation feasible.

The likelihood ratio trick

The policy represented by π_θ is assumed to be a differentiable function whenever it is non-zero, but computing the gradient of the policy with respect to theta, $\nabla_\theta \pi_\theta(s,a)$, may not be straightforward. We can multiply and divide by policy $\pi_\theta(s,a)$ on both sides to get the following:

$$\nabla_\theta \pi_\theta(s,a) = \pi_\theta(s,a) \frac{\nabla_\theta \pi_\theta(s,a)}{\pi_\theta(s,a)}$$

From calculus, we know that the gradient of the log of a function is the gradient of the function over the function itself, which is mathematically given by the following:

$$\nabla_x \log f(x) = \frac{\nabla_x f(x)}{f(x)}$$

Therefore, we can write the gradient of the policy with respect to its parameters in the following form:

$$\pi_\theta(s, a) \frac{\nabla_\theta \pi_\theta(s, a)}{\pi_\theta(s, a)} = \pi_\theta(s, a) \underbrace{\nabla_\theta \log(\pi_\theta(s, a))}_{score\ function}$$

This is called the likelihood ratio trick, or the log derivative trick, in machine learning.

The policy gradient theorem

Because policy $\pi_\theta(s, a)$ is a probability distribution function that describes the probability distribution over actions given the state and parameters θ by definition, the double summation terms over the states and the actions can be expressed as the expectation of the score function scaled by reward R_s^a over distribution π_θ. This is mathematically equivalent to the following:

$$\underbrace{\sum_s d^{\pi_\theta} \sum_a \pi_\theta(s, a) \underbrace{\nabla_\theta \log(\pi_\theta(s, a))}_{score\ function} R_s^a}_{Likelihood\ ratios\ trick} = \mathbb{E}_{\pi_\theta(s,a)} [\nabla_\theta \log(\pi_\theta(s, a)) R_s^a]$$

Note that in the preceding equation, R_s^a is the step reward for taking action a from state s.

The policy gradient theorem generalizes this approach by replacing the instantaneous step reward R_s^a with the long-term action value $Q^{\pi_\theta(s,a)}$ and can be written as follows:

$$\nabla_\theta J(\theta) = \mathbb{E}_{\pi_\theta} [\nabla_\theta \log \pi_\theta(s, a)] Q^{\pi_\theta}(s, a)$$

This result is a very useful one and forms the basis of several variations of the policy gradient method.

With this understanding of policy gradients, we will dive into actor-critic algorithms and their variations in the following few sections.

Actor-critic algorithm

Let's start with a diagrammatic representation of the actor-critic architecture, as shown in the following diagram:

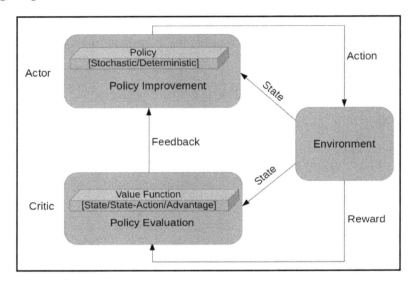

There are two components in the actor-critic algorithm, as evident from the name and the preceding diagram. The actor is responsible for acting in the environment, which involves taking actions, given observations about the environment and based on the agent's policy. The actor can be thought of as the policy holder/maker. The critic, on the other hand, takes care of estimating the state-value, or state-action-value, or advantage-value function (depending on the variant of the actor-critic algorithm used). Let's consider a case where the critic is trying to estimate the action value function $Q^{\pi_\theta}(s, a))$. If we use a set of parameters w to denote the critic's parameters, the critic's estimates can be essentially written as:

$$Q_w(s, a) \approx Q^{\pi_\theta}(s, a)$$

Replacing the true action-value function with the critic's approximation of the action-value function (the last equation in the policy gradient theorem section) in the results of the policy gradient theorem from the previous section leads us to the approximate policy gradient given by the following:

$$\nabla_\theta J(\theta) \approx \mathbb{E}_{\pi_\theta}[\nabla_\theta \log \pi_\theta(s, a)]Q_w(s, a)$$

In practice, we further approximate the expectation using stochastic gradient ascent (or descent with a -ve sign).

Advantage actor-critic algorithm

The action-value actor-critic algorithm still has high variance. We can reduce the variance by subtracting a baseline function, *B(s)*, from the policy gradient. A good baseline is the state value function, $V^{\pi_\theta}(s)$. With the state value function as the baseline, we can rewrite the result of the policy gradient theorem as the following:

$$\nabla_\theta J(\theta) = \mathbb{E}_{\pi_\theta}[\nabla_\theta \log \pi_\theta(s, a)]Q^{\pi_\theta}(s, a) = \mathbb{E}[\nabla_\theta \log(\pi_\theta(s, a)](Q^{\pi_\theta}(s, a) - V^{\pi_\theta}(s))$$

We can define the advantage function $A^{\pi_\theta}(s, a)$ to be the following:

$$A^{\pi_\theta}(s, a) = Q^{\pi_\theta}(s, a) - V^{\pi_\theta}(s)$$

When used in the previous policy gradient equation with the baseline, this gives us the advantage of the actor-critic policy gradient:

$$\nabla_\theta J(\theta) = \mathbb{E}_{\pi_\theta}[\nabla_\theta \log \pi_\theta(s, a)]A^{\pi_\theta}(s, a)$$

Recall from the previous chapters that the 1-step Temporal Difference (TD) error for value function $V^{\pi_\theta}(s)$ is given by the following:

$$\delta^{\pi_\theta} = r + \gamma V^{\pi_\theta}(s') - V^{\pi_\theta}(s)$$

If we compute the expected value of this TD error, we will end up with an equation that resembles the definition of the action-value function we saw in Chapter 2, *Reinforcement Learning and Deep Reinforcement Learning*. From that result, we can observe that the TD error is in fact an unbiased estimate of the advantage function, as derived in this equation from left to right:

$$\mathbb{E}_{\pi_\theta}[\delta^{\pi_\theta}|s, a] = \underbrace{\mathbb{E}_{\pi_\theta}[r + \gamma V^{\pi_\theta}(s')] - V^{\pi_\theta}(s)}_{Action-Value\ function} = \underbrace{Q^{\pi_\theta}(s, a) - V^{\pi_\theta}(s)}_{Advantage\ function} = A^{\pi_\theta(s,a)}$$

With this result and the previous set of equations in this chapter so far, we have enough theoretical background to get started with our implementation of our agent! Before we get into the code, let's understand the flow of the algorithm to get a good picture of it in our minds.

The simplest (general/vanilla) form of the advantage actor-critic algorithm involves the following steps:

1. Initialize the (stochastic) policy and the value function estimate.
2. For a given observation/state s_t, perform the action, a_t, prescribed by the current policy, $\pi_t(s, a)$.
3. Calculate the TD error based on the resulting state, s_{t+1} and the reward obtained using the 1-step TD learning equation:

$$\delta_t = \underbrace{r_t + \gamma * V_t(s_{t+1})}_{TD-Target} - V_t(s_t)$$

4. Update the actor by adjusting the action probabilities for state s_t based on the TD error:
    - If $\delta_t > 0$, increase the probability of taking action a_t because a_t was a good decision and worked out really well
    - If $\delta_t < 0$, decrease the probability of taking action a_t because a_t resulted in a poor performance by the agent
5. Update the critic by adjusting its estimated value of s_t using the TD error:
    - $V_t(s_t) = V_t(s_t) + \alpha * \delta_t$, where α is the critic's learning rate
6. Set the next state s_{t+1} to be the current state s_t and repeat step 2.

n-step advantage actor-critic algorithm

In the advantage actor-critic algorithm section, we looked at the steps involved in implementing the algorithm. In step 3, we noticed that we have to calculate the TD error based on the 1-step return (TD target). It is like letting the agent take a step in the environment and then based on the outcome, calculating the error in the critic's estimates and updating the policy of the agent. This sounds straightforward and simple, right? But, is there any better way to learn and update the policy? As you might have guessed from the title of this section, the idea is to use the n-step return, which uses more information to learn and update the policy compared to 1-step return-based TD learning. n-step TD learning can be seen as a generalized version and the 1-step TD learning used in the actor-critic algorithm, as discussed in the previous section, is a special case of the n-step TD learning algorithm with n=1. Let's look at a quick illustration to understand the n-step return calculation and then implement a Python method to calculate the n-step return, which we will use in our agent implementation.

n-step returns

n-step returns are a simple but very useful concept known to yield better performance for several reinforcement learning algorithms, not just with the advantage actor-critic-based algorithm. For example, the best performing algorithm to date on the Atari suite of *57* games, which significantly outperforms the second best algorithm, uses n-step returns. We will actually discuss that agent algorithm, called Rainbow, in `Chapter 10`, *Exploring the learning environment landscape: Roboschool, Gym-Retro, StarCraft-II, DMLab.*

Let's first get an intuitive understanding of the n-step return process. Let's use the following diagram to illustrate one step in the environment. Assume that the agent is in state s_1 at time t=1 and decides to take action a_1, which results in the environment being transitioned to state s_2 at time t=t+1= 1+1 = 2 with the agent receiving a reward of r_1:

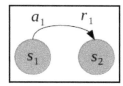

We can calculate the 1-step TD return using the following formula:

$$G_{t=1}^{(n=1)} = r_1 + \gamma V_t(s_2)$$

Here, $V_t(s_2)$ is the value estimate of state s_2 according to the value function (critic). In essence, the agent takes a step and uses the received return and the discounted value of the agent's estimate of the value of the next/resulting state to calculate the return.

If we let the agent continue interacting with the environment for a few more steps, the trajectory of the agent can be simplistically represented using the following diagram:

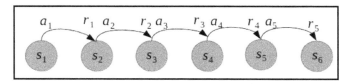

This diagram shows a 5-step interaction between the agent and the environment. Following a similar approach to the 1-step return calculation in the previous paragraph, we can calculate the 5-step return using the following formula:

$$G_{t=1}^{(n=5)} = r_1 + \gamma r_2 + \gamma^2 r_3 + \gamma^3 r_4 + \gamma^4 r_5 + \gamma^5 V_t(s_6)$$

We can then use this as the TD target in step 3 of the advantage actor-critic algorithm to improve the performance of the agent.

> You can see how the performance of the advantage actor-critic agent with the 1-step return compares to the performance with the n-step return by running the `ch8/a2c_agent.py` script with the `learning_step_thresh` parameter in the `parameters.json` file set to 1 (for the 1-step return) and 5 or 10 (for the n-step return) in any of the Gym environments.
> For example, you can run `(rl_gym_book) praveen@ubuntu:~/HOIAWOG/ch8$python a2c_agent.py --env Pendulum-v0` with `learning_step_thresh=1`, monitor its performance using Tensorboard using the command `(rl_gym_book) praveen@ubuntu:~/HOIAWOG/ch8/logs$tensorboard --logdir=.`, and then after a million or so steps you can compare the performance of the agent trained with `learning_step_thresh=10`. Note that the trained agent model will be saved at `~/HOIAWOG/ch8/trained_models/A2_Pendulum-v0.ptm`. You can rename it or move it to a different directory before you start the second run to start the training from scratch!

To make the concept more explicit, let's discuss how we will use this in step 3 and in the advantage actor-critic algorithm. We will first use the n-step return as the TD target and calculate the TD error using the following formula (step 3 of the algorithm):

$$\delta_t = \underbrace{G_{t=1}^{(n=5)}}_{TD-Target} - V_t(s_t) = \underbrace{r_1 + \gamma r_2 + \gamma^2 r_3 + \gamma^3 r_4 + \gamma^4 r_5 + \gamma^5 V_t(s_6)}_{TD-Target} + V_t(s_t)$$

We will then follow step 4 in the algorithm discussed in the previous subsection and update the critic. Then, in step 5, we will update the critic using the following update rule:

$$V_t(s_1) = V_t(s_1) + \alpha * \delta_t$$

We will then move on to step 6 of the algorithm to continue with the next state, s_2, using 5-step transitions from s_2 until s_7 and calculating the 5-step return, then repeat the procedure for updating $V_t(s_2)$.

Implementing the n-step return calculation

If we pause for a moment and analyze what is happening, you might see that we are probably not making full use of the 5-step long trajectory. With access to the information from the agent's 5-step long trajectory starting from state s_1, we only ended up learning one new piece of information, which is all about s_1 to update the actor and the critic ($V_t(s_1)$). We can actually make the learning process more efficient by using the same 5-step trajectory to calculate updates for each of the state values present in the trajectory, with their respective n values based on the end of the trajectory. For example, in a simplified trajectory representation, if we considered state s_5, with the forward-view of the trajectory enclosed inside the bubble, as shown in this diagram:

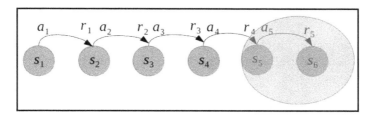

We can use the information inside the bubble to extract the TD learning target for state s_5. In this case, since there is only one step of information available from s_5, we will be calculating the 1-step return, as shown in this equation:

$$G_{t=5}^{(n=1)} = r_5 + \gamma V_t(s_6)$$

As we discussed before, we can use this value as the TD target in equation to get another TD error value, and use the second value to update the actor and $V_t(s_5)$, in addition to previous updates ($V_t(s_1)$). Now, we have got one more piece of information for the agent to learn from!

If we apply the same intuition and consider state s_4, with the forward-view of the trajectory enclosed in the bubble, as shown in the following diagram:

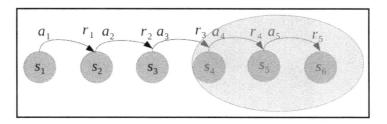

We can use the information inside the bubble to extract the TD learning target for s_4. In this case, there are two types of information available from s_4; therefore, we will calculate the 2-step return using the following equation:

$$G_{t=4}^{(n=2)} = r_4 + \gamma r_5 + \gamma^2 V_t(s_6)$$

If we look at this equation and the previous equation, we can observe that there is a relationship between $G_{t=4}^{(n=2)}$ and $G_{t=5}^{(n=1)}$, which is given by the following equation:

$$G_{t=4}^{(n=2)} = r_4 + \gamma r_5 + \gamma^2 V_t(s_6) = r_4 + \gamma \underbrace{(r_5 + \gamma V_t(s_6))}_{G_{t=5}^{(n=1)}} = r_4 + \gamma * G_{t=5}^{(n=1)}$$

This gives us another piece of information for the agent to learn from. Likewise, we can extract more information from this one trajectory of the agent. Extending the same concept for s_3, s_2 and s_1, we can arrive at the following relationship:

$$G_{t=3}^{(n=3)} = r_3 + \gamma r_4 + \gamma^2 r_5 + \gamma^3 V_t(s_6) = r_3 + \gamma \underbrace{(r_4 + \gamma (r_5 + \gamma V_t(s_6)))}_{G_{t=4}^{(n=2)}} = r_3 + \gamma * G_{t=4}^{(n=2)}$$

Likewise, in short, we can observe the following:

$$G_{t=2}^{(n=4)} = r_2 + \gamma * G_{t=3}^{(n=3)}$$

And finally, we can also observe the following:

$$G_{t=1}^{(n=5)} = r_1 + \gamma * G_{t=2}^{(n=4)}$$

Simply put, we can start from the last step in the trajectory, calculate the n-step return until the end of the trajectory, and then move back to the previous step to calculate the return using the previously calculated value.

The implementation is straightforward and simple, and it is advisable to try to implement this on your own. It is provided as follows for your reference:

```
def calculate_n_step_return(self, n_step_rewards, final_state, done,
gamma):
        """
        Calculates the n-step return for each state in the input-
trajectory/n_step_transitions
        :param n_step_rewards: List of rewards for each step
```

```
        :param final_state: Final state in this
n_step_transition/trajectory
        :param done: True rf the final state is a terminal state if not,
False
        :return: The n-step return for each state in the n_step_transitions
        """
        g_t_n_s = list()
        with torch.no_grad():
            g_t_n = torch.tensor([[0]]).float() if done else
self.critic(self.preproc_obs(final_state)).cpu()
            for r_t in n_step_rewards[::-1]: # Reverse order; From r_tpn to
r_t
                g_t_n = torch.tensor(r_t).float() + self.gamma * g_t_n
                g_t_n_s.insert(0, g_t_n) # n-step returns inserted to the
left to maintain correct index order
            return g_t_n_s
```

Deep n-step advantage actor-critic algorithm

We observed that the actor-critic algorithm combines value-based methods and policy-based methods. The critic estimates the value function and the actor follows the policy, and we looked at how we can update the actor and the critic. From our previous experience in Chapter 6, *Implementing an Intelligent Agent for optimal discrete control using Deep Q Learning*, we naturally got the idea of using a neural network to approximate the value function and therefore the critic. We can also use a neural network to represent policy π_θ, in which case parameters θ are the weights of the neural network. Using deep neural networks to approximate the actor and the critic is exactly the idea behind deep actor-critic algorithms.

Implementing a deep n-step advantage actor critic agent

We have prepared ourselves with all the background information required to implement the deep n-step advantage actor-critic (A2C) agent. Let's look at an overview of the agent implementation process and then jump right into the hands-on implementation.

The following is the high-level flow of our A2C agent:

1. Initialize the actor's and critic's networks.
2. Use the current policy of the actor to gather n-step experiences from the environment and calculate the n-step return.

3. Calculate the actor's and critic's losses.
4. Perform the stochastic gradient descent optimization step to update the actor and critic parameters.
5. Repeat from step 2.

We will implement the agent in a Python class named `DeepActorCriticAgent`. You will find the full implementation in this book's code repository under 8th chapter: `ch8/a2c_agent.py`. We will make this implementation flexible so that we can easily extend it further for the batched version, as well make an asynchronous version of the n-step advantage actor-critic agent.

Initializing the actor and critic networks

The `DeepActorCriticAgent` class's initialization is straightforward. We will quickly have a look into it and then see how we actually define and initialize the actor and critic networks.

The agent's initialization function is shown here:

```
class DeepActorCriticAgent(mp.Process):
    def __init__(self, id, env_name, agent_params):
        """
        An Advantage Actor-Critic Agent that uses a Deep Neural Network to
represent it's Policy and the Value function
        :param id: An integer ID to identify the agent in case there are
multiple agent instances
        :param env_name: Name/ID of the environment
        :param agent_params: Parameters to be used by the agent
        """
        super(DeepActorCriticAgent, self).__init__()
        self.id = id
        self.actor_name = "actor" + str(self.id)
        self.env_name = env_name
        self.params = agent_params
        self.policy = self.multi_variate_gaussian_policy
        self.gamma = self.params['gamma']
        self.trajectory = []  # Contains the trajectory of the agent as a
sequence of Transitions
        self.rewards = []  # Contains the rewards obtained from the env at
every step
        self.global_step_num = 0
        self.best_mean_reward = - float("inf")  # Agent's personal best mean
episode reward
        self.best_reward = - float("inf")
```

```
        self.saved_params = False # Whether or not the params have been
saved along with the model to model_dir
        self.continuous_action_space = True #Assumption by default unless
env.action_space is Discrete
```

You may wonder why the `agent` class is inheriting from the `multiprocessing.Process` class. Although for our first agent implementation we will be running one agent in one process, we can use this flexible interface to enable running several agents in parallel to speed up the learning process.

Let's move on to actor and critic implementations using neural networks defined with PyTorch operations. Following a similar code structure to what we used in our deep Q-learning agent in `Chapter 6`, *Implementing an Intelligent Agent for optimal discrete control using Deep Q Learning*, in the code base you will see that we are using a module named `function_approximator` to contain our neural network-based function approximator implementations. You can find the full implementations under the `ch8/function_approximator` folder in this book's code repository.

Since some environments have small and discrete state spaces, such as the `Pendulum-v0`, `MountainCar-v0`, or `CartPole-v0` environments, we will also implement shallow versions of neural networks along with the deep versions, so that we can dynamically choose a suitable neural network depending on the environment the agent is trained/tested on. When you look through the sample implementation of the neural networks for the actor, you will notice that in both the `shallow` and the `deep` function approximator modules, there is a class called `Actor` and a different class called `DiscreteActor`. This is again for generality purposes so that we can let the agent dynamically pick and use the neural network most suitable for representing the actor, depending on whether the environment's action space is continuous or discrete. There is one more variation for the completeness and generality of our agent implementation that you need to be aware of: both the `shallow` and the `deep` function approximator modules in our implementations have an `ActorCritic` class, which is a single neural network architecture that represents both the actor and the critic. In this way, the feature extraction layers are shared between the actor and the critic, and different heads (final layers) in the same neural network are used to represent the actor and the critic.

Sometimes, the different parts of the implementation might be confusing. To help avoid confusion, here is a summary of the various options in our neural network-based actor-critic implementations:

Module/class	Description	Purpose/use case	
1. `function_approximator.shallow`	Shallow neural network implementations for actor-critic representations.	Environments that have low-dimensional state/observation spaces.	
1.1 `function_approximator.shallow.Actor`	Feed-forward neural network implementation that produces two continuous values: mu (mean) and sigma for a Gaussian distribution-based policy representation.	Low-dimensional state/observation space and continuous action space.	
1.2 `function_approximator.shallow.DiscreteActor`	Feed-forward neural network that produces a logit for each action in the action space.	Low-dimensional state/observation space and discrete action space.	
1.3 `function_approximator.shallow.Critic`	Feed-forward neural network that produces a continuous value.	Used to represent the critic/value function for environments with low-dimensional state/observation space	
1.4 `function_approximator.shallow.ActorCritic`	Feed-forward neural network that produces mu (mean), sigma for a Gaussian distribution, and a continuous value.	Used to represent the actor and the critic in the same network for environments with low-dimensional state/observation space. It is possible to modify this to a discrete actor-critic network.	
2. `function_approximator.deep`	Deep neural network implementations for actor, critic representation.	Environments that have high-dimensional state/observation spaces.	
2.1 `function_approximator.deep.Actor`	Deep convolutional neural network that produces the mu (mean) and sigma for a Gaussian distribution-based policy representation.	High-dimensional state/observation space and continuous action space.	

2.2 `function_approximator.deep.DiscreteActor`	Deep convolutional neural network that produces a logit for each action in the action space.	High-dimensional state/observation space and discrete action-space.	
2.3 `function_approximator.deep.Critic`	Deep convolutional neural network that produces a continuous value.	Used to represent the critic/value-function for environments with high-dimensional state/observation space.	
2.4 `function_approximator.deep.ActorCritic`	Deep convolutional neural network that produces mu (mean), sigma for a Gaussian distribution as well as a continuous value.	Used to represent the actor and the critic in a same network for environments with high-dimensional state/observation space. It is possible to modify this to a discrete actor-critic network.	

Let's now look at the first part of the `run()` method, where we initialize the actor and the critic network based on the type of the environment's state and action spaces, as well as based on whether the state space is low-dimensional or high-dimensional based on the previous table:

```
from function_approximator.shallow import Actor as ShallowActor
from function_approximator.shallow import DiscreteActor as
ShallowDiscreteActor
from function_approximator.shallow import Critic as ShallowCritic
from function_approximator.deep import Actor as DeepActor
from function_approximator.deep import DiscreteActor as DeepDiscreteActor
from function_approximator.deep import Critic as DeepCritic

def run(self):
        self.env = gym.make(self.env_name)
        self.state_shape = self.env.observation_space.shape
        if isinstance(self.env.action_space.sample(), int): # Discrete
action space
            self.action_shape = self.env.action_space.n
            self.policy = self.discrete_policy
            self.continuous_action_space = False

        else: # Continuous action space
            self.action_shape = self.env.action_space.shape[0]
            self.policy = self.multi_variate_gaussian_policy
        self.critic_shape = 1
```

```
            if len(self.state_shape) == 3: # Screen image is the input to the
agent
                if self.continuous_action_space:
                    self.actor= DeepActor(self.state_shape, self.action_shape,
device).to(device)
                else: # Discrete action space
                    self.actor = DeepDiscreteActor(self.state_shape,
self.action_shape, device).to(device)
                self.critic = DeepCritic(self.state_shape, self.critic_shape,
device).to(device)
            else: # Input is a (single dimensional) vector
                if self.continuous_action_space:
                    #self.actor_critic = ShallowActorCritic(self.state_shape,
self.action_shape, 1, self.params).to(device)
                    self.actor = ShallowActor(self.state_shape,
self.action_shape, device).to(device)
                else: # Discrete action space
                    self.actor = ShallowDiscreteActor(self.state_shape,
self.action_shape, device).to(device)
                self.critic = ShallowCritic(self.state_shape,
self.critic_shape, device).to(device)
            self.actor_optimizer = torch.optim.Adam(self.actor.parameters(),
lr=self.params["learning_rate"])
            self.critic_optimizer = torch.optim.Adam(self.critic.parameters(),
lr=self.params["learning_rate"])
```

Gathering n-step experiences using the current policy

The next step is to perform what are called *rollouts* using the current policy of the agent to collect n number of transitions. This process is basically letting the agent interact with the environment and generating new experiences in terms of state transitions, usually represented as a tuple containing the state, action, reward obtained, and next state, or in short (s_t, a_t, r_t, s_{t+1}), as illustrated in the following diagram:

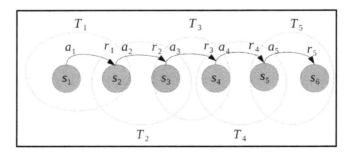

In the example shown in the preceding diagram, the agent would fill its `self.trajectory` with a list of the five transitions like this: `[T1, T2, T3, T4, T5]`.

In our implementation, we will use a slightly modified transition representation to reduce redundant calculations. We will use the following definition to represent a transition:

```
Transition = namedtuple("Transition", ["s", "value_s", "a",
"log_prob_a"])
```
Here, `s` is the state, `value_s` is the critic's prediction of the value of state `s`, `a` is the action taken, and `log_prob_a` is the logarithm of the probability of taking action `a` according to the actor/agent's current policy.

We will use the `calculate_n_step_return(self, n_step_rewards, final_state, done, gamma)` method we implemented previously to calculate the n-step return based on the `n_step_rewards` list containing the scalar reward values obtained at each step in the trajectory and the `final_state` used to calculate the critic's estimate value of the final/last state in the trajectory, as we discussed earlier in the n-step return calculation section.

Calculating the actor's and critic's losses

From the description of the n-step deep actor-critic algorithm we went over previously, you may remember that the critic, represented using a neural network, is trying to solve a problem that is similar to what we saw in `Chapter 6`, *Implementing an Intelligent Agent for Optimal Discrete Control using Deep Q-Learning*, which is to represent the value function (similar to the action-value function we used in this chapter, but a bit simpler). We can use the standard **Mean Squared Error** (**MSE**) loss or the smoother L1 loss/Huber loss, calculated based on the critic's predicted values and the n-step returns (TD targets) computed in the previous step.

For the actor, we will use the results obtained with the policy gradient theorem, and specifically the advantage actor-critic version, where the advantage value function is used to guide the gradient updates of the actor policy. We will use the TD_error, which is an unbiased estimate of the advantage value function.

In summary, the critic's and actor's losses are as follows:

- *critic_loss* $= MSE(G_t^{(n)}, critic\_prediction)$
- *actor_loss* $= log(\pi_\theta(s)[a]) * TD\_error$

With the main loss calculation equations captured, we can implement them in code using the `calculate_loss(self, trajectory, td_targets)` method, as illustrated by the following code snippet:

```
def calculate_loss(self, trajectory, td_targets):
    """
    Calculates the critic and actor losses using the td_targets and
self.trajectory
    :param td_targets:
    :return:
    """
    n_step_trajectory = Transition(*zip(*trajectory))
    v_s_batch = n_step_trajectory.value_s
    log_prob_a_batch = n_step_trajectory.log_prob_a
    actor_losses, critic_losses = [], []
    for td_target, critic_prediction, log_p_a in zip(td_targets,
v_s_batch, log_prob_a_batch):
        td_err = td_target - critic_prediction
        actor_losses.append(- log_p_a * td_err) # td_err is an unbiased
estimated of Advantage
        critic_losses.append(F.smooth_l1_loss(critic_prediction,
td_target))
        #critic_loss.append(F.mse_loss(critic_pred, td_target))
    if self.params["use_entropy_bonus"]:
        actor_loss = torch.stack(actor_losses).mean() -
self.action_distribution.entropy().mean()
    else:
        actor_loss = torch.stack(actor_losses).mean()
    critic_loss = torch.stack(critic_losses).mean()

    writer.add_scalar(self.actor_name + "/critic_loss", critic_loss,
self.global_step_num)
    writer.add_scalar(self.actor_name + "/actor_loss", actor_loss,
self.global_step_num)

    return actor_loss, critic_loss
```

Updating the actor-critic model

After we have calculated the losses for the actor and critic, the next and final step in the learning process is to update the actor and critic parameters based on their losses. Since we use the awesome PyTorch library, which takes care of the partial differentiation, back-propagation of errors, and gradient calculations automatically, the implementation is simple and straightforward using the results from the previous steps, as shown in the following code sample:

```
def learn(self, n_th_observation, done):
        td_targets = self.calculate_n_step_return(self.rewards,
n_th_observation, done, self.gamma)
        actor_loss, critic_loss = self.calculate_loss(self.trajectory,
td_targets)

        self.actor_optimizer.zero_grad()
        actor_loss.backward(retain_graph=True)
        self.actor_optimizer.step()

        self.critic_optimizer.zero_grad()
        critic_loss.backward()
        self.critic_optimizer.step()

        self.trajectory.clear()
        self.rewards.clear()
```

Tools to save/load, log, visualize, and monitor

In the previous sections, we walked through the core part of the agent's learning algorithm implementation. Apart from those core parts, there are a few utility functions that we will use to train and test the agent in different learning environments. We will reuse the components that we already developed in Chapter 6, *Implementing an Intelligent Agent for optimal discrete control using Deep Q Learning,*such as the utils.params_manager, and also the save() and load() methods, which respectively save and load the agent's trained brain or model. We also will make use of the logging utilities to log the agent's progress in a format that is usable with Tensorboard for a nice and quick visualization, as well as for debugging and monitoring to see whether there is something wrong with our agent's training process.

With that, we can complete our implementation of the n-step advantage actor-critic agent! You can find the full implementation in the ch8/a2c_agent.py file. Before we see how we can train the agent, in the next section we will quickly look at one of the extensions we can apply to the deep n-step advantage agent to make it perform even better on multi-core machines.

An extension - asynchronous deep n-step advantage actor-critic

One easy extension that we can make to our agent implementation is to launch several instances of our agent, each with their own instance of the learning environment, and send back updates from what they have learned in an asychronous manner, that is, whenever they are available, without any need for time syncing. This algorithm is popularly known as the A3C algorithm, which is short for asynchronous advantage actor-critic.

One of the motivations behind this extension stems from what we learned in Chapter 6, *Implementing an Intelligent Agent for optimal discrete control using Deep Q Learning*, with the use of the experience replay memory. Our deep Q-learning agent was able to learn considerably better with the addition of experience replay memory, which in essence helped in decorrelating the dependencies in the sequential decision making problem, and letting the agent extract more juice/information from its past experience. Similarly, the idea behind using multiple actor-learner instances running in parallel is found to be helpful in breaking the correlation between the transitions, and also helps in the exploration of different parts of the state space in the environment, as each actor-learner process has its own set of policy parameters and environment instance to explore. Once the agent instances running in parallel have some updates to send back, they send them over to a shared, global agent instance, which then acts as the new parameter source for the other agent instances to sync from.

We can use Python's PyTorch multiprocessing library to implement this extension. Yes! You guessed it right. This was the reason our DeepActorCritic agent in our implementation subclassed torch.multiprocessing.Process right from the start, so that we can add this extension to it without any significant code refactoring. You can look at the ch8/README.md file in the book's code repository for more resources on exploring this architecture if you are interested.

We can easily extend our n-step advantage actor-critic agent implementation in a2c_agent.py to implement the synchronous deep n-step advantage actor-critic agent. You can find the asynchronous implementation in ch8/async_a2c_agent.py.

Training an intelligent and autonomous driving agent

We now have all the pieces we need to accomplish our goal for this chapter, which is to put together an intelligent, autonomous driving agent, and then train it to drive a car autonomously in the photo-realistic CARLA driving environment that we developed as a learning environment using the Gym interface in the previous chapter. The agent training process can take a while. Depending on the hardware of the machine that you are going to train the agent on, it may take anywhere from a few hours for simpler environments (such as Pendulum-v0, CartPole-v0, and some of the Atari games) to a few days for complex environments (such as the CARLA driving environment). In order to first get a good understanding of the training process and how to monitor progress while the agent is training, we will start with a few simple examples to walk through the whole process of training and testing the agent. We will then look at how easily we can move it to the CARLA driving environment to train it further.

Training and testing the deep n-step advantage actor-critic agent

Because our agent's implementation is generic (as discussed using the table in step 1 in the previous section), we can use any learning environment that has Gym-compatible interfaces to train/test the agent. You can experiment and train the agent in a variety of environments that we discussed in the initial chapters of this book, and we will also be discussing some more interesting learning environments in the next chapter. Don't forget about our custom CARLA car driving environment!

We will pick a few environments as examples and walk through how you can launch the training and testing process to get you started experimenting on your own. First, update your fork of the book's code repository and cd to the ch8 folder, where the code for this chapter resides. As always, make sure to activate the conda environment we created for this book. After this, you can launch the training process for the n-step advantage actor critic agent using the a2c_agent.py script, as illustrated here:

```
(rl_gym_book) praveen@ubuntu:~/HOIAWOG/ch8$ python a2c_agent --env
Pendulum-v0
```

You can replace `Pendulum-v0` with any Gym-compatible learning environment name that is set up on your machine.

This should launch the agent's training script, which will use the default parameters specified in the `~/HOIAWOG/ch8/parameters.json` file (which you can change to experiment). It will also load the trained agent's brain/model for the specified environment from the `~/HOIAWOG/ch8/trained_models` directory, if available, and continue training. For high-dimensional state space environments, such as the Atari games, or other environments where the state/observation is an image of the scene or the screen pixels, the deep convolutional neural network we discussed in one of the previous sections will be used, which will make use of the GPU on your machine, if available, to speed up computations (you can disable this by setting `use_cuda = False` in the `parameters.json` file if you want). If you have multiple GPUs on your machine and would like to train different agents on different GPUs, you can specify the GPU device ID as a command line argument to the `a2c_agent.py` script using the `--gpu-id` flag to ask the script to use a particular GPU for training/testing.

Once the training process starts, you can monitor the agent's process by launching `tensorboard` using the following command from the `logs` directory:

```
(rl_gym_book) praveen@ubuntu:~/HOIAWOG/ch8/logs$ tensorboard --logdir .
```

After launching `tensorboard` using the preceding command, you can visit the web page at `http://localhost:6006` to monitor the progress of the agent. Sample screenshots are provided here for your reference; these were from two training runs of the n-step advantage actor-critic agent, with different values for *n* steps, using the `learning_step_threshold` parameter in the `parameters.json` file:

Actor-critic (using separate actor and critic network):

1. - `Pendulum-v0` ; n-step (learning_step_threshold = 100)

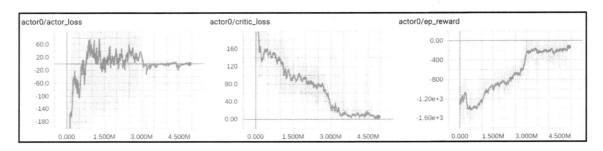

2. - `Pendulum-v0`; n-step (learning_step_threshold = 5)

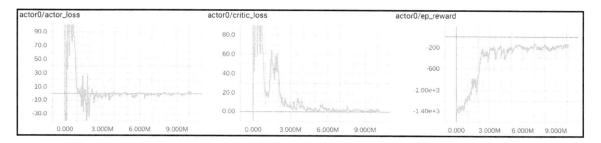

- Comparing 1 (100-step AC in green) and 2 (5-step AC in grey) on `Pendulum-v0` for 10 million steps:

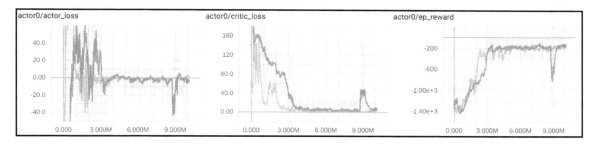

The training script will also output a summary of the training process to the console. If you want to visualize the environment to see what the agent is doing or how it is learning, you can add the `--render` flag to the command while launching the training script, as illustrated in the following line:

```
(rl_gym_book) praveen@ubuntu:~/HOIAWOG/ch8$ python a2c_agent --env
CartPole-v0 --render
```

As you can see, we have reached a point where you are just one command away from training, logging, and visualizing the agent's performance! We have made very good progress so far.

You can run several experiments with different sets of parameters for the agent, on the same environment or on different environments. The previous example was chosen to demonstrate its performance in a simpler environment so that you can easily run full-length experiments and reproduce and compare the results, irrespective of the hardware resources you may have. As part of the book's code repository, trained agent brains/models are provided for some environments so that you can quickly start and run the script in test mode to see how a trained agent performs at the tasks. They are available in the `ch8/trianed_models` folder in your fork of the book's repository, or at the upstream origin here: `https://github.com/PacktPublishing/Hands-On-Intelligent-Agents-with-OpenAI-Gym/tree/master/ch8/trained_models`. You will also find other resources, such as illustrations of learning curves in other environments and video clips of agents performing in a variety of environments, in the book's code repository for your reference.

Once you are ready to test the agent, either using your own trained agent's brain model or using one of the pre-trained agent brains, you can use the `--test` flag to signify that you would like to disable learning and run the agent in testing mode. For example, to test the agent in the `LunarLander-v2` environment with rendering of the learning environment turned on, you can use the following command:

```
(rl_gym_book) praveen@ubuntu:~/HOIAWOG/ch8$ python a2c_agent --env
LunarLander-v2 --test --render
```

We can interchangeably use the asynchronous agent that we discussed as an extension to our base agent. Since both the agent implementations follow the same structure and configuration, we can easily switch to the asynchronous agent training script by just using the `async_a2c_agent.py` script in place of `a2c_agent.py`. They even support the same command line arguments to make our work simpler. When using the `asyn_a2c_agent.py` script, you should make sure to set the `num_agents` parameter in the `parameters.json` file, based on the number of processes or parallel instances you would like the agent to use for training. As an example, we can train the asynchronous version of our agent in the `BipedalWalker-v2` environment using the following command:

```
(rl_gym_book) praveen@ubuntu:~/HOIAWOG/ch8$ python async_a2c_agent --env
BipedalWalker-v2
```

As you may have realized, our agent implementation is capable of learning to act in a variety of different environments, each with its own set of tasks to be completed, as well as their own state, observation and action spaces. It is this versatility that has made deep reinforcement learning-based agents popular and suitable for solving a variety of problems. Now that we are familiar with the training process, we can finally move on to training the agent to drive a car and follow the lanes in the CARLA driving simulator.

Training the agent to drive a car in the CARLA driving simulator

Let's start training an agent in the CARLA driving environment! First, make sure your GitHub fork is up to date with the upstream master so that you have the latest code from the book's repository. Since the CARLA environment we created in the previous chapter is compatible with the OpenAI Gym interface, it is actually easy to use the CARLA environment for training, just like any other Gym environment. You can train the n-step advantage actor-critic agent using the following command:

```
(rl_gym_book) praveen@ubuntu:~/HOIAWOG/ch8$ python a2c_agent --env Carla-v0
```

This will launch the agent's training process, and like we saw before, a summary of the progress will be printed to the console window, along with the logs written to the `logs` folder, which can be viewed using `tensorboard`.

During the initial stages of the training process, you will notice that the agent is driving the car like crazy!

After several hours of training, you will see that the agent learns to control the car and successfully drives down the road while staying in the lane and avoiding crashing into other vehicles. A trained model for the autonomous driver agent is available in the `ch8/trained_models` folder for you to quickly take the agent on a test drive! You will also find more resources and experimental results in the book's code repository to help with your learning and experimentation. Happy experimenting!

Summary

In this chapter, we got hands-on with an actor-critic architecture-based deep reinforcement learning agent, starting from the basics. We started with the introduction to policy gradient-based methods and walked through the step-by-step process of representing the objective function for the policy gradient optimization, understanding the likelihood ratio trick, and finally deriving the policy gradient theorem. We then looked at how the actor-critic architecture makes use of the policy gradient theorem and uses an actor component to represent the policy of the agent, and a critic component to represent the state/action/advantage value function, depending on the implementation of the architecture. With an intuitive understanding of the actor-critic architecture, we moved on to the A2C algorithm and discussed the six steps involved in it. We then discussed the n-step return calculation using a diagram, and saw how easy it is to implement the n-step return calculation method in Python. We then moved on to the step-by-step implementation of the deep n-step advantage actor-critic agent.

We also discussed how we could make the implementation flexible and generic to accommodate a variety of environments, which may have different state, observation and action space dimensions, and also may be continuous or discrete. We then looked at how we can run multiple instances of the agent in parallel on separate processes to improve the learning performance. In the last section, we walked through the steps involved in the process of training the agents, and once they are trained, how we can use the `--test` and `--render` flags to test the agent's performance. We started with simpler environments to get accustomed to the training and monitoring process, and then finally moved on to accomplishing the goal of this chapter, which was to train an intelligent agent to drive a car autonomously in the CARLA driving simulator! I hope you learned a lot going through this relatively long chapter. At this point, you have experience understanding and implementing two broad classes of high-performance learning agent algorithms from this chapter and `Chapter 6`, *Implementing an Intelligent Agent for Optimal Discrete Control using Deep Q-Learning*. In the next chapter, we will explore the landscape of new and promising learning environments, where you can train your custom agents and start making progress towards the next level.

9
Exploring the Learning Environment Landscape - Roboschool, Gym-Retro, StarCraft-II, DeepMindLab

You have come a long way in your quest to get hands-on experience in building intelligent agents to solve a variety of challenging problems. In the previous chapters, we looked into several environments that are available in OpenAI Gym. In this chapter, we will look beyond the Gym and look at some of the other well developed environments that you can use to train your intelligent agents or run experiments.

Before we look at other open source libraries that provide good learning environments for developing intelligent agents, let's have a look at a recent class of environments added to the OpenAI Gym library. If, like me, you are interested in robotics, you will like this one a lot. Yes! It is the robotics class of environments, which provides very useful environments for robotic manipulation tasks such as fetching, sliding, pushing, and so on with a robotic arm. These robotics environments are based on the MuJoCo engine and you may recall from Chapter 3, *Getting Started with OpenAI Gym and Deep Reinforcement Learning*, that the MuJoCo engine requires a paid license, unless you are a student and using MuJoCo for personal or class use. A summary of these robotics environments is shown in the following screenshot, with the environment names and a brief description for each, so that you can check them out if you are interested in exploring such problems:

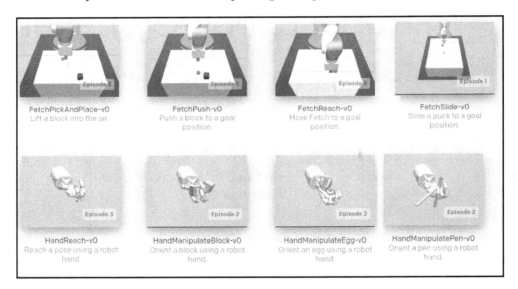

Gym interface-compatible environments

In this section, we will have a deeper look into environments that are compatible with the Gym interface out of the box. You should be able to use any of the agents we developed in the previous chapters in these environments. Let's get started and look at a few very useful and promising learning environments.

Roboschool

Roboschool (https://github.com/openai/roboschool) provides several environments for controlling robots in simulation. It was released by OpenAI and the environments have the same interface as the OpenAI Gym environments that we have been using in this book. The Gym's MuJoCo-based environments offer a rich variety of robotic tasks, but MuJoCo requires a license for use after the free trial. Roboschool provides eight environments that quite closely match the MuJoCo ones, which is a good news as it offers a free alternative. Apart from these eight environments, Roboschool also offers several new and challenging environments.

The following table shows a quick comparison between the MuJoCo Gym environments and the Roboschool environments:

Brief description	MuJoCo environment	Roboschool environment
Make a one-legged 2D robot hop forward as fast as possible	Hopper-v2	RoboschoolHopper-v1
Make a 2D robot walk	Walker2d-v2	RoboschoolWalker2d-v1
Make a four-legged 3D robot walk	Ant-v2	RoboschoolAnt-v1

	Humanoid-v2	RoboschoolHumanoid-v1
Make a bipedal 3D robot walk forward as fast as possible without falling	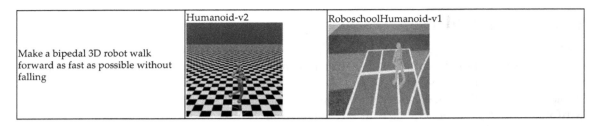	

A full list of environments that are available as part of the Roboschool library, with their state and action spaces, is provided in the following table for your quick reference:

Env ID	Roboschool env	obs space	action space
RoboschoolInvertedPendulum-v1		Box(5,)	Box(1,)
RoboschoolInvertedPendulumSwingup-v1		Box(5,)	Box(1,)
RoboschoolInvertedDoublePendulum-v1		Box(9,)	Box(1,)
RoboschoolReacher-v1		Box(9,)	Box(2,)
RoboschoolHopper-v1		Box(15,)	Box(3,)
RoboschoolWalker2d-v1		Box(22,)	Box(6,)
RoboschoolHalfCheetah-v1		Box(26,)	Box(6,)
RoboschoolAnt-v1		Box(28,)	Box(8,)

Env ID	Roboschool env	obs space	action space
RoboschoolHumanoid-v1		Box(44,)	Box(17,)
RoboschoolHumanoidFlagrun-v1		Box(44,)	Box(17,)
RoboschoolHumanoidFlagrunHarder-v1		Box(44,)	Box(17,)
RoboschoolPong-v1		Box(13,)	Box(2,)

Quickstart guide to setting up and running Roboschool environments

Roboschool environments make use of the open source Bulletphysics engine instead of the proprietary MuJoCo engine. Let's quickly have a look at a Roboschool environment so that you know how to use any environment from the Roboschool library if you happen to find it useful for your work. To get started, we will have to first install the Roboschool Python library in our rl_gym_book conda environment. Because the library depends on several components, including the Bulletphysics engine, there are several installation steps involved, which are listed in the official Roboschool GitHub repository here: https://github.com/openai/roboschool. To make things simpler, you can use the script in the book's code repository at ch9/setup_roboschool.sh to automatically compile and install the Roboschool library for you. Follow these steps to run the script:

1. Activate the rl_gym_book conda environment using source activate rl_gym_book.
2. Navigate to the ch9 folder with cd ch9.
3. Make sure that the script's execution bit is set as chmod a+x setup_roboschool.sh.
4. Run the script with sudo:./setup_roboschool.sh.

This should install the required system dependencies, fetch and compile a compatible source code of the bullet3 physics engine; pull the Roboschool source code to the `software` folder under your home directory; and finally compile, build, and install the Roboschool library in the `rl_gym_book` conda environment. If the setup completes successfully, you will see the following message printed on the console:

```
Setup completed successfully. You can now import roboschool and use it. If
you would like to \test the installation, you can run: python
~/roboschool/agent_zoo/demo_race2.py"
```

You can run a quickstart demo script using the following command:

```
`(rl_gym_book) praveen@ubuntu:~$ python
~/roboschool/agent_zoo/demo_race2.py`
```

This will launch a funny-to-watch robo-race in which you will see a hopper, half-cheetah, and humanoid running a race! The interesting aspect is that each of the robots is being controlled by a reinforcement learning-based trained policy. The race will look similar to this snapshot:

Once it has been installed, you can create a Roboschool environment and use one of the agents we developed in an earlier chapter to train and run on these environments.

You can use the `run_roboschool_env.py` script in this chapter's code repository at `https://github.com/PacktPublishing/Hands-On-Intelligent-Agents-with-OpenAI-Gym/tree/master/ch9` to check out any of the Roboschool environments. For example, to check out the `RoboschoolInvertedDoublePendulum-v1` environment, you can run the following script:

```
(rl_gym_book) praveen@ubuntu:~/HOIAWOG/ch9$python run_roboschool_env.py --
env RoboschoolInvertedDoublePendulum-v1
```

You can use any other Roboschool environment name from the previous table, as well as new Roboschool environments when they are made available.

Gym retro

Gym Retro (`https://github.com/openai/retro`) is a relatively new (released on May 25, 2018) Python library released by OpenAI (`https://blog.openai.com/gym-retro/`) as a research platform for developing reinforcement learning algorithms for game playing. Although the Atari suite of 60+ games was available in OpenAI Gym, the total number of games available was limited. Gym Retro supports the use of games developed for several console/retro gaming platforms, such as Nintendo's NES, SNES, Game Boy consoles, Sega Genesis, and Sega Master System to name a few. This is made possible with the use of emulators using the Libretro API:

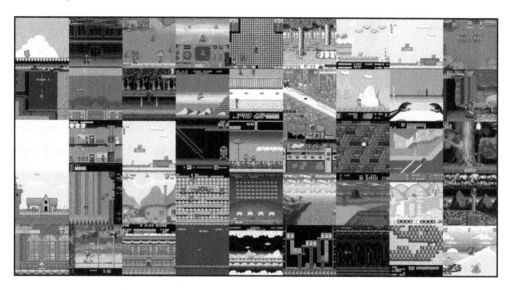

Gym Retro provides convenient wrappers to turn more than 1,000 such video games into Gym interface-compatible learning environments! Isn't that great! Several new learning environments but with the same interface, so that we can easily train and test the agents we have developed so far without any necessary changes to the code...

To get a feel for how easy it is to use the environments in Gym Retro, let's put the installation steps aside for a moment and quickly look at the code to create a new Gym Retro environment once it is installed:

```
import retro
env = retro.make(game='Airstriker-Genesis', state='Level1')
```

This code snipped will create an `env` object that has the same interfaces and methods, such as `step(...)`, `reset()` and `render()`, as all the Gym environments we have seen before.

Quickstart guide to setup and run Gym Retro

Let's try out the Gym Retro library quickly by installing the pre-built binaries using pip with the following command:

```
(rl_gym_book) praveen@ubuntu:~/rl_gym_book/ch9$ pip install gym-retro
```

Once the installation is successful, we can have a sneak peek into one of the available Gym Retro environments using the following script:

```python
#!/usr/bin/env python
import retro

if __name__ == '__main__':
    env = retro.make(game='Airstriker-Genesis', state='Level1')
    obs = env.reset()
    while True:
        obs, rew, done, info = env.step(env.action_space.sample())
        env.render()
        if done:
            obs = env.reset()
```

Running this script will bring up a window with the Airstriker game and show the spaceship taking random actions. The game window will look something like this:

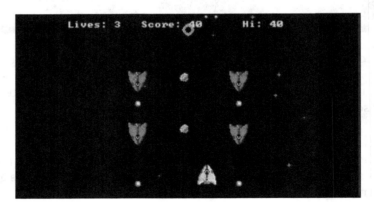

Before we move on, one thing to note is that the **ROM (Read-Only Memory)** file that contains the whole game data is not made freely available for all games. The ROMs for some non-commercial console games such as Airstriker (used in the previous script), Fire, Dekadrive, Automaton, Fire, Lost Marbles, and so on are included with the Gym Retro library and are free to use. Other games, such as the Sonic series (Sonic The Hedgehog, Sonic The Hedgehog 2, Sonic 3 & Knuckles) require ROMs to be purchased for legal use from places such as Steam. This is a barrier for hobbyists, students, and other enthusiasts who wish to develop algorithms using such environments. But at least this barrier is relatively small, as it costs about USD 1.69 on Steam for the Sonic The Hedgehog ROM. Once you have the ROM files for the games, the Gym Retro library provides a script to import them into the library like so:

```
(rl_gym_book) praveen@ubuntu:~/rl_gym_book/ch9$ python -m retro.import
/PATH/TO/YOUR/ROMs/DIRECTORY
OpenAI Universe
```

Note that when creating a new Gym Retro environment, we need the name of the game as well as the state of the game retro.make(game='NAME_OF_GAME', state='NAME_OF_STATE')

To get a list of available Gym Retro environments, you can run the following command:

```
(rl_gym_book) praveen@ubuntu:~/rl_gym_book/ch9$ python -c "import retro;
retro.list_games()"
```

And to get a list of available game states, you can run the following Python script:

```
#!/usr/bin/evn python
import retro
for game in retro.list_games():
    print(game, retro.list_states(game))
```

So far, we have gotten ourselves familiar with the Gym Retro library. Let's analyze what advantages or new features this library provides us in addition to what we have already seen and used. First, the Gym Retro library utilizes newer games consoles (such as the SEGA Genesis) than the Atari console. For comparison, the SEGA Genesis games console has 500 times as much RAM as the Atari console, enabling better visuals and a greater range of controls. This provides us with learning environments that are relatively sophisticated, and some more complex tasks and challenges for our intelligent agents to learn and solve. Second, several of these console games are progressive in nature, where the complexity of the game typically increases with every level and the levels have several similarities in some aspects (such as the goal, object appearances, physics, and so on) while also providing diversity in other aspects (such as the layout, new objects, and so on). Such a training environment with levels of progressively increasing difficulty help in developing intelligent agents that can learn to solve tasks in general without being very task/environment-specific (such as overfitting in supervised learning). Agents can learn to transfer their skills and learning from one level to another, and then to another game. This area is under active research and is usually known as curriculum learning, staged learning, or incremental evolution. After all, ultimately we are interested in developing intelligent agents that can learn to solve tasks in general and not just the specific tasks the agent was trained on. The Gym Retro library provides some useful, though game-only, environments to facilitate such experiments and research.

Other open source Python-based learning environments

In this section, we will discuss recent Python-based learning environments that provide a good platform for intelligent agent development but don't necessarily have a Gym-compatible environment interface. Although they do not provide Gym-compatible interfaces, the environments we will be discussing in this section were carefully selected to make sure that either a Gym wrapper (to make it compatible with the Gym interface) is available, or they are easy to implement in order to use and experiment with the agents we have developed through this book. As you can guess, this list of good Python-based learning environments for developing intelligent agents will grow in the future, as this area is being very actively researched at the moment. The book's code repository will have information and quickstart guides for new environments as they become available in the future. Sign up for update notifications at the book's GitHub repository to get those updates. In the following sub-sections, we will discuss some of the most promising learning environments that are readily available for use.

StarCraft II - PySC2

StarCraft II is very popular, in fact one of the most successful real-time strategy games ever, and is played by millions of people worldwide. It even has a world championship league (https://wcs.starcraft2.com/en-us/)! The environment is quite complex and the main goal is to build an army base, manage an economy, defend the base, and destroy enemies. The player controls the base camp and the army from a third-person view of the scene. If you are not familiar with StarCarft, you should watch a few games online to get a feel for how complex and fast-paced the game is.

For humans to play this real-time strategy game well, it takes a lot of practice (several months even; in fact, professional players train for several years), planning, and quick responses. Although software agents can press several software buttons per frame to make pretty fast moves, speed of action is not the only factor that contributes to victory. The agent has to multi-task and micro-manage the army units, and maximize their score, which is several orders of magnitude more complex than the Atari games.

Blizzard, the company that made StarCraft II, released the StarCraft II API, which provides the necessary hooks to interface with the StarCraft II game and control it without limitations. That enables several new possibilities, such as the development of the intelligent agents that we are after. They even have a separate **End User License Agreement** (**EULA**) for open use of the environment under an AI and machine learning license! This was a very welcome move by a company such as Blizzard, which is in the business of making and selling games. The open source the **StarCraft2** (**SC2**) client protocol implementation and provides the Linux installation package, along with several accessories such as the map packs, free to download from their GitHub page at https://github.com/Blizzard/s2client-proto. On top of that, Google DeepMind has open sourced their PySC2 library, which exposes the SC2 client interfaces through Python and provides a wrapper that makes it an RL environment.

The following screenshot shows the PySC2 UI, with the feature layers available as observations to the agents shown on the right and a simplified overview of the game scene on the left:

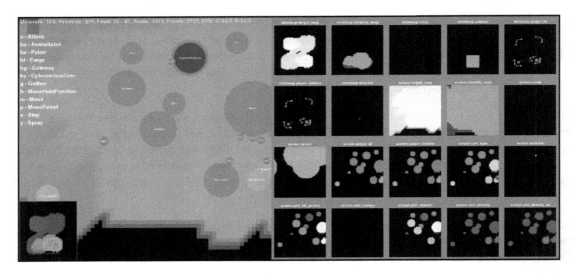

If you are interested in these types of environment, and especially if you are a game developer, you might be interested in the Dota 2 environment as well. Dota 2 is a real-time strategy game, like StarCraft II, and is played between two teams of five players with each player controlling a hero character. You can learn more about how OpenAI developed a team of five neural network-based agents that have learned to work in a team, played 180 years' worth of games in a day, learned to overcome several challenges (including high-dimensional and continuous state and action spaces, and long-term horizons), all while playing against themselves using self-play! You can read more about the five-agent team at https://blog.openai.com/openai-five/.

Quick start guide to setup and run StarCraft II PySC2 environment

We will look at how you can quickly set up and get started with the StarCraft II environment. As always, use the README files in the code repository for the latest up-to-date instructions, as things as the links and the versions may change. If you have not done so already, star and watch the book's code repository to get notified about changes and updates.

Downloading the StarCraft II Linux packages

Download the latest Linux packages for the StarCraft game from
https://github.com/Blizzard/s2client-proto#downloads and extract it onto your hard disk at
~/StarCraftII. For example, to download version 4.1.2 to your ~/StarCraftII/ folder,
you can use the following command:

```
wget http://blzdistsc2-a.akamaihd.net/Linux/SC2.4.1.2.60604_2018_05_16.zip
-O ~/StarCraftII/SC2.4.1.2.zip
```

Let's unzip and extract the files to the ~/StarCraftII/ directory:

```
unzip ~/StarCraftII/SC2.4.1.2.zip -d ~/StarCraftII/
```

Note that, as mentioned on the download page, the files are password protected with the
password 'iagreetotheeula.

By typing that, Blizzard ensures we agree to be bound by the terms of their AI and machine
learning license, found on the download page.

Downloading the SC2 maps

We will need the StarCraft II map packs and the mini games pack to get started.

Download the map packs from https://github.com/Blizzard/s2client-proto#map-packs

Extract them to your ~/StarCraftII/Maps directory.

As an example, let's download the Ladder maps released for 2018 season 2 using the
following command:

```
wget
http://blzdistsc2-a.akamaihd.net/MapPacks/Ladder2018Season2_Updated.zip -O
~/StarCraftII/Maps/Ladder2018S2.zip
```

Let's unzip the maps to the ~/StarCraftII/Maps directory:

```
unzip ~/StarCraftII/Maps/Ladder2018S2.zip -d ~/StarCraftII/Maps/
```

Next, we will download and unzip the mini game map files:

```
wget
https://github.com/deepmind/pysc2/releases/download/v1.2/mini_games.zip -O
~/StarCraftII/Maps/mini_games1.2.zip

unzip ~/StarCraftII/Maps/mini_games1.2.zip -d ~/StarCraftII/Maps
```

Installing PySC2

Let's install the PySC2 library for the RL environment interface, along with the required dependencies. This step is going to be straightforward, as there is a PyPi Python package for the PySC2 library:

```
(rl_gym_book) praveen@ubuntu:~/HOIAWOG/ch9$ pip install pysc2
```

Playing StarCraftII yourself or running sample agents

To test whether the installation went fine and to see what the StarCarftII learning environment looks like, you can quickly start up a randomly-acting agent on the Simple64 map or the CollectMineralShards map using the following command:

```
(rl_gym_book) praveen@ubuntu:~/HOIAWOG/ch9$ python -m pysc2.bin.agent --map
Simple64
```

You can also load another available map for the environment. For example, the following command loads the CollectMineralShards map:

```
(rl_gym_book) praveen@ubuntu:~/HOIAWOG/ch9$ python -m pysc2.bin.agent --map
CollectMineralShards
```

This should bring up a UI showing you the actions taken by the random agent, which gives you an idea of what the valid actions are and helps you to visualize what is going on in the environment as the agent is acting.

To play the game yourself, PySC2 offers a human agent interface, which is quite useful for debugging (and, if you are interested, playing!) purposes. The following is the command to run and play the game yourself:

```
(rl_gym_book) praveen@ubuntu:~/HOIAWOG/ch9$ python -m pysc2.bin.play --map
Simple64
```

You can also run a sample agent that is scripted to collect mineral shards, which is one of the tasks in the game, using the following command:

```
(rl_gym_book) praveen@ubuntu:~/HOIAWOG/ch9$ python -m pysc2.bin.agent --map
CollectMineralShards --agent
pysc2.agents.scripted_agent.CollectMineralShards
```

Watch the book's code repository for new agent source code and instructions to train and test new agents with advanced skills. You can also customize the agents we developed in the previous chapter to learn to play StarCraftII. If you do, send a pull request to the book's code repository, shoot the author an email, or shout it out so that everyone knows what cools things you have done!

DeepMind lab

DeepMind Lab (https://github.com/deepmind/lab) is a 3D learning environment that provides a suite of environments with challenging tasks, such as 3D navigation through mazes and puzzle solving. It is built based on a handful of pieces of open source software, including the famous Quake III Arena.

The environment interface is very similar to the Gym interface that we have used extensively in this book so far. To get a feel for what the environment interface actually looks like, have a look at the following code snippet:

```
import deepmind_lab
num_steps = 1000
config = {
    'width': 640,
    'height': 480,
    'fps': 30
}
...
env = deepmind_lab.Lab(level, ['RGB_INTERLEAVED'], config=config,
renderer='software')

for step in range(num_steps)
if done:
    env.reset()
obs = env.observations()
action = agent.get_action(...)
reward = env.step(action, num_steps=1)
done = not env.is_running()
```

This code, though not one-to-one compatible with the OpenAI Gym interface, provides a very similar interface.

DeepMind Lab learning environment interface

We will briefly discuss the environment interface for **DeepMind Lab (DM Lab)**, so that you are familiar with it, can see the similarities with the OpenAI Gym interface, and can start experimenting with agents in DM Lab environments!

reset(episode=-1, seed=None)

This is similar to the `reset()` method we saw in the Gym interface, but unlike Gym environments, DM Lab's `reset` method call does not return the observation. We will see later how to get observations, so for now, we will discuss DM Lab's `reset(episode=-1, seed=None)` method. It resets the environment to an initial state and needs to be called at the end of every episode, in order for a new episode to be created. The optional `episode` argument takes an integer value to specify the level in a specific episode. If the `episode` value is not set, or is set to `-1`, the levels are loaded in numerical order. The `seed` argument is also optional and is used to seed the environment's random number generator for reproducibility purposes.

step(action, num_steps=1)

This is similar to the Gym interface's `step(action)` method, but like with the `reset(...)` method, the call to this method does not return the next observation (or reward, done, and info). Calling this method advances the environment by `num_steps` number of frames, executing the action defined by `action` in every frame. This action-repeat behavior is useful in cases where we would like the same action to be applied for four or so consecutive frames, which was actually found by several researchers to help with learning. There are Gym environment wrappers that accomplish this action-repeat behavior.

observations()

This is the method we would use after the call to `reset(...)` or `step(action)` to receive the observations from DM Lab environments. This method returns a Python dictionary object with every type of observation that we specified from the list of available types for the environment. For example, if we wanted **RGBD (Red-Green-Blue-Depth)** information about the environment as the observation type, we can specify that when we initialize the environment using the `'RGBD'` key, we can then retrieve this information from the returned observation dictionary using the same `'RGBD'` key. A simple example to illustrate this is shown here:

```
env = deepmind_lab.Lab('tests/empty_room_test', ['RGBD'])
```

```
env.reset()
obs = env.observations()['RGBD']
```

There are also other observation types that are supported by DM Lab environments. We can use `observation_spec()` to get a list of supported observation types, which we will discuss very shortly.

is_running()

This method is analogous (in the opposite sense) to the `done` Boolean returned by the Gym interface's `step(action)` method.

This method will return `False` when the environment is done with an episode or stops running. It will return `True` as long as the environment is running.

observation_spec()

This method is similar to `env.observation_space()`, which we used with the Gym environments. This method returns a list specifying all the available observations supported by the DM Lab environment. It also includes specifications about level-dependent custom observations.

The specifications contain the name, type, and shape of the tensor or string that will be returned if that specification name is specified in the observation list (such as the `'RGBD'` example previously). For example, the following code snippet lists two items in the list that will be returned to give you an idea about what the specs contain:

```
{
    'dtype': <type 'numpy.uint8'>, ## Array data type
    'name': 'RGBD',               ## Name of observation.
    'shape': (4, 180, 320)        ## shape of the array. (Heights, Width,
Colors)
}


{
    'name': 'RGB_INTERLEAVED', ## Name of observation.
    'dtype': <type 'numpy.uint8'>, ## Data type array.
    'shape': (180, 320, 3) ## Shape of array. (Height, Width, Colors)
}
```

To quickly understand how this method can be used, let's look at the following lines of code and the output:

```
import deepmind_lab
import pprint
```

```
env = deepmind_lab.Lab('tests/empty_room_test', [])
observation_spec = env.observation_spec()
pprint.pprint(observation_spec)
# Outputs:
[{'dtype': <type 'numpy.uint8'>, 'name': 'RGB_INTERLEAVED', 'shape': (180,
320, 3)},
 {'dtype': <type 'numpy.uint8'>, 'name': 'RGBD_INTERLEAVED', 'shape': (180,
320, 4)},
 {'dtype': <type 'numpy.uint8'>, 'name': 'RGB', 'shape': (3, 180, 320)},
 {'dtype': <type 'numpy.uint8'>, 'name': 'RGBD', 'shape': (4, 180, 320)},
 {'dtype': <type 'numpy.uint8'>, 'name': 'BGR_INTERLEAVED', 'shape': (180,
320, 3)},
 {'dtype': <type 'numpy.uint8'>, 'name': 'BGRD_INTERLEAVED', 'shape': (180,
320, 4)},
 {'dtype': <type 'numpy.float64'>, 'name': 'MAP_FRAME_NUMBER', 'shape':
(1,)},
 {'dtype': <type 'numpy.float64'>, 'name': 'VEL.TRANS', 'shape': (3,)},
 {'dtype': <type 'numpy.float64'>, 'name': 'VEL.ROT', 'shape': (3,)},
 {'dtype': <type 'str'>, 'name': 'INSTR', 'shape': ()},
 {'dtype': <type 'numpy.float64'>, 'name': 'DEBUG.POS.TRANS', 'shape':
(3,)},
 {'dtype': <type 'numpy.float64'>, 'name': 'DEBUG.POS.ROT', 'shape': (3,)},
 {'dtype': <type 'numpy.float64'>, 'name': 'DEBUG.PLAYER_ID', 'shape':
(1,)},
# etc...
```

action_spec()

Similar to the `observation_spec()` the `action_spec()` method returns a list containing the min, max, and a name for each of the elements in the space. The `min` and `max` values respectively represent the minimum and maximum value that the corresponding element in the action space can be set to. The length of this list will equal the dimension/shape of the action space. This is analogous to `env.action_space`, which we have been using with the Gym environments.

The following code snippet gives us a quick look into what the return values from a call to this method will look like:

```
import deepmind_lab
import pprint

env = deepmind_lab.Lab('tests/empty_room_test', [])
action_spec = env.action_spec()
pprint.pprint(action_spec)
# Outputs:
```

```
# [{'max': 512, 'min': -512, 'name': 'LOOK_LEFT_RIGHT_PIXELS_PER_FRAME'},
#  {'max': 512, 'min': -512, 'name': 'LOOK_DOWN_UP_PIXELS_PER_FRAME'},
#  {'max': 1, 'min': -1, 'name': 'STRAFE_LEFT_RIGHT'},
#  {'max': 1, 'min': -1, 'name': 'MOVE_BACK_FORWARD'},
#  {'max': 1, 'min': 0, 'name': 'FIRE'},
#  {'max': 1, 'min': 0, 'name': 'JUMP'},
#  {'max': 1, 'min': 0, 'name': 'CROUCH'}]
```

num_steps()

This utility method is like a counter that counts the number of frames executed by the environment since the last `reset()` call.

fps()

This utility method returns the number of frames (or environment steps) executed per actual (wall-clock) second. This is useful to keep track of the environment execution speeds and how fast the agent can sample from the environment.

events()

This utility method can be useful for debugging as it returns a list of events that have occurred since the last call to `reset()` or `step(...)`. The returned tuple contains a name and a list of observations.

close()

Like the `close()` method available with Gym environments, this method also closes the environment instance and releases the underlying resources, such as the Quake III Arena instance.

Quick start guide to setup and run DeepMind Lab

With the familiarity we got after the brief discussion about the DeepMind Lab environment interface in the previous section, we are ready to get some hands on experience with this learning environment. In the following sub-sections, we will go through the steps to setup DeepMind Lab and run a sample agent.

Setting up and installing DeepMind Lab and its dependencies

The DeepMind Lab library uses Bazel as the build tool, which in turn requires Java. The book's code repository has a script that you can run to easily set up DeepMind Lab. You can find the script under the chapter9 folder at `https://github.com/PacktPublishing/Hands-On-Intelligent-Agents-with-OpenAI-Gym/tree/master/ch9`. You can run the script using the following command:

```
(rl_gym_book) praveen@ubuntu:~/HOIAWOG/ch9$./setup_deepmindlab.sh
```

This script will take some time to finish, but will automatically install all the necessary packages and libraries, including Bazel and its dependencies, and set everything up for you.

Playing the game, testing a randomly acting agent, or training your own!

Once the installation is complete, you can test the game using your keyboard inputs by running the following commands:

```
(rl_gym_book) praveen@ubuntu:~/HOIAWOG/ch9$ cd deepmindlab
```

```
(rl_gym_book) praveen@ubuntu:~/HOIAWOG/ch9/deepmindlab$ bazel run :game --
--level_script=tests/empty_room_test
```

You can also test it with the help of a randomly acting agent using the following command:

```
(rl_gym_book) praveen@ubuntu:~/HOIAWOG/ch9/deepmindlab$ bazel run
:python_random_agent --define graphics=sdl -- --length=5000
```

To get started with your own agent development, you can use the example agent script that was already configured to interact with the DeepMind Lab environment. You can find the script at `~/HOIAWOG/ch9/deepmindlab/python/random_agent.py`. To start training that agent, you can use the following command:

```
(rl_gym_book) praveen@ubuntu:~/HOIAWOG/ch9/deepmindlab$ bazel run
:python_random_agent
```

Summary

In this chapter, we looked at several interesting and valuable learning environments, saw how their interfaces are set up, and even got hands-on with those environments using the quickstart guides for each environment and the setup scripts available in the book's code repository. We first looked at environments that have interfaces compatible with the OpenAI Gym interface that we are now very familiar with. Specifically in this category, we explored the Roboschool and Gym Retro environments.

We also looked at other useful learning environments that did not necessarily have a Gym-compatible environment interface, but had a very similar API and so it was easy to adapt our agent code or implement a wrapper around the learning environment to make it compatible with the Gym API. Specifically, we explored the famous real-time strategy game-based StarCraft II environment and the DeepMind Lab environment. We also very briefly touched upon the DOTA2 environment, which has been used to train both single agents and a team of agents, trained by OpenAI, which successfully defeated amateur human players, and even some professional gaming teams, in the DOTA 2 contest.

We saw the different sets of tasks and environments available in each of these learning environment libraries and tried out examples to get a feel for the environment, and also to get an idea about how we can use the agents we developed in the previous chapters to train and solve the challenging tasks in these relatively new learning environments.

10
Exploring the Learning Algorithm Landscape - DDPG (Actor-Critic), PPO (Policy-Gradient), Rainbow (Value-Based)

In the previous chapter, we looked at several promising learning environments that you can use to train agents to solve a variety of different tasks. In Chapter 7, *Creating Custom OpenAI Gym Environments – CARLA Driving Simulator*, we also saw how you can create your own environments to solve the task or problem that you may be interested in developing a solution for, using intelligent and autonomous software agents. That provides you with directions on where you can head after finishing in order to explore and play around with all the environments, tasks, and problems we discussed in this book. Along the same lines, in this chapter, we will discuss several promising learning algorithms that serve as future references for your intelligent agent development endeavors.

So far in this book, we have gone through the step-by-step process of implementing intelligent agents that can learn to improve and solve discrete decision making/control problems (Chapter 6, *Implementing an Intelligent Agent for Optimal Discrete Control Using Deep Q-Learning*) and continuous action/control problems (Chapter 8, *Implementing an Intelligent Autonomous Car Driving Agent Using the Deep Actor-Critic algorithm*). They served as good starting points in the development of such learning agents. Hopefully, the previous chapters gave you a holistic picture of an autonomous intelligent software agent/system that can learn to improve given the task or problem at hand. We also looked at the overall pipeline with useful utilities and routines (such as logging, visualization, parameter management, and so on) that help when developing, training, and testing such complex systems. We saw two main classes of algorithms: deep Q-learning (and its extensions) and deep actor-critic (and their extensions)-based deep reinforcement learning algorithms. They are good baseline algorithms and in fact are still referenced in state-of-the art research papers in this area. This area of research has been under active development in recent years, and several new algorithms have been proposed. Some have better sample complexity, which is the number of samples the agent collects from the environment before it reaches a certain level of performance. Some other algorithms have stable learning characteristics and find optimal policies, given enough time, for most problems with little or no tuning. Several new architectures, such as IMPALA and Ape-X, have also been introduced and enable highly scaleable learning algorithm implementations.

We will have a quick look at these promising algorithms, their advantages, and their potential application types. We will also look at code examples for the key components that these algorithms add to what we already know. Sample implementations of these algorithms are available in this book's code repository under the ch10 folder at https:// github.com/PacktPublishing/Hands-On-Intelligent-Agents-with-OpenAI-Gym.

Deep Deterministic Policy Gradients

Deep Deterministic Policy Gradient (DDPG) is an off-policy, model-free, actor-critic algorithm and is based on the **Deterministic Policy Gradient (DPG)** theorem (proceedings.mlr.press/v32/silver14.pdf). Unlike the deep Q-learning-based methods, actor-critic policy gradient-based methods are easily applicable to continuous action spaces, in addition to problems/tasks with discrete action spaces.

Core concepts

In Chapter 8, *Implementing an Intelligent Autonomous Car Driving Agent Using the Deep Actor-Critic algorithm*, we walked you through the derivation of the policy gradient theorem and reproduced the following for bringing in context:

$$\nabla_\theta J(\theta) = \mathbb{E}_{\pi_\theta} \left[\nabla_\theta \log \pi_\theta(s, a) \right] Q^{\pi_\theta}(s, a)$$

You may recall that the policy we considered was a stochastic function that assigned a probability to each action given the **state** (**s**) and the parameters (θ). In deterministic policy gradients, the stochastic policy is replaced by a deterministic policy that prescribes a fixed policy for a given state and set of parameters θ. In short, DPG can be represented using the following two equations:

This is the policy objective function:

$$J(\mu_\theta) = \mathbb{E}_{s \sim \rho^\mu} \left[r(s, \mu_\theta(s)) \right]$$

Here, $\mu_\theta : S \to A$ is the deterministic policy parametrized by θ, r(s,a) is the reward function for taking action *a* in state s, and ρ^μ is the discounted state distribution under the policy.

The gradient of the deterministic policy objective function is proven (in the paper linked before) to be:

$$\nabla_\theta J(\mu_\theta) = \mathbb{E}_{s \sim \rho^\mu} \left[\nabla_\theta Q^\mu(s, \mu_\theta(s)) \right]$$

We now see the familiar action-value function term, which we typically call the critic. DDPG builds on this result and uses a deep neural network to represent the action-value function, like we did in Chapter 6, *Implementing an Intelligent Agent for Optimal Discrete Control Using Deep Q-Learning*, along with a few other modifications to stabilize the training. Specifically, a Q-target network is used (like what we discussed in Chapter 6, *Implementing an Intelligent Agent for Optimal Discrete Control Using Deep Q-Learning*), but now this target network is slowly updated rather than keeping it fixed for a few update steps and then updating it. DDPG also uses the experience replay buffer and uses a noisy version of μ_θ, represented using the equation $\mu_{exploration} = \mu_\theta(s) + \mathcal{N}$, to encourage exploration as the policy. μ_θ is deterministic.

There is an extension to DDPG called D4PG, short for Distributed Distributional DDPG. I can guess what you might be thinking: DPG -> DDPG -> {Missing?}-> DDDDPG. Yes! The missing item is for you to implement.

The D4PG algorithm applies four main improvements to the DDPG algorithm, which are listed here briefly if you are interested:

- Distributional critic (the critic now estimates a distribution for Q-values rather than a single Q-value for a given state and action)

- N-step returns (similar to what we used in Chapter 8, *Implementing an Intelligent Autonomous Car Driving Agent Using the Deep Actor-Critic algorithm*, n-step TD returns are used instead of the usual 1-step return)

- Prioritized experience replay (this is used to sample experiences from the experience replay memory)

- Distributed parallel actors (utilizes K independent actors, gathering experience in parallel and populating the experience replay memory)

Proximal Policy Optimization

Proximal Policy Optimization (**PPO**) is a policy gradient-based method and is one of the algorithms that have been proven to be stable as well as scalable. In fact, PPO was the algorithm used by the OpenAI Five team of agents that played (and won) against several human DOTA II players, which we discussed in our previous chapter.

Core concept

In policy gradient methods, the algorithm performs rollouts to collect samples of transitions and (potentially) rewards, and updates the parameters of the policy using gradient descent to minimize the objective function. The idea is to keep updating the parameters to improve the policy until a good policy is obtained. To improve the training stability, the **Trust Region Policy Optimization** (**TRPO**) algorithm enforces a **Kullback-Liebler** (**KL**) divergence constraint on the policy updates, so that the policy is not updated too much in one step when compared to the old policy. TRPO was the precursor to the PPO algorithm. Let's briefly discuss the objective function used in the TRPO algorithm in order to get a better understanding of PPO.

Off-policy learning

As we know, in the case of off-policy learning, the agent follows a behavioral policy that is different from the policy that the agent is trying to optimize. Just to remind you, Q-learning, which we discussed in `Chapter 6`, *Implementing an Intelligent Agent for Optimal Discrete Control Using Deep Q-Learning*, along with several extensions, is also an off-policy algorithm. Let's denote the behavior policy using $\beta(a|s)$. Then, we can write the objective function of the agent to be the total advantage over the state-visitation distribution and actions given by the following:

$$J(\theta) = \sum_{s \in S} \rho^{\pi_{\theta_{old}}} \sum_{a \in A} \left(\pi_\theta(a|s) \hat{A}_{\theta_{old}}(s, a) \right)$$

Here, θ_{old} is the policy parameters before the update and $\rho^{\pi_{\theta_{old}}}$ is the state visitation probability distribution under the old policy parameters. We can multiply and divide the terms in the inner summation by the behavior policy $\beta(a|s)$, with the idea being the use of importance sampling to account for the fact that the transitions are sampled using the behavior policy $\beta(a|s)$:

$$J(\theta) = \sum_{s \in S} \rho^{\pi_{\theta_{old}}} \sum_{a \in A} \left(\beta(a|s) \frac{\pi_\theta(a|s)}{\beta(a|s)} \hat{A}_{\theta_{old}}(s, a) \right)$$

The changed terms in the preceding equation compared to the previous equation are shown in red.

We can write the previous summations over a distribution as an expectation, like so:

$$J(\theta) = \mathbb{E}_{s \sim \rho^{\pi_{\theta_{old}}}} \sum_{a \in A} (\beta(a|s) \frac{\pi_\theta(a|s)}{\beta(a|s)} \hat{A}_{\theta_{old}}(s,a)) = \mathbb{E}_{s \sim \rho^{\pi_{\theta_{old}}}, \, a \sim \beta} [\frac{\pi_\theta(a|s)}{\beta(a|s)} \hat{A}_{\theta_{old}}(s,a)]$$

On-policy

In the case of on-policy learning, the behavior policy and the target policy for the agent are one and the same. So, naturally the current policy (before the update) that the agent is using to collect samples is going to be $\pi_{\theta_{old}}$, which is the behavior policy, and therefore the objective function becomes this:

$$J(\theta) = \mathbb{E}_{s \sim \rho^{\pi_{\theta_{old}}}, \, a \sim \pi_{\theta_{old}}} [\frac{\pi_\theta(a|s)}{\pi_{\theta_{old}}} \hat{A}_{\theta_{old}}(s,a)]$$

 The changed terms in the preceding equation compared to the previous equation are shown in red.

TRPO optimizes the previous object function with a *trust region* constraint, which using the KL divergence metric given by the following equation:

$$\mathbb{E}_{s \sim \rho^{\pi_{theta_{old}}}} [D_{KL}(\pi_{\theta_{old}}(.|s)||\pi_{theta}(.|s))] \leq \delta$$

This is the constraint that makes sure that the new update to the policy is not diverging too much from the current policy. Although the idea behind TRPO was neat and intuitively simple, the implementation and gradient updates involved complexities. PPO simplifies the approach using a clipped surrogate objective that was effective and simple as well. Let's get a deeper understanding of the core concepts behind PPO using the math behind the algorithm. Let the probability ratio of taking action a given state s between the new policy π_θ and the old policy $\pi_{\theta_{old}}$ be defined as follows:

$$r(\theta) = \frac{\pi_\theta(a|s)}{\pi_{\theta_{old}}(a|s)}$$

Substituting this into the on-policy objective function equation of TRPO that we discussed earlier results in the objective function:

$$J^{TRPO}(\theta) = \mathbb{E}[r(\theta)\hat{A}_{\theta_{old}}(s,a)]$$

Simply removing the KL divergence constraint will result in instability, due to the large number of parameter updates that may result. PPO imposes the constraint by forcing $r(\theta)$ to lie within the interval $[1 - \epsilon, 1 + \epsilon]$, where ϵ is a tunable hyperparameter. Effectively, the objective function used in PPO takes the minimum value between the original parameter values and the clipped version, which can mathematically be described as shown here:

$$J^{PPO}(\theta) = \mathbb{E}[min(r(\theta)\hat{A}_{\theta_{old}}(s,a), clip(r(\theta), 1 - \epsilon, 1 + \epsilon)\hat{A}_{\theta_{old}}(s,a))]$$

This results in a stable learning objective with monotonically improving policy.

Rainbow

Rainbow (`https://arxiv.org/pdf/1710.02298.pdf`) is an off-policy deep reinforcement learning algorithm based on DQN. We looked at and implemented deep Q-learning (DQN) and some of the extensions to DQN in Chapter 6, *Implementing an Intelligent Agent for Optimal Discrete Control Using Deep Q-Learning*. There have been several more extensions and improvements to the DQN algorithm. Rainbow combines six of those extensions and shows that the combination works much better. Rainbow is a state-of-the art algorithm that currently holds the record for the highest score on all Atari games. If you are wondering why the algorithm is named *Rainbow*, it is most probably due to the fact that it combines seven (the number of colors in a rainbow) extensions to the Q-learning algorithm, namely:

- DQN
- Double Q-Learning
- Prioritized experience replay
- Dueling networks
- Multi-step learning/n-step learning
- Distributional RL
- Noisy nets

Core concept

Rainbow combines DQN with six selected extensions that were shown to address the limitations of the original DQN algorithm. We will briefly look at the six extensions to understand how they contributed to the overall performance boost and landed Rainbow in the top spot on the Atari benchmark, and also how they proved to be successful in the OpenAI Retro contest.

DQN

By now, you should be very familiar with DQN, as we went through the step-by-step implementation of a deep Q-learning agent in `Chapter 6`, *Implementing an Intelligent Agent for Optimal Discrete Control Using Deep Q-Learning*, where we discussed DQN in detail and how it extends standard Q-learning with a deep neural network function approximation, replay memory, and a target network. Let's recall the Q-learning loss that we used in the deep Q-learning agent in `Chapter 6`, *Implementing an Intelligent Agent for Optimal Discrete Control Using Deep Q-Learning*:

$$q_{loss} = (R_{t+1} + \gamma_{t+1} \max_{a' \in \mathbb{A}} q_{\bar{\theta}}(S_{t+1}, a') - q_\theta(S, A_t))^2$$

This is basically the mean squared error between the TD target and DQN's Q-estimate, as we noted in `Chapter 6`, *Implementing an Intelligent Agent for Optimal Discrete Control Using Deep Q-Learning*, where $q_{\bar{\theta}}$ is the slow-moving target network and q_θ is the main Q network.

Double Q-Learning

In Double Q-Learning, there are two action-value/Q functions. Let's call them Q1 and Q2. The idea in double Q-learning is to *decouple action selection from the value estimation*. That is, when we want to update Q1, we select the best action according to Q1, but use Q2 to find the value of the selected action. Similarly, when Q2 is being updated, we select the action based on Q2, but use Q1 to determine the value of the selected action. In practice, we can use the main Q network q_θ as Q1 and the slow-moving target network $q_{\bar{\theta}}$ as Q2, which gives us the following Double Q-Learning loss equation (the differences from the DQN equation are shown in red):

$$q_{loss,double} = (R_{t+1} + \gamma_{t+1} q_{\bar{\theta}}(S_{t+1}, \arg\max_{a'} q_\theta(S_{t+1}, a')) - q_\theta(S_t, A_t))^2$$

The motivation behind this change in the loss function is that Q-learning is affected by overestimation bias, and this can harm learning. The overestimation is due to the fact that the expectation of a maximum is greater than or equal to the maximum of the expectation (often the inequality is the one that holds) which arises due to the maximization step in the Q-learning algorithm and DQN. The change introduced by double Q-learning was shown to reduce overestimations that were harmful to the learning process, thereby improving performance over DQN.

Prioritized experience replay

When we implemented deep Q-learning in `Chapter 6`, *Implementing an Intelligent Agent for Optimal Discrete Control Using Deep Q-Learning*, we used an experience replay memory to store and retrieve sampled transition experience. In our implementation, and in the DQN algorithm, the experiences from the replay memory buffer are sampled uniformly. Intuitively, we would want to sample those experiences more frequently, as there is much to learn. Prioritized experience replay samples transition with probability p_t relative to the last encountered absolute TD error, given by the following equation:

$$ p_t \propto \left| R_{t+1} + \gamma_{t+1} \max_{a'} q_{\bar{\theta}}\left(S_{t+1}, a'\right) - q_\theta\left(S_t, A_t\right) \right|^w $$

Here, w is a hyperparameter that determines the shape of the distribution. This makes sure that we sample those transitions in which the predictions of the Q-values were more different from the correct values. In practice, new transitions are inserted into the replay memory with maximum priority to signify the importance of recent transition experiences.

Dueling networks

Dueling networks is a neural network architecture designed for value-based reinforcement learning. The name *dueling* stems from the main feature of this architecture, which is that there are two streams of computations, one for the value function and the other for the advantage. The following diagram, from a research paper (https://arxiv.org/pdf/1511.06581.pdf), shows the comparison of the dueling network architecture (the network shown at the bottom of the diagram) with the typical DQN architecture (shown at the top of the diagram):

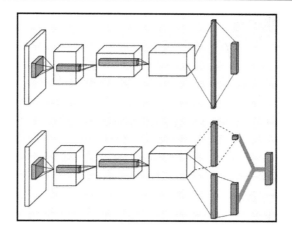

The convolutional layers that encode features are shared by both the value and advantage streams, and are merged by a special aggregation function, as discussed in the paper that corresponds to the following factorization of the action values:

$$q_\theta(s, a) = v_\eta(f_\xi(s)) + a_\psi(f_\xi(s), a) - \frac{\sum_{a'} a_\psi(f_\xi(s), a')}{N_{actions}}$$

η, ξ, and ψ are, respectively, the parameters of the value stream, the shared convolutional encoder, and the advantage stream, and $\theta = \{\eta, \xi, \psi\}$ is their concatenation.

Multi-step learning/n-step learning

In `Chapter 8`, *Implementing an Intelligent Autonomous Car Driving Agent Using the Deep Actor-Critic algorithm*, we implemented the n-step return TD return method and discussed how forward-view multi-step targets can be used in place of a single/one-step TD target. We can use that n-step return with DQN, and that is essentially the idea behind this extension. Recall that the truncated n-step return from state S_t is given as follows:

$$G_t^{(n)} = R_t^{(n)} = \sum_{k=0}^{n-1} \gamma_t^{(k)} R_{t+k+1}$$

Using this equation, a multi-step variant of DQN can be defined to minimize the following loss (the differences from the DQN equation are shown in red):

$$q_{loss,n-step} = (R_t^{(n)} + \gamma_t^{(n)} \max_{a'} q_{\bar{\theta}}(S_{t+n}, a') - q_\theta(S_t, A_t))^2$$

This equation shows the change introduced to DQN.

Distributional RL

The distributional RL method (https://arxiv.org/abs/1707.06887) is about learning to approximate the distribution of returns rather than the expected (average) return. The distributional RL method proposes the use of probability masses placed on a discrete support to model such distributions. This, in essence, means that rather than trying to model one action-value given the state, a distribution of action-values for each action given the state is sought. Without going too much into the details (as that would require a lot of background information), we will look at one of the key contributions of this method to RL in general, which is the formulation of the Distributional Bellman equation. As you may recall from the previous chapters of this book, the action-value function, using a one-step Bellman backup for it, can be returned as follows:

$$Q(S_t, A_t) = r + \gamma Q(S_{t+1}, A_{t+1})$$

In the case of Distributional Bellman equations, the scalar quantity $Q(S, A)$ is replaced by a random variable $Z(S, A)$, which gives us the following equation:

$$Z(S_t, A_t) = r + \gamma Z(S_{t+1}, A_{t+1})$$

Because the quantity is no longer a scalar, the update equation needs to be dealt with more car than just adding the discounted value of the next state-action-value to the step-return. The update step of the distributional bellman equation can be understood easily with the help of the following diagram (stages from left to right):

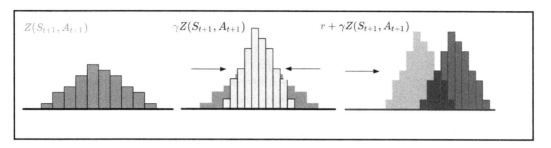

In the previous illustration, the distribution of the next state action-value is depicted in red on the left, which is then scaled by the discount factor γ (middle), and finally the distribution is shifted by r to yield the Distributional Bellman update. After the update, the target distribution Z' that results from the previous update operation is projected onto the supports of the current distribution Z by minimizing the cross entropy loss between Z and Z'.

With this background, you can briefly glance through the pseudo code of the C51 algorithm from the Distributional RL paper, which is integrated into the Rainbow agent:

Algorithm 1 Categorical Algorithm

---

input A transition $x_t, a_t, r_t, x_{t+1}, \gamma_t \in [0,1]$
    $Q(x_{t+1}, a) := \sum_i z_i p_i(x_{t+1}, a)$
    $a^* \leftarrow \arg\max_a Q(x_{t+1}, a)$
    $m_i = 0, \quad i \in 0, \ldots, N-1$
    for $j \in 0, \ldots, N-1$ **do**
        # Compute the projection of $\hat{T}z_j$ onto the support $\{z_i\}$
        $\hat{T}z_j \leftarrow [r_t + \gamma_t z_j]_{V_{MIN}}^{V_{MAX}}$
        $b_j \leftarrow (\hat{T}z_j - V_{MIN})/\Delta z$ # $b_j \in [0, N-1]$
        $l \leftarrow \lfloor b_j \rfloor, u \leftarrow \lceil b_j \rceil$
        # Distribute probability of $\hat{T}z_j$
        $m_l \leftarrow m_l + p_j(x_{t+1}, a^*)(u - b_j)$
        $m_u \leftarrow m_u + p_j(x_{t+1}, a^*)(b_j - l)$
    end for
output $-\sum_i m_i \log p_i(x_t, a_t)$ # Cross-entropy loss

Noisy nets

If you recall, we used an ϵ-greedy policy for the deep Q-learning agent in `Chapter 6`, *Implementing an Intelligent Agent for Optimal Discrete Control Using Deep Q-Learning*, to take action based on the action-values learned by the deep Q-network, which basically means taking the action with the highest action-value for a given state most of the time, except when, for some tiny fraction of the time (that is, with a very small probability ϵ), the agent selects a random action. This may prevent the agent from exploring more reward states, especially if the action-values it has converged to are not the optimal action-values. The limitations of exploring using ϵ-greedy policies were evident from the performance of the DQN variants and the value-based learning methods in the Atari game Montezuma's Revenge, where a long sequence of actions have to be executed in the right way to collect the first reward. To overcome this exploration limitation, Rainbow uses the idea of noisy nets—which are a simple but effective method proposed in 2017.

The main idea behind noisy nets is a noisy version of the linear neural network layer that combines a deterministic and a noisy stream, as exemplified in the following equation for the case of the linear neural network layer:

$$y = \underbrace{(b + Wx)}_{\substack{Deterministic \\ (usual\ linear\ layer)}} + \underbrace{(b_{noisy} \odot \epsilon^b + (W_{noisy} \odot \epsilon^w)x)}_{Stochastic\ (Noisy\ linear\ layer)}$$

Here, b_{noisy} and W_{noisy} are the parameters of the noisy layer, which are learned along with the other parameters of the DQN using gradient descent. The $\odot$ represents the element-wise product operation and ϵ^b and ϵ^w are zero-mean random noise. We can use the noisy linear layer in place of the usual linear layer in our DQN implementation, which will have the added advantage of exploring better. Because b_{noisy} and W_{noisy} are learnable parameters, the network can learn to ignore the noisy stream. Because this happens over time for each of the neurons, the noisy stream decays at different rates in different parts of the state space, allowing better exploration with a form of self-annealing.

The Rainbow agent implementation combines all of these methods to achieve state-of-the art results with better performance than any other method on the Atari suite of 57 games. Overall, the performance of the Rainbow agent against the previous best-performing agent algorithms on the combined benchmark for Atari games is summarized in the following graph from the Rainbow paper:

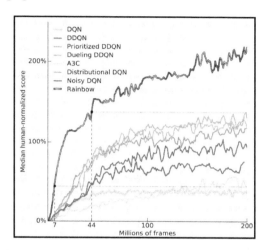

From the plot, it is clearly evident that the methods incorporated into the Rainbow agent lead to substantially improved performance across 57 different Atari games.

Quick summary of advantages and applications

A few of the key advantages of the Rainbow agent are summarized here for your quick reference:

- Combines several notable extensions to Q-learning developed over the past several years
- Achieves state-of-the art results in the Atari benchmarks
- n-step targets with a suitably tuned value for *n* often leads to faster learning
- Unlike other DQN variants, the Rainbow agent can start learning with 40% less frames collected in the experience replay memory
- Matches the best performance of DQN in under 10 hours (7 million frames) on a single-GPU machine

The Rainbow algorithm has become the most sought after agent for discrete control problems where the action space is small and discrete. It has been very successful with other game environments, such as Gym-Retro, and notably a tweaked version of the Rainbow agent placed second in the OpenAI Retro contest held in 2018, which is a transfer learning contest where the task is to learn to play the retro Genesis console games Sonic The Hedgehog, Sonic The Hedgehog II, and Sonic & Knuckles on some levels, and then be able to play well on other levels that the agent was not trained on. Considering the fact that in typical reinforcement learning settings, agents are trained and tested in the same environment, the retro contest measured the learning algorithm's ability to generalize its learning from previous experience. In general, the Rainbow agent is the best first bet to try on any RL problem/task in a discrete action space.

Summary

Being the final chapter of this book, this chapter provided summaries of key learning algorithms that are currently state of the art in this domain. We looked at the core concepts behind three different state-of-the-art algorithms, each with their own unique elements and their own categories (actor-critic/policy based/value-function based).

Specifically, we discussed the deep deterministic policy gradient algorithm, which is an actor-critic architecture method that uses a deterministic policy rather than the usual stochastic policy, and achieves good performance on several continuous control tasks.

We then looked at the PPO algorithm, which is a policy gradient-based method that uses a clipped version of the TRPO objective and learns a monotonically better and stable policy, and has been successfully used in very high-dimensional environments such as DOTA II.

Finally, we looked at the Rainbow algorithm, which is a value-based method and combines several extensions to the very popular Q-learning algorithm, namely DQN, double Q-learning, prioritized experience replay, dueling networks, multi-step learning/n-step learning, distributional reinforcement learning, and noisy-network layers. The Rainbow agent achieved significantly better performance in the Atari benchmark suite of 57 games and also performed very well in transfer learning tasks in the OpenAI Retro contest.

With that, we are into the last paragraph of this book! I hope you enjoyed your journey through the book, learned a lot, and acquired a lot of hands-on skills to implement intelligent agent algorithms and the necessary building blocks to train and test the agents on the learning environment/problem of your choice. You can use the issue-tracking system in the book's code repository to report issues with the code, or if you would like to discuss a topic further, or need any additional references/pointers to move to the next level.

Other Books You May Enjoy

If you enjoyed this book, you may be interested in these other books by Packt:

Deep Reinforcement Learning Hands-On
Maxim Lapan

ISBN: 978-1-78883-424-7

- Understand the DL context of RL and implement complex DL models
- Learn the foundation of RL: Markov decision processes
- Evaluate RL methods including Cross-entropy, DQN, Actor-Critic, TRPO, PPO, DDPG, D4PG and others
- Discover how to deal with discrete and continuous action spaces in various environments
- Defeat Atari arcade games using the value iteration method
- Create your own OpenAI Gym environment to train a stock trading agent
- Teach your agent to play Connect4 using AlphaGo Zero
- Explore the very latest deep RL research on topics including AI-driven chatbots

Reinforcement Learning with TensorFlow
Sayon Dutta

ISBN: 978-1-78883-572-5

- Implement state-of-the-art Reinforcement Learning algorithms from the basics
- Discover various techniques of Reinforcement Learning such as MDP, Q Learning and more
- Learn the applications of Reinforcement Learning in advertisement, image processing, and NLP
- Teach a Reinforcement Learning model to play a game using TensorFlow and the OpenAI gym
- Understand how Reinforcement Learning Applications are used in robotics

Leave a review - let other readers know what you think

Please share your thoughts on this book with others by leaving a review on the site that you bought it from. If you purchased the book from Amazon, please leave us an honest review on this book's Amazon page. This is vital so that other potential readers can see and use your unbiased opinion to make purchasing decisions, we can understand what our customers think about our products, and our authors can see your feedback on the title that they have worked with Packt to create. It will only take a few minutes of your time, but is valuable to other potential customers, our authors, and Packt. Thank you!

Index

A

actor-critic algorithm 170
advantage actor-critic algorithm 171, 172
agent
  performance, recording 82
  performance, testing 82
Application Programming Interface (API) 9
Arcade Learning Environment (ALE) 11
Artificial Intelligence (AI)
  about 22, 23
  machine learning 23
asynchronous deep n-step advantage actor-critic 186
Atari Alien environment, nomenclature
  Alien-ram-v0 55
  Alien-ram-v4 55
  Alien-ramDeterministic-v0 56
  Alien-ramDeterministic-v4 56
  Alien-ramNoFrameskip-v0 56
  Alien-v0 56
  Alien-v4 56
  AlienDeterministic-v0 56
  AlienDeterministic-v4 56
  AlienNoFrameskip-v0 56
  AlienNoFrameskip-v4 56
Atari games
  deep Q-learner, training 132
Atari Gym environment
  about 121
  custom Gym environment wrappers, implementing 122
  customizing 122
  wrappers, applying 131

C

CARLA simulator
  reference 145
compatible environments, Gym interface
  about 194
  Gym retro 199
  Roboschool 195, 196
Compute Unified Device Architecture (CUDA)
  installing 48, 49
  reference 48
conda environment
  creating 40
configuration parameters
  JSON file, using 112
  managing 111
  parameters manager 112
Convolutional Neural Network (CNN) 106
CUDA Deep Neural Network (cuDNN) 49
custom Gym environment wrappers
  Atari screen image frames, preprocessing 124
  AtariRescale 122
  ClipRewardEnv 122
  episodic life 129
  EpisodicLifeEnv 123
  fire, on reset 128
  FireResetEnv 123
  implementing 122
  max frame 130
  MaxAndSkipEnv 123
  NoopResetEnv 123
  NormalizedEnv 123
  observations, normalizing 125
  random no-ops, on reset 127
  reward, clipping 123
  skip-frame 130
custom Gym environment

template, creating 143

D

deep convolutional Q-network
  agent's learning process, logging 109
  agent's learning process, visualizing 109
  implementing, in PyTorch 106
  target Q-network, using 107
Deep Deterministic Policy Gradient (DDPG)
  about 216
  concepts 217
deep n-step advantage actor critic agent
  actor networks, initializing 178, 181
  actor's losses, calculating 183
  actor-critic model, updating 184
  asynchronous deep n-step advantage actor-critic
  186
  critic networks, initializing 178, 181
  critic's losses, calculating 183
  implementing 177, 178
  n-step experiences, gathering with current policy
  182
  tools 185
deep n-step advantage actor-critic algorithm
  about 166, 177
  actor-critic algorithm 170
  advantage actor-critic algorithm 171
  policy gradients 166, 167, 168
deep Q-learner
  hyperparameters 136
  implementing 133
  performance, testing in Atari games 138, 139
  training process, launching 137
  training, for Atari games 132
deep Q-learning agent
  complex problems, solving with raw pixel input
  114, 120
  configuration parameters, managing 111
  hyperparameters, managing 111
  implementing 105
deep reinforcement learning
  about 32, 34
  Compute Unified Device Architecture (CUDA),
  installing 48, 49
  libraries, installing 47

practical applications 34
prerequisite system packages, installing 48
PyTorch, installing 49, 50
tools, installing 47
DeepFace system
  reference 24
DeepMind Lab, methods
  close() 211
  events() 211
  fps() 211
  is_running() 209
  num_steps() 211
  observation_spec() 209
  observations() 208
  reset(episode=-1, seed=None) 208
  step(action, num_steps=1) 208
DeepMind lab
  about 207
  dependencies 212
  executing 211
  game, playing 212
  installing 212
  learning environment interface 208
  randomly acting agent, testing 212
  reference 207
  setting up 211
Deterministic Policy Gradient (DPG)
  about 216
  reference 216
distributional RL
  about 226, 227
  reference 226
Double Q-Learning 223
DQN 223
dueling networks 224
dynamic programming 31

E

End User License Agreement (EULA) 203
environment types, OpenAI Gym
  algorithmic environments 11
  Atari environments 11
  board games 11
  Box2D 12
  classic control 12

Doom 13
MineCraft 14
MuJoCo 15
Soccer 15
Toy text 16
epsilon-greedy action policy
  epsilon decay schedule, implementing 104, 105
  revisiting 103
experience replay
  about 98
  experience memory, implementing 99
  implementing, for Q-learner class 101
  prioritized experience replay 224

G

Generative Adversarial Networks
  reference 24
Gym environments, methods
  _close() 142
  _configure 142
  _render() 142
  _seed 142
  action_space 142
  observation_space 142
  reset() 142
  step(...) 142
Gym environments
  anatomy 142
  custom environments, registering with OpenAI
    Gym 145
  template, creating for custom Gym environment
    implementation 143
Gym interface
  about 58, 59, 60, 61, 62, 63
  compatible environments 194
Gym retro
  about 199
  executing 200, 201
  reference 199
  setting up 200, 201

H

Hands On Intelligent Agents With OpenAI Gym
  (HOIAWOG) 38
heating, ventilation, and air conditioning (HVAC)

systems 165
hyperparameters, deep Q-learner
  epsilon_max 137
  epsilon_min 137
  gamma 136
  load_dir 137
  load_trained_model 137
  lr 136
  max_num_episodes 136
  replay_batch_size 136
  replay_memory_capacity 136
  save_dir 137
  seed 137
  target_network_update_freq 136
  use_cuda 137
  use_target_network 136
hyperparameters
  managing 111

I

ImageNet Large Scale Visual Recognition
  Challenge (ILSVRC) 18
independent and identically distributed (i.i.d) 98
intelligent agent 8
intelligent and autonomous driving agent
  deep n-step advantage actor-critic agent, testing
    187, 188, 190
  deep n-step advantage actor-critic agent, training
    187, 188, 190
  training 187
  training, in CARLA driving simulator 191

J

JavaScript Object Notation (JSON) file 112

K

Kullback-Liebler (KL) 219

L

learning environment
  about 8
  varieties 9

M

machine learning
 about 23
 reinforcement learning 25
 supervised learning 24
 types 23
 unsupervised learning 24
macOS
 OpenAI Gym, installation 43
Markov Decision Process (MDP)
 about 30, 99
 Markov Decision Process 31
 Markov Process 31
 Markov Reward Process (MRP) 31
Mean Squared Error (MSE) 183
Monte Carlo (MC) learning 31
Mountain Car problem
 about 70
 environment 70, 71
 solving, with Q-Learner implementation 83, 85, 86, 87
Multi-Joint dynamics with Contact (MuJoCo)
 about 43
 installing 44
 reference 44
multi-step learning/n-step learning 225

N

n-step advantage actor-critic algorithm
 about 172
 n-step return calculation, implementing 175, 176
 n-step returns 173, 174
natural intelligence 23
neural networks
 Q-functions, approximating 92
 shallow Q-network, implementing with PyTorch 93
noisy nets 228, 229
nomenclature
 about 55
 exploring 53
NumPy
 Q-learning agent, implementing 76

O

open source Python-based learning environments
 about 202
 DeepMind lab 207
 StarCraft II 203
OpenAI Gym environment
 creating 18, 19, 20
 exploring 53, 55, 57
 visualizing 20
OpenAI Gym, features
 comparability 17
 progress, monitoring 17
 reproducibility 17
 simple environment interface 16
OpenAI Gym-compatible CARLA driving simulator environment
 actions, sending CARLA simulation server 157
 actions, sending to control agents 154
 camera data, accessing 154
 cameras, adding to vehicle 150
 configuration 147, 148
 continuous action space 155
 creating 145, 146, 147
 customizing, with CarlaSettings object 150
 discrete action space 156
 end of episodes, determining 159
 initialization 147, 148
 reset method, implementing 149
 sensor data, accessing 154
 sensors, adding to vehicle 150
 step function, implementing 153
 testing 160, 161, 162
OpenAI Gym
 about 9
 completing 47
 custom environments, registering 145
 environment types 11
 installation, for macOS 43
 installation, for Ubuntu 43
 learning environments, installing 43
 MuJoCo, installation 44
 prerequisites 39, 40
 reference 16
 setup, completing 44, 46

toolkit 18

P

policy gradients
  about 166, 167, 168
  likelihood ratio trick 168
  policy gradient theorem 169
Proximal Policy Optimization (PPO)
  about 218
  concept 219
  off-policy learning 219, 220
  on-policy learning 220, 221
PySC2
  installing 206
Python Package Index (PyPI)
  installing 41, 42
Python
  conda environment, creating 40
  installing 39, 40
  Q-learning agent, implementing 76
  using 39
PyTorch
  deep convolutional Q-network, implementing 106
  installing 49, 50
  reference 49
  shallow Q-network, implementing 93

Q

Q-learning 32
Q-learning agent
  epsilon-greedy action policy, revisiting 103
  experience replay 98
  hyperparameters, defining 76
  implementing 72, 73, 74, 75
  implementing, with Python and Numpy 76
  improving 91
  Q-functions, approximating with neural networks 92
  Q_Learner class's __init__ method, implementing 77
  Q_Learner class's discretize method, implementing 78
  Q_learner class's learn method, implementing 79
  Q_Learner class, implementation 80, 81

Q_Learner's get_action method, implementing 79
  revisiting 75

R

Rainbow
  about 222
  advantages 229
  applications 230
  concept 222
  distributional RL 226, 227
  Double Q-Learning 223
  DQN 223
  dueling networks 224
  multi-step learning/n-step learning 225
  noisy nets 228, 229
  prioritized experience replay 224
  reference 222
Random Access Memory (RAM) 55
Rectified Linear Unit (ReLU or relu) 94
reinforcement learning
  about 22, 25
  agent 26
  agent, training 81
  environment 26
  model 29
  policy 30
  practical applications 34
  practical aspects 25
  rewards 26
  state 27, 28
  value function 29
RGBD (Red-Green-Blue-Depth) 208
Roboschool
  about 195
  environments 196
  environments, executing 197, 198
  environments, setting up 197
  reference 195, 197
  versus MuJoCo 195
ROM (Read-Only Memory) 201

S

SARSA 32
SC2 maps

reference 205
shallow Q-network
  Cart Pole problem, solving 95, 98
  implementing 94
  implementing, with PyTorch 93
Single Layer Perceptron (SLP) 93
space, type
  Box 64
  Dict 64
  Discrete 64
  MultiBinary 64
  MultiDiscrete 64
  Tuple 64
spaces 63, 64, 65, 66, 67
StarCraft II
  about 203
  Linux packages, downloading 205
  PySC2 environment, executing 204
  PySC2 environment, setting up 204
  PySC2, installing 206
  reference 203
  sample agents, executing 206

SC2 maps, downloading 205
StarCraft2 (SC2) 203
supervised learning 24

T

Temporal Difference (TD) 31, 103
Text-To-Speech (TTS) 92
Trust Region Policy Optimization (TRPO) 219

U

Ubuntu
  OpenAI Gym, installation 43
unsupervised learning 24

V

value function, reinforcement learning
  about 29
  action-value function 30
  state-value function 29
ViZDoom
  about 13
  reference 13

www.ingramcontent.com/pod-product-compliance
Lightning Source LLC
Chambersburg PA
CBHW080636060326
40690CB00021B/4952